NEVER SUCH INNOCENCE

NEVER SUCH INNOCENCE

A NEW ANTHOLOGY OF GREAT WAR VERSE

Edited and introduced by

MARTIN STEPHEN

Buchan & Enright, Publishers
London

First published in 1988 by
Buchan & Enright, Publishers (Fountain Press Ltd)
45 The Broadway, Tolworth, Surrey KT6 7DW

British Library Cataloguing in Publication Data

Stephen, Martin
    Never such innocence: a new anthology of great war verse
    1. World War, 1914-1918 — Poetry
    2. English poetry — 20th century
    1. Title
    821'.912'080358   PR1195.W65

    ISBN 0-907675-67-0

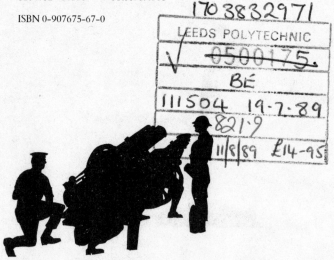

Typeset by Leaper & Gard Ltd., Bristol, England.
Printed in Great Britain by Biddles Ltd, Guildford

CONTENTS

⁺NOTE: where, after a poem, the writer's name is followed by a cross, it indicates that the poet was killed or died during the Great War.

ACKNOWLEDGEMENTS

Grateful thanks are due to the following for their kind permission to reprint copyright poems in this collection:

'Somewhere East of Suez' by H.W. Berry, reproduced by permission of *Punch*; 'The Unreturning Spring' by Lawrence Binyon (from *The Four Years*, London, Elkin Matthews, 1919), by permission of Mrs Nicolete Gray and The Society of Authors on behalf of the Lawrence Binyon Estate; 'From the Front: The Song of the Trench, December 1914' by Captain C.W. Blackall (from *Songs from the Trenches*, London, Bodley Head, 1915) by permission of The Bodley Head Ltd; 'Concert Party: Busseboom', 'Escape' and 'The Guard's Mistake' by Edmund Blunden (from *Undertones of War*, Oxford, Oxford University Press, 1928, 1956) by permission of A.D. Peters & Co. Ltd; 'The Gift' by Francis Brett Young (from *Poems 1916-18*, London, Collins, 1919) by permission of David Higham Associates Ltd; Extract from 'Death of John Rump' and two 'Fragments' by Rupert Brooke (from *Rupert Brooke: a Reappraisal and Selection* by Timothy Rogers, London, Routledge & Kegan Paul, 1971) by permission of Associated Book Publishers (UK) Ltd; 'The Kirk Bell' and 'On Leave' by John Buchan (from *Poems Scots and English*, London, Nelson, 1917) by permission of A.P. Watt Ltd on behalf of the Rt Hon. the Lord Tweedsmuir of Elsfield, CBE; 'The Infantryman' by E.F. Clarke, by permission of *Punch*; 'The Sailing of the Fleet' by N.M.F. Corbett (from *A Naval Motley: Verses Written at Sea during the War and before it*, London, Methuen, 1916), by permission of Methuen & Co.; 'Harrow and Flanders' by Lord Crewe, by kind permission of *The Harrovian* Newspaper; 'A Fleeting Passion', 'The Bird of Paradise', 'The Heap of Rags' and 'The Birds of Steel' by W.H. Davies (from *The Bird of Paradise*, London, Methuen, 1914; now to be found in *The Complete Poems of W.H. Davies*, London, Jonathan Cape), by permission of Jonathan Cape Ltd; 'The Turkish Trench Dog' by Geoffrey Dearmer (from *Poems*, London, Heinemann, 1918), reprinted by permission of William Heinemann Ltd; 'A Grand Night' by D.J. Enright (from *The Terrible Shears*, London, Chatto & Windus, 1973; now to be found in the author's *Collected Poems*, Oxford, Oxford University Press, 1981, 1987), by permission of the author and Watson, Little Ltd; 'The Forest of the Dead' by James Griffyth Fairfax (from *Mesopotamia*, London, Murray, 1919), by permission of John Murray (Publishers) Ltd; 'Eyes in the Air' by Gilbert Frankau (from *The Judgement of Valhalla*, London, Chatto & Windus, 1918), by permission of the Author's Estate and Chatto & Windus Ltd; 'Headquarters' by Gilbert Frankau (from *The City of Fear*, London, Chatto & Windus, 1917), by permission of Aitken & Stone Ltd for the Estate of Gilbert Frankau; 'A Soldier' by Robert Frost (from *The Poetry of Robert Frost*, ed. Edward Connery Lathem, London, Jonathan Cape, 1971), by permission of the Estate of Robert Frost and Jonathan Cape Ltd; 'Geraniums', 'Troopship: mid-Atlantic', 'Ambulance Train', 'The Question', 'Retreat', and 'A Lament' by Wilfrid Wilson Gibson (from *Collected Poems 1905-1925*, London, Macmillan, 1926), by permission of Michael Gibson Esq and Macmillan, London and Basingstoke; 'The Flapper' and 'Back to the Land' by C.L. Graves, by permission of *Punch*; 'Crucifix Corner' and 'I Saw French Once' by Ivor Gurney, copyright © Robin Haines, Sole Trustee of the Gurney Estate, 1982, reprinted from *Collected Poems of Ivor Gurney*, edited and with an introduction by P.J. Kavanagh (Oxford, Oxford University Press, 1982) by permission of Oxford University Press; 'The German Graves', 'The Cookers', 'Dead-Mule Tree', 'Untitled' and 'After the Battle' by A.P. Herbert (all from *Punch*, except 'Untitled', which was first printed in *Somme* by Lyn Macdonald, London, Michael Joseph, 1983), by permission of A.P. Watt Ltd on behalf of Lady Herbert; 'The Sand of Palestine' by T. Hodgkinson, by permission of *Punch*; extract from 'The Bull' by Ralph Hodgson (from *Poems*, London, Macmillan, 1917; now to be found in *Collected Poems*, London, Macmillan, 1961), by permission of Mrs Hodgson and Macmillan, London and Basingstoke; 'The Mystery Ships' by R.A. Hopwood, by permission of *Punch*; 'Six Young Men' by Ted Hughes (from *The Hawk in the Rain*, London, Faber and Faber, 1957), reprinted by permission of Faber and Faber Ltd; 'High Wood' by Philip Johnstone (from *The Nation* of 16 February 1918), by permission of the *New Statesman*; 'MCMXIV' by Philip Larkin (from *The Whitsun Weddings*, London, Faber and Faber, 1964), by permission of Faber and Faber Ltd; 'German Prisoners' by Joseph Johnston Lee (from *Work-a-Day Warriors*, London, Murray, 1917), by permission of John Murray (Publishers) Ltd; 'Many Sisters to Many Brothers' by Rose Macaulay (from *Poems of Today*, London, Sidgwick & Jackson, 1919), by permission of Sidgwick & Jackson Ltd; 'Another Epitaph on an Army of Mercenaries' by Hugh MacDiarmid, reprinted with permission of Macmillan Publishing Company, New York, from *Collected Poems* by Hugh MacDiarmid (New York, 1962), © Christopher Murray Grieve 1948, 1962; 'Matey', 'The Star-Shell' and 'Marching' by Patrick MacGill (from *Soldier Songs*, London, Barrie & Jenkins) by permission of Chris MacGill Esq and the Estate of Patrick MacGill; 'A Square Dance' by Roger McGough (from *Penguin Modern Poets* No. 10, London, Penguin, 1967), by permission of A.D. Peters & Co. Ltd; 'Sinn Fein' by Isobel Marchbank, by permission of *Punch*; 'The General' by George Kenneth Menzies, by permission of *Punch*; 'Gold Braid' and 'From a Full Heart' by A.A. Milne, by permission of *Punch*; 'The Nurse' by Miss G.M. Mitchell (from *Poems from Punch, 1909-1920*, London, Macmillan, 1922), by permission of *Punch*; 'Commandeered' by Lucy Gertrude Moberley (from *Blue Cross Fund: A Book of Poems for the Blue Cross Fund [to help horses in war time]*, London, Jarrold, 1917), by permission of Jarrold, Norwich; 'Vitaï Lampada' by Sir Henry Newbold (from *Poems: New and Old*, London, Murray, 1912; later to be found in *Selected Poems of Henry Newbolt*, ed. Patrick Dickinson, London, Hodder & Stoughton, 1981), by kind permission of Peter Newbolt Esq; 'Comrades: An Episode' by Robert Nichols (from *Ardours and Endurances*, London, Chatto & Windus, 1917) by permission of the Estate of the Author and Chatto & Windus Ltd; 'Kilmeny', 'The Search-Lights', and 'A Victory Dance' by Alfred Noyes (from *Collected Poems*, London, Methuen, 1950), by permission of Methuen & Co.; 'Three Hills' by Everard Owen (from *Three Hills and other Poems*, London, Sidgwick & Jackson, 1916) by permission of Sidgwick & Jackson Ltd; 'It Was a Navy Boy' by Wilfred Owen (first printed in *The Poems of Wilfred Owen*, ed. Jon Stallworthy, London, Hogarth Press, 1985), by permission of the Estate of the Author, Professor Jon Stallworthy, and The Hogarth Press Ltd; 'The Burdened Ass', 'A Telephone Message', and 'Where are You Sleeping Tonight, My Lad?' by John Oxenham (from *All's Well* and *The King's High Way*, London, Methuen, both 1916), by permission of Methuen & Co.; 'The Profiteer' by Ezra Pound (from 'Canto XXXVIII' in *The Cantos of Ezra Pound*, London, Faber and Faber, 1954), by permission of Faber and Faber Ltd; extracts from 'Gallipoli' by Sidney Walter Powell (from *One-Way Street and other poems*, London, Harrap, 1934; now to be found in the reprint of Powell's *Adventurers of a Wanderer*, London, Jonathan Cape, 1928, new edn London, Century Hutchinson, 1986) by kind permission of Colonel G.S. Powell, MC, for the Executors of Sidney Walter Powell; 'The Happy Warrior' and 'To a Conscript of 1940' by Herbert Read (from *Collected Poems*, London, Faber and Faber, 1946, 1966) by permission of David Higham Associates Ltd; 'Repetition' by Anthony Rhodes (from *Sword of Bone*, new edn, London, Buchan & Enright, 1986), by kind permission of the author; 'Moonrise Over Battlefield' by Edgell Rickword (from *Collected Poems*, London, Bodley Head, 1947), by permission of The Bodley Head Ltd; 'Night on the Convoy', 'To any Dead Officer', 'The Death-Bed', 'Stretcher Case', 'The Dug-Out', 'Concert Party', 'Picture Show', 'Everyone Sang', 'Reconciliation', 'Repression of War

Experience', 'Aftermath', and 'To One Who Was With Me in the War' by Siegfried Sassoon (from *War Poems*, London, Faber and Faber, 1919; now to be found in *The War Poems of Siegfried Sassoon*, ed. Rupert Hart-Davis, London, Faber and Faber, 1983), by kind permission of George Sassoon Esq; 'The Great War' by Vernon Scannell (from *A Sense of Danger*, London, Putnam, 1962; now to be found in *Collected Poems 1952-1980*, London, Robson, 1980) by permission of Robson Books Ltd; 'The Volunteer', 'A Pot of Tea', 'Grand-Père', and 'Going Home' by Robert Service (from *Rhymes of a Red Cross Man*, New York, Dodd Mead, 1916; London, Fisher Unwin, 1916), by permission of and © the Estate of Robert Service and Feinman and Krasilovsky PC, New York; 'The Halt' by Edward Shanks (from *Poems 1912-32*, London, Macmillan, 1933), by permission of Macmillan, London and Basingstoke; 'Judas and the Profiteer' by Osbert Sitwell (from *Argonaut and Juggernaut*, London, Chatto & Windus, 1919) by permission of David Higham Associates Ltd; 'The Next War' by Osbert Sitwell (from *Selected Poems Old and New*, London, Duckworth, 1943), by permission of David Higham Associates Ltd; 'Admiral Dugout' by Cicely Fox Smith, by permission of *Punch*; 'Chloe' and 'Elegy On The Death of Bingo, Our Trench Dog' by E. de Stein, by permission of *Punch*; 'From Albert to Bapaume' by Alec Waugh (from *Resentment*, London, Grant Richards, 1918), by permission of A.D. Peters & Co. Ltd; 'The Q-Boat' by H.E. Wilkes, by permission of *Punch*; 'Mine-Sweeping Trawlers' by Edward Hilton Young (from *A Muse at Sea*, London, Sidgwick & Jackson, 1919), by permission of Sidgwick & Jackson Ltd.

We have made very considerable efforts to trace all the poets represented here whose work is still in copyright, or their descendants, literary executors, and publishers. Sadly, after so great a lapse of time this has not always proved possible. We would be glad to hear from copyright-holders whom we have been unable to trace.

Further bibliographical details, as well as biographies of the poets, will be found at the end of this book, where there is also an Index of Titles and First Lines.

The editor of a poetry anthology is a parasite, feeding not only off the creative writing of other people, but also off the suggestions and contributions made by a host of friends and contacts. My warmest thanks go to those who have helped to compile this collection; needless to say, they are not responsible for the quality of the final product and any failings it might show. The book would never have happened without Eric Norris of Pioneer Books, Toby Buchan, and Dominique Enright. I am also deeply indebted to Michael Ffinch, author of *G.K. Chesterton: A Biography*; Lawrence James, author of *The Savage Wars* and *Mutiny: in the British and Commonwealth Forces, 1797-1956*; Jack and Imogen Thomas for their delvings in the Haileybury College library; Hilda Spear, Jon Stallworthy, Ursula Bickersteth, Laurence Cotterell, Maeve and Eliot Jeffrey, David Summerscale, Alan MacKichan, and the many other people who have provided information, support, and encouragement. My thanks also go to Jean Gooder of Newnham College, Cambridge, and Nick de Somogyi of Pembroke College, Cambridge, and to the long-suffering staff of the Cambridge University Library, the Lancaster University Library, and the Imperial War Museum, and to Ruth Kelso of the British Library. For their provision of idyllic writing facilities — and much more — my thanks also to George and Betty Fisher. The greater part of my thanks and gratitude go to Jenny, Neill, Simon, and Henry, whose judgements on the poems contained here were often more telling than my own. A final word of thanks must go to Catherine Reilly, whose *English Poetry of the First World War: A Bibliography* (George Prior, 1978) is one of the most inspired works any editor could hope to find.

PREFACE

The First World War was, in the words of John Terraine, 'unquestionably a major watershed in history'. It did not turn the lights out all over Europe so much as turn them full on, a harsh and lurid glare illuminating the bitter harvest of the Industrial Revolution. The First World War was the point at which that revolution came of age. Starting in Great Britain in the middle of the eighteenth century, the Industrial Revolution began to turn society on its head. It pushed the British, then a predominantly rural population, into becoming urban dwellers. It revolutionised manufacturing, transport, communications, the production of wealth, and placed immense pressure on the country's whole power base. It helped to make an empire, and to sustain it when it had been made.

Its impact on warfare was even more startling: at Rorke's Drift in 1879, for instance, a handful of British soldiers armed with Martini-Henry rifles held off an overwhelmingly superior force of Zulu warriors. Industry had replaced the slow, cumbersome and inaccurate muzzle-loading musket with the breech-loading rifle. Bullet and propellant were now housed in one single cartridge; in the Martini-Henry, each round had to be hand-loaded into the breech, which was prone to jamming, but the weapon was lethal in the hands of disciplined troops. Lethal as it was, it was a mere curtain-raiser for one of the finest infantry rifles ever produced, the bolt-action, magazine-fed Lee-Enfield, which was standard issue in the British Army by the time the First World War started in 1914 (and remained so until the 1960s). Similar weapons could be found in every European army of the time. With the Lee-Enfield, trained troops could maintain fifteen rounds of aimed fire a minute; the best reached thirty rounds a minute. Such rifles gave the ordinary infantryman more killing power than ever before in the history of warfare.

One rung higher up the ladder of technological development was the machine-gun. Properly handled and positioned, a machine-gun could decimate a whole battalion, if that battalion was advancing against it in close order over open ground. Even further up the ladder was the exploding artillery shell, which could contain simple high explosive, shrapnel, smoke or gas and could be fused to suit an almost infinite number of circumstances, and which with advances in propellant technology could be fired more accurately over greater ranges, and far more frequently than any previous projectile. At the very foot of the ladder was simple barbed wire. The industrial plant that could produce the howitzer had no difficulty in producing wire with barbed pieces wrapped around it. Simple as it was, it presented an impenetrable barrier — men would be held 'on the wire' while the rifle, the machine-gun, and the bomb did their work among them. Under intense bombardment barbed wire could be broken, but equally the effect might be to crumple it up into even more confused and impenetrable barriers.

Technological development did not stop at weaponry or defensive ironmongery. The European powers, and latterly the United States, had massive manufacturing capability, and when this was turned on to a war economy it became almost inevitable that the war would be long and hard, just as technical advances made it inevitable that the fighting would be bitter and bloody. The advent of new techniques and weapons — wireless-telegraphy, vastly improved engines, new mobile weapons such as the tank and the aeroplane — and the capacity of the warring powers to keep their armies supplied with everything from writing paper to aircraft engines, inevitably extended the war and the ability of the soldiers to fight it. Above all, the great weight of the civilian populations, male and female, was called on and used in addition to the large numbers of people in uniform, ensuring that this was indeed 'total' war.

The impact of the Industrial Revolution went even deeper than this, however. It had brought with it — perhaps had even been caused by — a vast increase in population. The population of a great capital city in 1914 might have equalled that of a whole nation in medieval times. Industrialisation and the corresponding Agricultural Revolution had freed huge numbers of people from the need to work on the land. These extra numbers could be marshalled into vast armies without the nation having to starve as a result; the wealth of the industrialised society could pay for them, arm them, feed them, and clothe them. The railways could bring them to a given point faster and more efficiently than ever before and, provided the troops did not venture into areas where lines had never been laid, or had been uprooted, the railways could keep them supplied with the appalling number of items, from food to lavatory paper, that they needed to fight and survive. Queen Elizabeth I never travelled further than the Midlands; Queen Victoria, not renowned for living it rough, had a home at Balmoral in Aberdeenshire, more than 500 miles north of

London. The Industrial Revolution unified the country with a practical communications network in a way that had never been possible before. With that unification, it became possible to unite the nation behind a war effort as it had never been united before.

The root cause of the carnage that marked the First World War came not with what the Industrial Revolution had done by 1914, but with what it had *not* done. It had vastly increased the defensive capability of the average infantryman, something which the opposing armies found out almost by accident when the early western offensive of 1914 collapsed into the mud of Flanders, and trenches were built as temporary expedients. The methods by which an army could break through a well-defended trench line were partly tactical, but also partly technological, and in 1914 that technology was in its infancy. Motorised transport, tanks and aircraft would in the end make trench warfare obsolete, but, even where they existed, they were not employed in any effective manner in the early years of the Great War. In 1914, very few senior officers in any European army had the vision to cope with the changing nature of warfare. The factors governing military conflict had changed little since the Napoleonic and imperial wars. There had been very little reason for them to have done so. European wars had always been fought with the bludgeon rather than the scalpel, and some sources suggest that the actual *proportion* of casualties to total number of combatants was not significantly higher in the First World War than in any other major conflict. The aim of war has always been to kill as many of the enemy as possible, and success is measured in those terms. It was the sheer numbers involved in the First World War that tipped it over the edge of acceptability. It can be argued that the generals of that war were no better and no worse than the majority of their ancestors. After all, Henry V had shown himself to be a fool by getting his army into a position whereby they had to fight at Agincourt, and in the Crimea not only the fighting leadership but also the commissariat failed at least as badly as they ever did in France between 1914 and 1913. Trench warfare and staggering casualties had been seen before in both the American Civil War and the Crimea.

The relative ability of the First World War generals may be in question; the result of the war is not. The superbly trained British Expeditionary Force was all but wiped out in helping the French hold the Germans before the latter reached Paris. Many more angels, and devils too, were created at the Battle of Mons than were ever seen in the sky over the battlefield, but such early actions were mere skirmishes compared with the battles that were to follow. Caught by surprise, Britain nevertheless managed to recruit and train the largest volunteer army in its history. Nearly 60,000 of these men were to become casualties on the first day of the Somme offensive in 1916. It is these men and this battle (actually a series of offensives launched over a number of months) that, ever since, have come to symbolise the war in the popular imagination. Weighted down with over 60 pounds of equipment, hundreds of thousands of troops went 'over the top', marching slowly forward in close-knit waves, in one instance kicking footballs ahead of them — all to be ripped apart by German rifle- and machine-gun fire. With the death of that army something went out of the heart of England. For many people the anguish and the truth about the First World War are forever symbolised by the work of Wilfred Owen, Siegfried Sassoon, Isaac Rosenberg, and the other famous 'trench poets'. So great is the association that, in Britain at least, the term 'war poets' can only mean the poets of the Great War.

Or so the story goes ...

To question that image of the First World War is regarded nowadays almost as sacrilege. Yet even a cursory glance at history suggests that in our reaction to the war, we show a response quite out of proportion to the known facts. The Industrial, French and Russian revolutions arguably had more political impact. The Second World War cost far more lives in Europe and as a whole. A great many more of these lives were those of innocent civilians. The Second War forced a radical and persistently dangerous division of Europe. Most of all, the Second World War ended with the detonation of atomic bombs over Hiroshima and Nagasaki. If it is true that a whole, tragic generation was wiped out in the Great War, then the Second World War told us to prepare for a whole planet to be wiped out.

My own battle with the conventional image of the First World War started with a doctoral thesis on its poetry. My particular hero at the time was Isaac Rosenberg, who in the balmy days of 1972 could still be described as the undiscovered genius of the First World War. I carried into my research all the features that were, and possibly still are, the product of a standard education in English Literature at a standard British university.

Doubts began to come at an early stage. My research task was to explore the links between pre-war poetry and that written in the First World War. The dominant group of poets in England, in the years before 1914 at least, was the Georgian Poetry movement, with Edward Marsh as its administrator and Rupert Brooke as its chief young star. There was a disturbing disparity between what the critics appeared to be saying the Georgians had written, and what was actually there on the pages of the anthologies which had spearheaded the movement. Partly out of literary interest, and partly because I was involved in some research into military history at the same time, I began to meet with and talk to survivors of the fighting in the First World War, the most prestigious of whom was the writer and historian Charles Carrington (author, under the name Charles Edmonds, of *A Subaltern's War*), the most lowly a man who had served for a few weeks in the trenches with a Lancashire regiment. The turning-point, for me, came in an interview with a Norfolk gentleman-farmer who had served for the whole war with the artillery. He listened carefully as I waxed enthusiastic about Wilfred Owen and Siegfried Sassoon. Yes, he agreed, they were fine men, and fine poets. But, he added, I was not to think that they were altogether representative. He asked if I watched the ceremonies on Armistice Day. Had I ever wondered what it was that drew those increasingly ancient men out of their beds, and made them re-unite every year at chronic risk to life and health? He was like them. He remembered the war with sadness, sometimes with repulsion, but more often with pride. They had taken on the most professional army in Europe, and beaten it in a fair fight. They had also taken on German militarism, and, in his opinion, if the politicians had not messed it up in 1918 there might have been no Second World War.

There was a flavour and a feeling in these remarks with which I was wholly unfamiliar. It was not that they ignored the horrors or the follies of the First World War, rather that they produced from them a mood that was neither markedly left- nor right-wing, and which was certainly not reflected in any poetry anthology with which I was familiar. It raised a niggling doubt in my mind about the conventional image of Great War poetry, a doubt that was to grow stronger as the years went on. Wilfred Owen clearly despised the war from the core of his being, yet something dragged him back to fight and die in it even when an honourable escape had been offered to him. Siegfried Sassoon appears to have been willing to have been shot as a traitor, but he was a courageous, indeed heroic officer who went back to active service *after* his famous public declaration against the war. Two of the finest pacifist poets of the First World War were awarded the Military Cross for gallantry in action. Yet judging by the poems which appeared in most anthologies, these men should never have joined up, and never have carried on fighting. Even after reading three biographies of him, I was still unclear as to why that most unlikely of soldiers, Isaac Rosenberg, should have joined up. Rosenberg has been set up by posterity as something of the 'working-class hero' of the First World War. He was, in fact, no such thing. Rather he was a unique and sometimes pathetic figure whose Judaic and working-class background gave him a vision of a world in which suffering was normal. He mined Judaism for his symbolism, but was neither a practising Jew nor a convincing symbol of the working classes. He was a bohemian and an artist who spent much of his life revelling in the support and praise of that most middle-class of poetic movements, Georgian poetry.

If the sentiments found in many collections are the whole and only truth about that war, it is difficult to explain why there was no mass desertion, no sustained and extensive mutiny amongst British troops in the First World War. Yet these men and their officers — numbers which included scores of poets and writers — returned to the trenches and went into action again and again.

The result of all this is that the following pages therefore contain a rather more varied range of poems than is normal in anthologies of First World War verse. Many of the best-known poems by the famous poets are included, but rather less than in existing anthologies, and I have taken the opportunity of including some poems by well-known authors that do not normally feature on an editor's check-list. Occasionally the critical establishment (with some very notable exceptions) seems to have become locked with *rigor mortis* in its vision of the great poets of the First World War. Owen's 'Strange Meeting' is mildly obscure and symbolic, features that recommended it to a generation brought up on T.S. Eliot and W.H. Auden, but which may have rendered it more fashionable than meritorious. It is a very famous poem, but it is also a clumsy technical exercise in half-rhyme; in its stead I have included 'Spring Offensive', probably the last full and complete poem Owen ever wrote, partly because it seems altogether more certain and assured than 'Strange Meeting', but mainly because it reflects much more accurately a mood that was found amongst survivors of the war. It was a firm favourite with many of them. Siegfried Sassoon's 'hammer-blow' satirical poems* are left out of this selection. An age sick of war elevated them, quite understandably, so that they came to be seen as the figurehead for Sassoon's work. Nearly seventy years after the war ended they seem now to be a little one-dimensional, and sometimes built on very shaky moral and ethical grounds, particuarly where they seek to answer the senseless

---

* See, for instance, 'Blighters', 'Base Details', 'They' etc, all of which are to be found in more orthodox anthologies.

violence of the First World War with even more senseless violence. I have given preference to his more reflective and traditional monologue poems, in the main because they appear so much more moving than the graffiti-daub of the satirical poems. The element of personal choice cuts both ways. I have excluded certain poems because they do not seem to me always to reflect what was strongest and most lasting in an author's work. But above all this selection is intended to be representative, and with this decision comes the requirement to include poems which I personally find disturbing, such as Sir Henry Newbolt's 'Vitaï Lampada'.

It will be immediately obvious to those familiar with poetry of the Great War that four of the sixteen poets whose names are inscribed on the memorial in Westminster Abbey do not appear in this selection. I have respected Robert Graves's own desire for his war poetry not to be reprinted. (This, it must be said, seems a strange desire, for while the 1975 edition of Graves's *Collected Poems* — the last in his lifetime — contains none of his war poetry, almost all the other Great War anthologies do, as did some of his earlier collections. Modern editions containing his war poems must have obtained permission to print them from Graves, his agent, his publishers, or his Estate). Julian Grenfell and Richard Aldington are omitted because their relatively small number of major poems have achieved wide coverage elsewhere. David Jones's *In Parenthesis* is also extremely well known and, in my opinion, suffers in extract, although such extracts can be found in a number of anthologies. I hope that the difficult decision to exclude these authors has allowed the inclusion of less well known poets who are equally worthy of public attention. It is certainly true that a great deal of what *is* here is available nowhere else except in libraries and archives.

Perhaps the prevailing impression left after twelve years of reading dusty volumes of First World War poetry in university libraries is that the voice we most commonly hear, and the one with which we are most familiar, is actually the voice of outraged middle-class protest. The poets of the First World War who have achieved lasting fame were poets first, and soldiers a long way second. The recruiting, and, later, conscription, nets drew in men who in any previous ages, given their educations and backgrounds, would never have thought of enlisting, and as a result many more of these, even allowing for the vast scale, were poets than had been the case in previous wars. In addition, the war itself *caused* the writing of poetry by men who would almost certainly not have done so otherwise. The absence of an equal body of poetry about the war at sea, as compared with the war on land

and especially on the Western Front, is not because conditions for a stoker at Jutland or Scapa Flow were any less horrific than for a soldier in the trenches, but rather because the Royal Navy retained much more of a traditional intake during the war, and to have written poetry at Dartmouth then would be analogous to playing Jerry Lee Lewis at a harpsichord recital now. Wilfred Owen, Siegfried Sassoon, Edward Thomas, Robert Graves, and Edmund Blunden, like so many other poets of the war, came from an educated class with an awareness of literature. Their view of the war is admirable in both poetic and moral terms; it would, however, be wrong to assume that it is therefore typical or representative.

That familiar voice from the Great War is also the voice of the officers, something which is also true of some poetry which is occasionally hailed as being 'from the ranks'. Very often this proves to have been written by a middle-class mind which happened to be serving in the ranks, and which commented on the attitudes of the majority of the troops, rather than actually capturing them. Although trench life did sometimes breed a much closer understanding of the ordinary soldier on the part of the officers, there was at that time an unbridgeable gap between officers and men in all branches of the armed services. Owen did not wish to write anything to which a soldier might say 'no compris', but persistently did just that, and was horrified by the crudity and gross sentimentality of the ordinary soldier's attitude to the war. All this changed as more officers were promoted from the ranks, but in poetic terms the true voice of the infantryman is hard to find.

The most convenient image of Great War poetry is based on the shock-and-horror category of writing. It symbolises what in our national guilt we feel we *ought* to think about the First World War. It is gripping, immediate — and something of a *cul-de-sac*. It prompted W.B. Yeats's famous remark that passive suffering was not a fit subject for poetry, and Yeats was too shrewd a critic for the complaint not to have a germ of truth in it. The dominant mode of writing at the time when war broke out was pastoral. Edward Thomas and Edmund Blunden, in particular, continued to write about 'Nature' during the war, but the absence of death and muck and bullets in their work — especially Thomas's — has led to them sometimes being given second place in selections and anthologies. A weakness and a strength of the Nature poet was that his contemplation of something so vast as Nature sometimes made even the war seem a passing phase. This has not been a fashionable view, and it has led to the inevitable accusation that some of the Nature poets of the First World War were escapist. In

Edward Thomas's poetry, in the words of countrymen quoted in Ronald Blythe's *Akenfield*, and in a host of other writings, there is the feeling that, horrific as the war was, life still went on, the seasons were unchanging, and time and nature covered the scars of war. To Owen and Sassoon the war was an outrage, a crime against decency, civilisation, and humanity. To the aristocrat and the farm- or factory-worker (though for very different reasons) the war sometimes did not seem quite so appalling. The aristocracy had been conditioned since before Norman times to exchange their privileges for military service, and that had always carried with it the risk of mutilation and death. Such conditioning helped form the officer caste of the Regular Army. At times Julian Grenfell welcomed the war with boyish glee, and with the realisation that active service was just like school, only he did not have to wash nearly as often. To the farm-worker, who lived under conditions of feudal deprivation which nowadays are only a bad dream, war may have been frightful, but not nearly so frightful as it was for those from sheltered backgrounds. When rural happiness could sometimes be measured in terms of a full stomach, something to smoke and drink, reasonable health, and a warm place to sleep, it took relatively little for the average infantryman to achieve a modicum of contentment in the Army, a fact frequently remarked on in tones of wonder by the essentially middle-class officers. The same often applied to the products of the industrial communities as well. Previous suffering did not make army life good; it made it more acceptable, in a way that Owen's poetry rarely conveys, for all his desire not to write anything to which a soldier might say 'no compris'.

There is no separate section devoted to religion in what follows, which might seem surprising, given the frequency with which religion is mentioned or used for imagery in the poetry of the Great War. It is the very universality of religious interest that makes it impossible to rope it off in a section of its own. Its influence permeates all types and styles of Great War poetry, and in terms of definition 'religious poetry' ceases to have any meaning in the Great War because of the variety of uses to which that religion could be put by poets. For many, it provided convenient symbols of suffering and sacrifice. For others it gave a historical context to the conflict, while some poets used it as a battering-ram, hurling conventional Sunday-morning Anglicanism at the bestialities of front-line life. Some poets mined it for its imagery, whilst those at home often attempted to justify the war in religious terms, or simply equate the teachings of Christianity with what was happening at the front.

The selection of poems given here therefore includes a separate section on poetry about nature and animals as it was applied to the war. At the expense of better-known work, it also includes poems by writers who have hitherto been considered rather second-division, and work by poets whose verse flickered into only the briefest fire of fame during and after the war. Much of the latter, and the poems culled from popular magazines, will never be great poetry, but it can have a heart and feel to it which go some way towards re-creating the feel and atmosphere of the First World War for those who fought in it, and thus for those who did not. There is a greater measure of more-or-less sentimental verse than is to be found in other anthologies. As Geoffrey Thurley has pointed out in his book *The Ironic Harvest*, we live in an age where savage irony can undercut any attempt to express simple strong emotion. For better or worse, many of those who joined up, fought, and either died or survived the First World War did so with attitudes markedly more simple and straightforward than our own. Those attitudes are given in this selection because they represent not what such people ought to have felt, but what they did feel.

MARTIN STEPHEN
July 1987

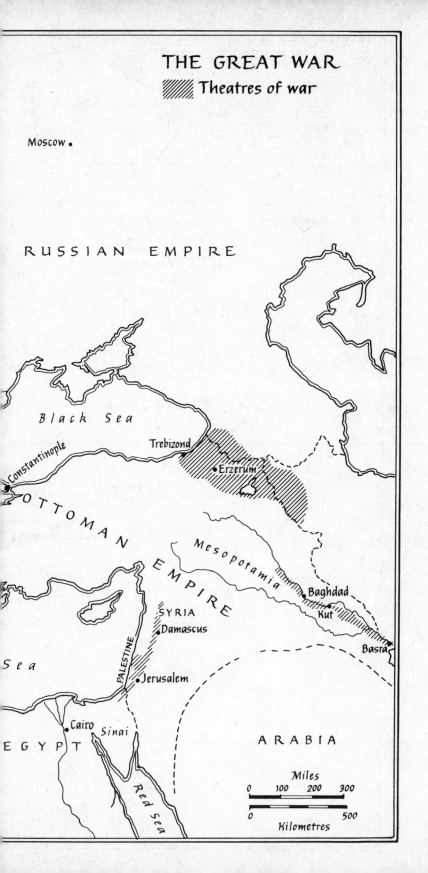

THE GREAT WAR
///// Theatres of war

Moscow •

RUSSIAN EMPIRE

Black Sea

Trebizond

Constantinople

•Erzerum

OTTOMAN EMPIRE

Mesopotamia

Baghdad

Kut

SYRIA

•Damascus

PALESTINE

Basra

Sea

•Jerusalem

•Cairo Sinai

EGYPT

ARABIA

Red Sea

Miles
0   100   200   300

0   500
Kilometres

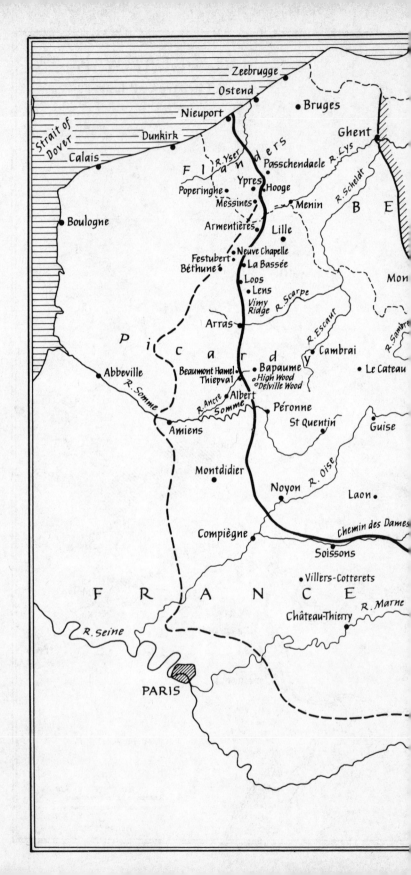

HOLLAND

Antwerp

R. Maas

Louvain

BRUSSELS

GERMANY

I U M

R. Meuse

Liège

Namur

Charleroi

Dinant

LUXEMBURG

Mézières

Sedan

R. Meuse

isne

Meuse - Argonne

Argonne Forest

Rheims

Verdun

Metz

ernay

Châlons

St Mihiel

Nancy

THE GREAT WAR
The Western Front

— — — Limit of German advance, 1914
———— Line of prolonged trench warfare
////// Final lines, November 1918

0   10   20   30 Miles

0   50 Kilometres

Troyes

I

'Honour's a name'

BEFORE THE WAR

The popularity of the work of the First World War trench poets, and even greater influence of the poets who wrote in the 1920s, have tended to blot out from public view the nature of pre-war poetry in Britain. This is hardly surprising. There had never been a war like the Great War, so the poetry that sprang directly out of it was very easily seen as 'different', and dealt with, critically, as if it had sprung up from nowhere. What came after the war had an even more profound effect. In the 1920s T.S. Eliot was launched on a career that was to make him the most influential poet of the twentieth century. Eliot, an American who took British citizenship, wrote in almost direct revolt against the simple and frequently pastoral poetry that had held sway in England until 1914. The more influential his poetry became, the more the literary establishment poured scorn on to pre-war British poetry, of which the most important part, by a wide margin, was the so-called Georgian school. Five *Georgian Poetry* anthologies were published between 1912 and 1922, under the editorship of a civil servant with private means, Edward Marsh. Post-Great War criticism, with a few honourable and notable exceptions, has been scathing about the Georgian poets. It has dismissed the movement as an enervated flicker of decaying Romanticism, trivialising nature and all else it dealt with in tired-out poetic form.

Here again, the truth is rather different. It is perfectly true that when the last *Georgian Poetry* anthology was published in 1922 it made weary reading, and showed all the signs of senile decay, but the first three anthologies were a very different story. By 1920 the war had killed many of the leading young Georgians, and the death of Rupert Brooke had knocked the stuffing out of Edward Marsh and allowed the movement to lose direction. A simple flick through the pages of a Georgian anthology reveals poets of startling poetic strength, poets such as D.H. Lawrence, Robert Graves, Siegfried Sassoon, Edmund Blunden, Walter de la Mare, Rupert Brooke, Wilfrid Gibson, James

Elroy Flecker, and Isaac Rosenberg. (Edward Thomas would have been on this list if the Georgian authors had had their way, and when Edward Marsh refused to include him they launched their own book virtually to publicise Thomas's work.) Georgian poetry is now beginning to be recognised as more than a poetic backwater, but the real nature of the poets' achievement has yet to be widely noticed. As some of the examples given below show, the Georgians could produce extremely bad poetry; so can any school of poets. They were very traditional in matters of form, and tended also to write very simply, that fact alone being enough to damn them in many literary circles nowadays. They also produced more than enough verse which dispels the often-accepted image of them as poets who hurled themselves into the war with a patriotic fervour based upon an insipid love affair with nature. They revolutionised and literalised the *content* of poetry, publishing among other things some of Graves's and Sassoon's most vicious attacks on the war. By stripping away the restrictions on what poets could write about, by demanding that poets write about only what they knew and had witnessed, and by developing an acute eye for visual detail, Georgian poetry provided an admirable training ground for the poets of the First World War. It was no accident that Owen's cry of triumph, uttered when he felt that he had achieved maturity as a poet, was 'I am held peer by the Georgians', or that two of his mentors, the two most responsible for encouraging him in his famous poems, were Georgians to the core — Siegfried Sassoon and Robert Graves. Nor was it an accident that the first major literary figures to recognise the genius of Isaac Rosenberg, and give him unstinted support and encouragement, were Lascelles Abercrombie and Gordon Bottomley, founder-figures of the Georgian poetry movement.

Rupert Brooke achieved fame through his patriotic sonnets, but was effectively a pre-war poet, summing up all that was best and worst in the Georgian movement. Some very fierce mothers protected the reputations of their poet-sons after the Great War, and none more than Mrs Brooke. Despite some noble work by Timothy Rogers, Brooke remains one of the most misrepresented figures of the Great War period, at least in the popular imagination. His relations with women were sufficient to give both him and them nervous break-downs, and even that most kind of biographers, Christopher Hassall, acknowledges that at times he teetered on the edge of total mental collapse. He appears at least to have dabbled in homosexuality, was anti-Semitic, and was a member of the Fabian Society. He loathed the same middle-classes who took him to his heart during and after the war. To many people, Brooke died too romantically* and too conveniently, and his reputation was too well protected, for the truth about him to have emerged satisfactorily. Such truth as can be discerned suggests that he was altogether a more surprising personality than his reputation might indicate.

The same could be said of many of the authors in the brief selection which follows, at least of their poems if not of their lives. Far from being obsessed with a pastoral idyll, poets such as W.H. Davies and Wilfrid Wilson Gibson show an obsession with urban casualties and the seediness of modern life. Gordon Bottomley presents a play in which there is a detailed description of body-lice crawling out of a cold, stiff corpse. With these must go an example of the other side of Georgian, and other, poetry, the inane babbling of Edmund Beale Sargant in 'The Cuckoo Wood', and Sir Henry Newbolt's 'Vitaï Lampada', a poem which suggests that massacre and a game of cricket are much the same thing.

Perhaps the most remarkable poet of all was Charles Hamilton Sorley. Whilst Rupert Brooke was raising hell and attracting a lion's share of attention, Sorley was proceeding through the English public-school system (his only volume of poems was entitled *Marlborough and Other Poems*) with considerably less fuss, and at times a great deal more insight. Sorley was killed in 1915 during the Battle of Loos. At a time when the bookshops were overflowing with slim volumes of poetry by dead soldiers, *Marlborough and Other Poems* went into several reprints, and was followed by a highly successful volume of *Letters*. Robert Graves considered Sorley to be one of only three great poets killed in the war, and his work commanded intense respect from Edmund Blunden. Sorley saw what the war would be more clearly than any other poet except Thomas Hardy. His poetry is remarkably clear and simple, but his iron-tight imagery and ability to control weird rhythms give his work a subtlety and complexity that is almost unique.

The purpose of this brief selection is merely to give a flavour of pre-war verse. I have excluded Walter de la Mare for reasons of space, hoping that his work is well-enough known already. With the exception of Sir Henry Newbolt and Sorley, all the poets in this section were published in the Georgian anthologies. It is sometimes difficult not to wonder whether some of those who have written about or referred to

---

* He received a commission in the Royal Naval Division in September 1914, and took part in the chaotic and abortive attempt to save Antwerp in October. Early in 1915 he sailed with the Division for the Dardanelles, but on 23 April died of blood poisoning (from an insect bite) on Skyros, where he is buried.

Georgian poetry ever opened one of these anthologies. These collections contain some appalling poetry, certainly, but it is hard to dismiss books which contained Rosenberg's first published work, some of Sassoon's most vitriolic anti-war poetry, and work by Robert Graves, Edmund Blunden, and John Masefield, in addition to the authors given here. Some of those authorities who deride Georgian poetry fail to recognise that virtually the only poets to give active support to Isaac Rosenberg, and the first to describe him as a genius, were those stalwarts of the Georgian movement, Lascelles Abercrombie and Gordon Bottomley. The only poet of the 'modern' movement with whom Rosenberg had any contact was Ezra Pound; his contribution to Rosenberg's career appears to have been limited to the suggestion that he should join up and fight in the Army.

Vitaï Lampada

There's a breathless hush in the Close to-night —
  Ten to make and the match to win —
A bumping pitch and a blinding light,
  An hour to play and the last man in.
And it's not for the sake of a ribboned coat,
  Or the selfish hope of a season's fame,
But his Captain's hand on his shoulder smote —
  'Play up! play up! and play the game!'

The sand of the desert is sodden red, —
  Red with the wreck of a square that broke; —
The Gatling's* jammed and the Colonel dead,
  And the regiment blind with dust and smoke.
The river of death has brimmed his banks,
  And England's far, and Honour a name,
But the voice of a schoolboy rallies the ranks:
  'Play up! play up! and play the game!'

This is the word that year by year,
  While in her place the School is set,

* Early machine-gun, employing revolving barrels driven by a hand-operated crank.

Every one of her sons must hear,
   And none that hears it dare forget.
This they all with a joyful mind
   Bear through life like a torch in flame,
And falling fling to the host behind —
   'Play up! play up! and play the game!'

SIR HENRY NEWBOLT

Death of John Rump

…It may have become apparent that personally I do not approve of John Rump. He was a failure. He might have been a thousand splendid things. He was — an English Gentleman. He might have seen — he was blind; have heard — he was deaf. Infinite chances lay about him — he was an English Gentleman.

Yet we may pity him now, lying there through that long March night, helpless in the hands of his like. In that stuffy room were no watching angels, no 'Justice and Mercy of God', no 'Death as an Emperor with all his Court'. No sublimity or solemnity of leaving this world was there; no awe and pomp of dying; but worry, heat and tangled bed-clothes; an incompetent doctor, and tired-eyed, gulping relations; injections of oxygen and God knows what; and, bared of gentility, John Rump, blue-lipped, fighting for breath, helpless and pitiable as a blind kitten in a water-butt, or an insect crushed underfoot; drugs and fuss, gasping and snivelling.

Outside, in the snow-covered town, perfectly silent under the faint approach of morning, were peace and mystery, colour and beauty and joy; things that John had never known.

Epilogue in Heaven

(Everywhere there is a subdued air of expectancy. The archangels, massed effectively at the back, are wearing scarlet for the occasion. The harps and trumpets tune up. St Cecilia waves the baton. The first semi-chorus of angels on the left sings:)

Home out of time and space,
   The wanderer is turning
      Immortal feet;

The white and eager face,
    The thirsting mouth and burning
        Eyes we'll regret, —
One that has found his grace,
    One that has staked his yearning,
        One out of imperfection grown complete.

(Second semi-chorus on the right)

What will he bear with him, what will he bring to us
    From the world where laughter and love are rife,
Great dreams to report to us, songs to sing to us,
    Spoils well won from the heart of the strife?
Will he come like a glad-eyed silent lover,
    Or slow and sorry that all is over,
Or sudden and splendid and swift as the spring to us,
    Fresh and laughing from lovely life?

(Full chorus)

As the ending to a story,
    As the light dies in the West
        When the birds turn home at even,
            Glad and splendid will he come,
He the victor into glory,
    He the weary to his rest,
        The immortal to his heaven,
            The wanderer home.

FIRST SERAPH (*pointing downwards*)   I see a speck immediately below.

MANY LITTLE CHERUBS   Bravo! Bravo! Bravo!

SECOND SERAPH   I see it too. A black speck. Very far!

CHERUBS   Huzza! Huzza! Huzza!

THIRD SERAPH (*excitedly*)   'Tis him! 'Tis him! upon his upward way!

CHERUBS   Hurray! Hurray! Hurray!

GOD (*rising*)
    I do espy him like a *fretful midge*,
    The while his wide and alternating vans

Winnow the buxom air. With flight serene
He wings amidst the watery Pleiades;
Now Leo feels his passage, and the Twins;
Orion now, and that unwieldy girth
Hight Scorpio; as when a trader bound
For Lamda or the isle of Mogador,
Freighted with ambergris and stilbrium,
And what rich odours ...

(The remaining 127 lines are lost in the increasing hubbub. Enter, from below on the left, JOHN RUMP in top-hat, frockcoat etc., bearing an umbrella. He stands impassive in the middle.)

GOD
  John Rump, of Balham, Leeds, and Canterbury,
  Why are you wearing hideous black clothes?

RUMP
  Because I am an English Gentleman.

GOD
  John Rump, we gave you life and all its wonder.
  What splendid things have you got to tell?

RUMP
  God, I have been an English Gentleman.

GOD
  Infinite splendour has been in your power;
  John Rump, what have you got to show for life?

RUMP
  God, I have been an English Gentleman.

GOD (*rising angrily*)
  Was it for this we sent you to the world,
  And gave you life and knowledge, made you man,
  Crowned you with glory? You could have worked and laughed,
  Sung, loved, and kissed, made all the world a dream,
  Found infinite beauty in a leaf or word ...
  ... Perish eternally, you and your hat!

RUMP (*not wincing*)
  You long-haired aesthetes, get you out of heaven!

I, John Rump, I, an English Gentleman,
Do not believe in you and all your gushing.
I am John Rump, this is my hat, and this
My umbrella. I stand here for sense,
Invincible, inviolable, eternal,
For safety, regulations, paving-stones,
Street lamps, police, and bijou-residences
Semi-detached. I stand for sanity,
Comfort, content, prosperity, top-hats,
Alcohol, collars, meat. Tariff Reform
Means higher wages and more work for all.

(As he speaks, GOD and the seraphic multitude grow faint, mistier and mistier, become ineffectually waving shadows, and vanish. The floor of Heaven rocks ... the thrones and the glassy sea ... all has vanished. JOHN RUMP remains, still and expressionless, leaning on his umbrella, growing larger and larger, infinitely menacing, filling the universe, blotting out the stars ...)

RUPERT BROOKE+

Heaven

Fish (fly-replete, in depth of June,
Dawdling away their wat'ry noon)
Ponder deep wisdom, dark or clear,
Each secret fishy hope or fear.
Fish say, they have their Stream and Pond;
But is there anything Beyond?
This life cannot be All, they swear,
For how unpleasant, if it were!
One may not doubt that, somehow, Good
Shall come of Water and of Mud;
And, sure, the reverent eye must see
A Purpose in Liquidity.
We darkly know, by Faith we cry,
The future is not Wholly Dry.
Mud unto mud! — Death eddies near —
Not here the appointed End, not here!
But somewhere, beyond Space and Time,

Is wetter water, slimier slime!
And there (they trust) there swimmeth One
Who swam ere rivers were begun,
Immense, of fishy form and mind,
Squamous, omnipotent, and kind;
And under that Almighty Fin,
The littlest fish may enter in.
Oh! never fly conceals a hook,
Fish say, in the Eternal Brook,
But more than mundane weeds are there,
And mud, celestially fair;
Fat caterpillars drift around,
And Paradisal grubs are found;
Unfading moths, immortal flies,
And the worm that never dies.
And in that Heaven of all their wish,
There shall be no more land, say fish.

RUPERT BROOKE+

Fragment

Isn't ligature — or is it ligament? — a lovely word?

'Is it prudent? is it Pure?
To go and break a ligature?'

'With lissom ligament
My lovely one she went
And trod the street
On quiet feet.'

RUPERT BROOKE+

Fragment

My lips (the inconstancy of man!)
Are yours no more. The legs that ran
Each dewy morn their love to wake,
Are now a steak, are now a steak! ...

The limbs that erstwhile charmed your sight,
Are now a savage's delight;
The ear that heard your whispered vow
Is one of many *entrées* now;
Broiled are the arms in which you clung
And devilled is the angelic tongue; ...
And oh! my anguish as I see
A Black Man gnaw your favourite knee!
Of the two eyes that were your ruin,
One now observes the other stewing.

RUPERT BROOKE+

The Sale of Saint Thomas
(Extract)

They say the land is full of apes, which have
Their own gods and worship; how ghastly, this! —
That demons (for it must be so) should build,
In mockery of man's upward faith, the souls
Of monkeys, those lewd mammets of mankind,
Into a dreadful farce of adoration!
And flies! a land of flies! where the hot soil
Foul with ceaseless decay steams into flies!
So thick they pile themselves in the air above
Their meal of filth, they seem like breathing heaps
Of formless life mounded upon the earth;
And buzzing always like the pipes and strings
Of solemn music made for sorcerers. —
I abhor flies, — to see them stare upon me

28

Out of their little faces of gibbous eyes;
To feel the dry cool skin of their bodies alight
Perching upon my lips! — O yea, a dream,
A dream of impious obscene Satan, this
Monstrous frenzy of life, the Indian being!
And there are men in the dream! What men are they?
I've heard, naught relishes their brains so much
As to tie down a man and tease his flesh
Infamously, until a hundred pains
Hound the desiring life out of his body,
Filling his nerves with such a fearful zest
That the soul overstrained shatters beneath it.
Must I preach God to these murderous hearts?
I would my lot had fallen to go and dare
Death from the silent dealing of Northern cold! —

LASCELLES ABERCROMBIE

King Lear's Wife
(Extract)

THE YOUNGER WOMAN
   Ah, you have always been a friend to me:
   Many's the time I have said I did not know
   How I could even have lived but for your kindness.
(The ELDER WOMAN draws down the bedclothes from the Queen's
body, loosens them from the bed, and throws them on the floor.)

THE ELDER WOMAN
   Pull her feet straight: is your mind wandering?
(She commences to fold the bedclothes, singing as she moves about.)
   A louse crept out of my lady's shift —
   Ahumm, Ahumm, Ahee—
   Crying 'Oi! Oi! We are turned adrift;
   The lady's bosom is cold and stiffed,
   And her arm-pit's cold for me.'
(While the ELDER WOMAN sings, the YOUNGER WOMAN straightens
the Queen's feet and ties them together, draws the pillows from under
her head, gathers her hair in one hand and knots it roughly; then she

loosens her nightgown, revealing a jewel hung on a cord round the Queen's neck.)

THE ELDER WOMAN (*running to the vacant side of the bed*)
    What have you there? Give it to me.

THE YOUNGER WOMAN   It is mine: I found it.

THE ELDER WOMAN   Leave it.

THE YOUNGER WOMAN   Let go.

THE ELDER WOMAN   Leave it, I say.
    Will you not? Will you not? An eye for a jewel, then!
(She attacks the face of the YOUNGER WOMAN with her disengaged hand.)

THE YOUNGER WOMAN
    Aie! Aie! Aie! Old thief! You are always thieving!
    You stole a necklace on your wedding day:
    You could not bear a child, you stole your daughter:
    You stole a shroud the morn your husband died:
    Last week you stole the Princess Regan's comb ...
(She stumbles into the chair by the bed, and, throwing her loose sleeves over her head, rocks herself and moans.)

THE ELDER WOMAN (*resuming her clothes-folding and her song*)
    'The lady's linen's no longer neat;' —
    Ahumm, Ahumm, Ahee —
    'Her savour is neither warm nor sweet;
    It's close for two in a winding sheet,
    And lice are too good for worms to eat;
    So here's no place for me.'

                                            GORDON BOTTOMLEY

A Fleeting Passion

Thou shalt not laugh, thou shalt not romp,
    Let's grimly kiss with bated breath;
As quietly and solemnly
    As Life when it is kissing Death.

Now in the silence of the grave,
　　My hand is squeezing that soft breast;
While thou dost in such passion lie,
　　It mocks me with its look of rest.

But when the morning comes at last,
　　And we must part, our passions cold,
You'll think of some new feather, scarf
　　　　To buy with my small piece of gold;
And I'll be dreaming of green lanes,
　　Where little things with beating hearts
Hold shining eyes between the leaves,
　　Till men with horses pass, and carts.

　　　　　　　　　　　W.H. DAVIES

The Bird of Paradise

Here comes Kate Summers, who, for gold,
　　Takes any man to bed:
'You knew my friend, Nell Barnes,' she said;
　　'You knew Nell Barnes — she's dead.

'Nell Barnes was bad on all you men,
　　Unclean, a thief as well;
Yet all my life I have not found
　　A better friend than Nell.

'So I sat at her side at last,
　　For hours, till she was dead;
And yet she had no sense at all
　　Of any word I said.

'For all her cry but came to this —
　　"Not for the world! Take care:
Don't touch that bird of paradise,
　　Perched on the bed-post there!"

'I asked her would she like some grapes,
　　Some damsons ripe and sweet;

31

A custard made with new-laid eggs,
    Or tender fowl to eat.

'I promised I would follow her,
    To see her in her grave;
And buy a wreath with borrowed pence,
    If nothing I could save.

'Yet still her cry but came to this —
    "Not for the world! Take care:
Don't touch that bird of paradise,
    Perched on the bed-post there!"'

W.H. DAVIES

The Heap of Rags

One night when I went down
Thames' side, in London Town,
A heap of rags saw I,
And sat me down close by.
That thing could shout and bawl,
But showed no face at all;
When any steamer passed
And blew a loud shrill blast,
That heap of rags would sit
And make a sound like it;
When struck the clock's deep bell,
It made those peals as well.
When winds did moan around,
It mocked them with that sound;
When all was quiet, it
Fell into a strange fit;
Would sigh, and moan and roar,
It laughed, and blessed, and swore.
Yet that poor thing, I know,
Had neither friend nor foe;
Its blessing or its curse
Made no one better or worse.

I left it in that place —
The thing that showed no face,
Was it a man that had
Suffered till he went mad?
So many showers and not
One rainbow in the lot;
Too many bitter fears
To make a pearl from tears.

W.H. DAVIES

Geraniums

Stuck in a bottle on the window-sill,
In the cold gaslight burning gaily red
Against the luminous blue of London night,
These flowers are mine: while somewhere out of sight
In some black-throated alley's stench and heat,
Oblivious of the racket of the street,
A poor old weary woman lies in bed.

Broken with lust and drink, blear-eyed and ill,
Her battered bonnet nodding on her head,
From a dark arch she clutched my sleeve and said:
'I've sold no bunch to-day, nor touched a bite ...
Son, buy six-pennorth; and 'twill mean a bed.'

So blazing gaily red
Against the luminous deeps
Of starless London night,
They burn for my delight:
While somewhere, snug in bed,
A worn old woman sleeps.

And yet to-morrow will these blooms be dead
With all their lively beauty; and to-morrow
May end the light lusts and the heavy sorrow
Of that old body with the nodding head.
The last oath muttered, the last pint drained deep,

33

She'll sink, as Cleopatra sank, to sleep;
Nor need to barter blossoms for a bed.

WILFRID WILSON GIBSON

Service of All the Dead

Between the avenues of cypresses,
All in their scarlet cloaks, and surplices
Of linen, go the chaunting choristers,
The priests in gold and black, the villagers.

And all along the path to the cemetery
The round, dark heads of men crowd silently,
And black-scarved faces of women-folk, wistfully
Watch at the banner of death, and the mystery.

And at the foot of a grave a father stands
With sunken head, and forgotten, folded hands;
And at the foot of a grave a woman kneels
With pale shut face, and neither hears nor feels

The coming of the chaunting choristers
Between the avenues of cypresses,
The silence of the many villagers,
The candle-flames beside the surplices.

D.H. LAWRENCE

The Bull
(Extract)

See an old unhappy bull,
Sick in soul and body both,
Slouching in the undergrowth
Of the forest beautiful,
Banished from the herd he led,
Bulls and cows a thousand head.

Cranes and gaudy parrots go
Up and down the burning sky;
Tree-top cats purr drowsily
In the dim day-green below;
And troops of monkeys, nutting, some,
All disputing, go and come;

And things abominable sit
Picking offal buck or swine,
On the mess and over it
Burnished flies and beetles shine,
And spiders big as bladders lie
Under hemlocks ten foot high;

And a dotted serpent curled
Round and round and round a tree,
Yellowing its greenery,
Keeps a watch on all the world,
All the world and this old bull
In the forest beautiful.

Bravely by his fall he came:
One he led, a bull of blood
Newly come to lustihood,
Fought and put his prince to shame,
Snuffed and pawed the prostrate head
Tameless even while it bled.

There they left him, every one,
Left him there without a lick,
Left him for the birds to pick,
Left him there for carrion,
Vilely from their bosom cast
Wisdom, worth and love at last.

RALPH HODGSON

A Call To Action

I

A thousand years have passed away,
    Cast back your glances on the scene,
Compare this England of to-day
    With England as she once has been.

Fast beat the pulse of living then:
    The hum of movement, throb of war
The rushing mighty sound of men
    Reverberated loud and far.

They girt their loins up and they trod
    The path of danger, rough and high;
For Action, Action was their god,
    'Be up and doing' was their cry.

A thousand years have passed away;
    The sounds of life are running low;
The world is sleeping out her day;
    The day is dying — be it so.

A thousand years have passed amain;
    The sands of life are running thin;
Thought is our leader — Thought is vain;
    Speech is our goddess — Speech is sin.

II

It needs no thought to understand,
    No speech to tell, nor sight to see
That there has come upon our land
    The curse of Inactivity.

We do not see the vital point
    That 'tis the eighth, most deadly, sin

To wail, 'The world is out of joint' —
　　And not attempt to put it in.

We see the swollen stream of crime
　　Flow hourly past us, thick and wide;
We gaze with interest for a time,
　　And pass by on the other side.

We see the tide of human sin
　　Rush roaring past our very door,
And scarcely one man plunges in
　　To drag the drowning to the shore.

We, dull and dreamy, stand and blink,
　　Forgetting glory, strength and pride,
Half-listless watchers on the brink,
　　Half-ruined victims of the tide.

III

We question, answer, make defence,
　　We sneer, we scoff, we criticise,
We wail and moan our decadence,
　　Enquire, investigate, surmise;

We preach and prattle, peer and pry
　　And fit together two and two:
We ponder, argue, shout, swear, lie —
　　We will not, for we cannot, DO.

Pale puny soldiers of the pen,
　　Absorbed in this your inky strife,
Act as of old, when men were men,
　　England herself and life yet life.

CHARLES HAMILTON SORLEY+
October 1912

Barbury Camp

We burrowed night and day with tools of lead,
Heaped the bank up and cast it in a ring
And hurled the earth above. And Caesar said,
'Why, it is excellent. I like the thing.'
We, who are dead,
Made it, and wrought, and Caesar liked the thing.

And here we strove, and here we felt each vein
Ice-bound, each limb fast-frozen, all night long.
And here we held communion with the rain
That lashed us into manhood with its thong,
Cleansing through pain.
And the wind visited us and made us strong.

Up from around us, numbers without name,
Strong men and naked, vast, on either hand
Pressing us in, they came. And the wind came
And bitter rain, turning grey all the land.
That was our game,
To fight with men and storms, and it was grand.

For many days we fought them, and our sweat
Watered the grass, making it spring up green,
Blooming for us. And, if the wind was wet,
Our blood wetted the wind, making it keen
With the hatred
And wrath and courage that our blood had been.

So, fighting men and winds and tempests, hot
With joy and hate and battle-lust, we fell
Where we fought. And God said, 'Killed at last
    then! What!
Ye that are too strong for heaven, too clean for hell
(God said) stir not.
This be your heaven, or, if ye will, your hell.'

So again we fight and wrestle, and again
Hurl the earth up and cast it in a ring.
But when the wind comes up, driving the rain
(Each rain-drop a fiery steed), and mists rolling
Up from the plain,
This wild procession, this impetuous thing,

Holds us amazed. We mount the wind-cars, then
Whip up the steeds and drive through all the world,
Searching to find somewhere some brethren,
Sons of the winds and waters of the world.
We, who were men,
Have sought, and found no men in all this world.

Wind, that has blown here always ceaselessly,
Bringing, if any man can understand,
Might to the mighty, freedom to the free;
Wind, that has caught us, cleansed us, made us
    grand,
Wind that is we
(We that were men) — make men in all this land,

That so may live and wrestle and hate that when
They fall at last exultant, as we fell,
And come to God, God may say, 'Do you come then
Mildly enquiring, is it heaven or hell?
Why! Ye were men!
Back to your winds and rain. Be these your heaven
    and hell!'

CHARLES HAMILTON SORLEY+
24 March 1913

Stones

This field is almost white with stones
    That cumber all its thirsty crust.
And underneath, I know, are bones,
    And all around is death and dust.

And if you love a livelier hue —
　　O, if you love the youth of year,
When all is clean and green and new,
　　Depart. There is no summer here.

Albeit, to me there lingers yet
　　In this forbidding stony dress
The impotent and dim regret
　　For some forgotten restlessness.

Dumb, imperceptibly astir,
　　These relics of an ancient race,
These men, in whom the dead bones were
　　Still fortifying their resting-place.

Their field of life was white with stones;
　　Good fruit to earth they never brought.
O, in these bleached and buried bones
　　Was neither love nor faith nor thought.

But like the wind in this bleak place,
　　Bitter and bleak and sharp they grew,
And bitterly they ran their race,
　　A brutal, bad, unkindly crew:

Souls like the dry earth, hearts like stone,
　　Brains like that barren bramble-tree:
Stern, sterile, senseless, mute, unknown —
　　But bold, O, bolder far than we!

　　　　　　　　CHARLES HAMILTON SORLEY+
　　　　　　　　　　14 July 1913

Rooks

There, where the rusty iron lies,
　　The rooks are cawing all the day.
Perhaps no man, until he dies,
　　Will understand them, what they say.

The evening makes the sky like clay.
    The slow wind waits for night to rise.
The world is half-content. But they

Still trouble all the trees with cries,
    That know, and cannot put away,
The yearning to the soul that flies
    From day to night, from night to day.

CHARLES HAMILTON SORLEY+
21 June 1913

The Cuckoo Wood

Cuckoo, are you calling me,
Or is it a voice of wizardry?
In these woodlands I am lost,
From glade to glade of flowers tost.
Seven times I held my way,
And seven times the voice did say,
Cuckoo! Cuckoo! No man could
Issue from this underwood,
Half of green and half of brown,
Unless he laid his senses down.
Only let him chance to see
The snows of the anemone
Heaped above its greenery;
Cuckoo! Cuckoo! No man could
Issue from the master wood.

Magic paths there are that cross;
Some beset with jewelled moss
And boughs all bare; where others run,
Bluebells bathe in mist and sun
Past a clearing filled with clumps
Of primrose round the nutwood stumps;
All as gay as gay can be,
And bordered with dog-mercury
The wizard flower, the wizard green,

Like a Persian carpet seen.
Brown, dead bracken lies between,
And wrinkled leaves, whence fronds of fern
Still untwist and upward turn.
Cuckoo! Cuckoo! No man could
Issue from this wizard wood,
Half of green, and half of brown,
Unless he laid his senses down.

Seven times I held my way
Where new heaps of brushwood lay,
All with withies loosely bound,
And never heard a human sound.
Yet men have toiled and men have rested
By yon hurdles darkly-breasted,
Woven in and woven out,
Piled four-square, and turned about
To show their white and sharpened stakes
Like teeth of hounds or fangs of snakes.
The men are homeward sped, for none
Loves silence and a sinking sun.
Cuckoo! Cuckoo! Woodmen know
Souls are lost that hear it so,
Seven times upon the wind,
To lull the watch-dogs of the mind.

EDMUND BEALE SARGANT

II

'We'll smash old Krupps!'

EARLY DAYS

Everywhere men were stirred by righteous passion, and thrust eagerly forward for sacrifice. Rupert Brooke spoke for an entire generation: 'Now, God be thanked Who has matched us with His hour.' He died soon afterwards, from the bite of a mosquito.

A.J.P. TAYLOR

On 28 June 1914, Archduke Francis Ferdinand, heir to the throne of Austria-Hungary, was shot dead in the streets of Sarajevo by a Serbian student. On 28 July Austria declared war on Serbia. Russia began to mobilise against Austria to support her Serbian allies. Austria called on Germany for support. On 3 August large German forces invaded Belgium, following thereby the Schlieffen Plan, which called for a massive thrust at France through Belgium in the early stages of a European war. On 4 August 1914 Britain declared war against Germany and her allies, in support of Belgium.

Over 6,000,000 men were mobilised by the European powers in the opening months of the First World War. The British Expeditionary Force which was sent over to France immediately war broke out numbered between 80,000 and 100,000 men. These were the 'Old Contemptibles', the pre-war, professional, Regular British Army, which was all but extinguished by the end of 1914. In Britain, 500,000 men volunteered for military service in the first month of Kitchener's appeal for volunteers. In the course of the war over 3,000,000 British men were to enlist voluntarily.

In 1914 the British Expeditionary Force went to war with two machine-guns per battalion. By 1918 each battalion had as standard issue over forty machine-guns.

23 August 1914:   British Expeditionary Force (two corps) meets six divisions of the German Army at the Battle of Mons. British withdraw; beginning of the Retreat from Mons.

43

26 August 1914: Lieutenant-General Sir Horace Smith-Dorrien disobeys orders for his II Corps to retreat because of risk of annihilation, and fights Battle of Le Cateau. German advance held up for twenty-four hours. British losses so far: 18,729 officers and men. Although his action has saved the Allied line, Smith-Dorrien's disobedience is held against him.

3-9 September 1914: Battle of the Marne. Germans beaten back by great French attack with BEF in support, retire to the line of the River Aisne, and start to dig trenches.

13-28 September 1914: First Battle of the Aisne. French and British forces make further assaults after the Marne, but despite some gains a stalemate soon develops. The opposing armies dig in and attempt to outflank each other, resulting in the 'Race to the Sea' — in the end, the trench system stretches from the Swiss frontier to the Channel Ports.

19 October-
21 November 1914: First Battle of Ypres. Number of British troops from Haig's I Corps killed, wounded, missing, or taken prisoner in excess of 13,000 men as repeated German attacks are driven off. Total German casualties at this stage of the war estimated at 250,000. The average strength of a BEF battalion, in August nearly 1,000 strong, is now down to one officer and thirty men surviving unwounded. British now hold a salient around Ypres, jutting out towards the German positions.

22 April-24 May 1915: Second Battle of Ypres. Germans launch a fresh offensive, using poison gas for the first time, which helps breach the British line. Canadian troops hold on, despite a second gas attack (and despite having no gas-masks), and though the salient shrinks repeated German assaults are driven off. Smith-Dorrien, who has ordered a 'voluntary retirement' in order to hold the position, which saves the line, is removed from his command with the words "Orace, you're for 'ome'. His successor, Plumer, carries out Smith-Dorrien's plan to good effect.

25 April 1915:	Beginning of combined British, Anzac and French operations at Gallipoli.
7 May 1915:	British liner *Lusitania* is torpedoed and sunk without warning off the Irish coast. 1,201 drown, including 158 Americans.
25 September-15 October 1915:	Battle of Loos. Casualties: 50,000 British (including the poet Charles Hamilton Sorley); 140,000 Germans; 190,000 French. The British use poison gas for the first time, but despite considerable early success, German counter-attacks restore the line.
December 1915-January 1916:	Gallipoli beaches evacuated.
January 1916:	Compulsory military service for single men between the ages of 18 and 40 introduced in Great Britain, effective from February.
21 February-18 December 1916:	Siege of Verdun. A series of attacks, counter-attacks and outflanking movements, always against the background of massive artillery battles, which becomes the bloodiest engagement in history and the longest battle of the Great War. French casualties are 542,000, German 434,000. Verdun holds — just — which probably saves France.
1 July 1916:	Battle of the Somme. Final casualties: British 420,000 (57,000 on first day of offensive); French 200,000; Germans 450,000. The battle eventually peters out in November, by which time the British advance, at its greatest, is some seven miles. 1 July 1916, in terms of casualties, has no parallel in British military history.

Poetry was an immensely popular medium in 1914; in the movement's heyday, a *Georgian Poetry* anthology could expect to sell over 20,000 hardback copies. On a less intellectual level, music-hall songs and an emphasis on reading and reciting for home entertainment had strengthened rather than interrupted the tradition of poetry as popular entertainment, which, in earlier centuries, had been symbolised by the semi-doggerel ballads widely available in the streets of London and other cities.

It is not surprising, therefore, that poets in 1914 rose to the challenge of the war by producing a large quantity of more-or-less patriotic verse. There are wide variations in quality and style. At ground level there were the soldiers' marching songs, often based upon music hall 'hits', which responded to the outbreak of war with a cheerful and frequently profane optimism. One famous German general revelled in the name von Kluck; it did not take the members of the British Expeditionary Force long to work out in verse what they were going to do to him. Higher on the ladder of intellect, if not of freshness, were the poets who responded to the war rather in the manner of a military brass band, allowing themselves a style that was both thumpingly rhythmical and brazen in its loudness. Then came the most famous of all, Rupert Brooke. His patriotic sonnets have been criticised both for the sentiments they express, and for the fact that, according to some readings, they appear to be about Rupert Brooke more than they are about England. Given the bellowing roars of outraged moral justification that typify the work of some other poets, the personal element in Brooke's sonnets might be seen as no bad thing. Whatever else they may be, Brooke's sonnets sum up admirably a mood that was felt by many people when war broke out. Authors as different as Rudyard Kipling, Isaac Rosenberg, Julian Grenfell, Thomas Hardy, Rupert Brooke and Edward Thomas all produced poems that in one way or another either welcomed the war, or gave it tacit approval. (Kipling's approval was not to outlast the death in action of his own son*; his 'Epitaphs of the War' are among the most bitter of short war verses.) Running like a thread through many of these poems is the feeling that somehow the war was a cleansing, purifying exercise. For Brooke the war may have at last offered certainty and direction to someone whose capacity to inflict injury on himself outweighed the damage he could do to others; for many of the others the war seemed to offer at last an ideal which could be embraced totally, a release from thought. It was as if the country had been bored with peace.

By no means all the poetry produced in the early years of the war supported it, however. Charles Sorley was more clear-sighted than most. He had actually been in Germany when war broke out, and cast

---

*Kipling's only son, John, was so short-sighted that only his famous father's influence secured him a commission in the Irish Guards. After his death, Kipling wrote:

'My son was killed while laughing at some jest. I would I knew/What it was, and it might serve me in a time when jests are few.' The truth, had Kipling known it, was more tragic. His son was seen by his comrades stumbling from the battlefield with a wound in his mouth, and in tears. He was never seen again, presumably buried or atomised by a shell.

an acutely objective eye over the whole business. Although, so far as I am aware, it has never been commented on, it seems highly likely that Sorley's sonnet 'When You See Millions of the Mouthless Dead' may have been written as a direct rebuttal of Brooke's patriotic sonnets. Sorley was certainly familiar with Brooke's work, and found himself very much at odds with the sentiments Brooke expressed in the patriotic sonnets.

In the summer of 1916 the product of Kitchener's recruitment drive, the New Army, was flung against the German lines on the Somme, with appalling casualties and minimal gains. This battle is often seen as the turning-point in the war, with disillusion and frustration rapidly setting in after it. It is a view which is sometimes more convenient than truthful. The offensives (and there had been many of them) mounted before July 1916 had been just as fruitless and just as painful as the Somme itself; it was merely that rather more men were involved on the Somme. If anything, conditions in the trenches had been worse in the early years of the war, for the Germans had been able to choose the higher, and therefore drier, ground when they had retreated to the Aisne in the autumn of 1914, and the British had not dug or built for a lengthy stay in the trenches. There is, however, a difference between the poetry written before 1916 and that written after it, although this is sometimes less than might be imagined. One reason for the difference is that many of the men who had been practising poets before the war did not start to see active service in the trenches until late 1915 or early 1916, and it is only then that the voice of middle-class protest begins to be heard at its strongest. Up until then there had been plenty of poetry that focused on the horrors of war, but much of its aim was accuracy rather than actual protest. It is doubtful whether a great deal of this poetry will ever rank as great literature. Clumsily, and with varying degrees of skill, soldiers and others in the war attempted in poetry to come to terms with what they experienced. Many turned to colloquial language and the monologue form of expression, perhaps following the example of John Masefield* before the war. Others ignored what we have come to see as the main features of the war, and wrote instead about essentials — drill, a full stomach, rum, tobacco, and tea. An accurate picture of the First World War recognises that warfare is long periods of boredom punctuated by spasms of intense terror. Over

---

*Masefield was an observer during part of the Somme battle, and at other times. His resultant writings — *The Old Front Line, Gallipoli* etc — sometimes take the form of mild propaganda, to which his letters give the lie.

those long periods* a soldier's happiness could be dictated by the quality of his rations, and above all by the staples, food, tobacco and rum, which did more to sustain the average front-line soldier than any protective jerkin or knitted comfort from home. Isaac Rosenberg devoted more space in his letters to complaining about his feet or begging for chocolate than he did complaining about being under fire. Charles Sorley seemed to be totally fixated by food, both before the war and during it. Underpinning these basic essentials was the comradeship that was perhaps the most binding and lasting feature of all in the Great War. G.K. Chesterton stated that the English were distinguishable from all other European races by their weakness for sentimentality, and there is plenty of that in the selection below. Yet in its own way the feelings expressed about a lost comrade or even a wounded German can be as moving as better poetry written in a finer style. A major effect of the war on the front-line soldier was to raise in importance simple things. A book such as *The Great War and Modern Memory* by Paul Fussell tells us that the First World War launched savage irony into our society, smashed faith, and taught the world to see betrayal and incompetence on top of, as well as under, every stone. For many people it was like that; for many it was not, and both view-points are given below.

It is difficult to write about some of the less well-known poets of the First World War without patronising them, but a significant quantity of what might be termed 'military verse' continued to be produced throughout the war. Military verse ignored the larger issues, viewed officers and the conduct of the war with healthy contempt, and persisted in seeing humour wherever and whenever it could be found. Sometimes the poetry printed in official or semi-official magazines, such as *The Listening Post*, itself patronises the soldiers and the Army, and is often written in a hearty, all-the-Tommies-are-so-marvellously-working-class-and-funny mode. Yet even populist publications can contain flashes of genuine humour and insight.

'Criticism' has sometimes been scathing — knowing what it now knows about the real nature of the war — about poetry which saw the carnage of the Western Front in terms of heroic sacrifice, honour or glory. There is certainly a strong body of poetry from the early years of the war which continues in the vein set by Sir Henry Newbolt's

---

*There is a popular notion that an infantryman spent his entire time in the front line, until relieved by death, wounds, leave or transfer. In fact, an infantryman was supposed to spend a week in the front line, a week in the reserve trenches, and a week at rest behind the lines, although the front-line tours, especially during offensives, could be and frequently were extended.

'Vitaï Lampada', seeing war as a continuation of cricket, and seeking to clap the English on the back for having been so clever as to invent cricket, because it trained men to throw grenades. Sometimes poetry such as this is distasteful, but distasteful or not it says a great deal about the genuinely held attitudes of many of those who went to war in 1914. At other times, criticism forgets what it is like to lose a husband, friend, or brother. Those who suffered savage losses in their circle of family or friends, and who responded by praising sacrifice and humour, were sometimes uttering a cry of agony as deep as those who used the occasion to damn war and pour out bitterness. It is merely that their anguish sought relief in the faith of that loss being in a good cause.

Major Owen Rutter's 'The Song of Tiadatha' is one of the great neglected classics of the war. Written by a serving officer, its gentle mockery, its warmth and sympathy, and its ability to produce flashes of sharp savagery, make it unique. The Tired Arthur who sits at the centre of the poem can appear at times to be Rupert Brooke's John Rump, at other times the officer Sassoon addresses in 'To Any Dead Officer'. Most of all he appears human, and instantly recognisable.

Occasionally I have included poems in this section that were written during or after 1916, when they seem to provide an interesting point of comparison with earlier work. Two examples are Owen's 'The Show' and Sassoon's 'Night on the Convoy'.

Joining Up
From '*The Song of Tiadatha*'

Then came war, and Tiadatha
Read his papers every morning
Read the posters on the hoardings,
Read 'Your King and Country want you.'
  'I must go,' said Tiadatha,
Toying with his devilled kidneys,
'Do my bit and join the Army.'
So he hunted up a great-aunt,
Who knew someone in the Service,
Found himself in time gazetted
To a temporary commission
In the 14th Royal Dudshires.

Straightway Tiadatha hied him
To the shop of Bope and Pradley,
Having seen their thrilling adverts
In the Tube and in the *Tatler*.
Pradley sold him all he needed,
Bope a lot of things he didn't,
Pressed upon him socks and puttees,
Haversacks and water-bottles.
Made him tunics for the winter,
Made him tunics for the summer,
And some very baggy breeches.
There he chose his cap of khaki,
Very light and very floppy
(Rather like a tam-ó-shanter),
And a supple chestnut Sam Browne,
Quite a pleasant thing in Sam Brownes,
Rather new but very supple.

Many pounds spent Tiadatha
On valises, baths and camp beds,
Spent on wash-hand stands and kit bags,

Macs and British warms and great-coats,
And a gent's complete revolver.
Then he went to Piccadilly,
Mr Wing, of Piccadilly,
Where he ordered ties and shirtings,
Cream and coffee ties and shirtings,
Ordered socks and underclothing,
Putting down the lot to Father.
Compass, torch and boots and glasses
All of these sought Tiadatha;
All day boys with loads were streaming
To and from the flat in Duke Street,
Like a chain of ants hard at it
Storing rations for the winter.

'One thing more,' cried Tiadatha,
'One thing more ere I am perfect.
I must have a sword to carry
In a jolly leather scabbard.'
So he called the son of Wilkin,
Wilkin's son who dwelt in Pall Mall,
Bade him make a sword and scabbard.
And the mighty son of Wilkin
Made a sword for Tiadatha,
From the truest steel he made it,
Slim and slender as a maiden,
Sharper than a safety razor,
Sighed a little as he made it,
Knowing well that Tiadatha
Probably would never use it.

Then at last my Tiadatha
Sallied forth to join the Dudshires,
Dressed in khaki, quite a soldier,
Floppy cap and baggy breeches,
Round his waist the supple Sam Browne,
At his side the sword and scabbard,
Took salutes from private soldiers
And saluted Sergeant-Majors

(Who were very much embarrassed),
And reported at Headquarters
Of the 14th Royal Dudshires.

Even as a fish whose lifetime
Has been spent in pleasant waters,
Shady waters of a river,
Feels when by some turn of fortune
He gets plopped into a cistern
At a comic dime museum,
Finds himself among strange fishes,
Finds his happy freedom vanished,
Even so felt Tiadatha
On the day he joined the Dudshires.
But he pulled himself together,
Found the Adjutant, saluted,
Saying briefly, 'Please I've come, sir.'
Such was Tiadatha's joining.

MAJOR OWEN RUTTER

Rumour
From '*The Song of Tiadatha*'

In the mighty British Army
Rumour is the only issue
That arrives at units larger
Than it leaves the Base Supply Park.
Up it comes without an indent
(Possibly in lieu of lime-juice),
Heaven only knows its maker;
Like a toy balloon it swells up,
Gently growing big and bigger;
At the Dump the Mr Knowalls
Have a blow to make it fatter,
Pass it on to Transport drivers,
Who in their turn puff their hardest,
Make it change its shape a little,

Hand it over with the rations.
Then the minions of the Q.M.
Do their little bit to help it,
After which the Sergeant-Major
Takes a lusty breath to fix it,
Sends it up into the trenches
As a full-blown army rumour.

MAJOR OWEN RUTTER

The two poems which follow show varieties of jingoistic tub-thumping. It should be no surprise that one of these comes from so fine a poet as James Elroy Flecker; very many poets had work such as these buried in their lockers by the end of the war. Of all the great poets of the war, only Charles Sorley and, to a lesser extent, Edward Thomas and Isaac Rosenberg, let their intelligence lead them to a view of the war that was in any way possessed of foresight. Even Rosenberg, in 'The Dead Heroes', shared and showed the sense of relief that was common amongst poets at the outbreak of the war. Like Rupert Brooke, Rosenberg was not immune to the lure of a 'cleansing' war.

Untitled

We mean to thrash these Prussian Pups,
We'll bag their ships, we'll smash old Krupps,*
We loathe them all, the dirty swine,
We'll drown the whole lot in the Rhine.

ANONYMOUS

God Save the King

God save our gracious King,
Nation and State and King,
    God save the King!
Grant him the Peace divine,

* German armaments manufacturer.

53

But if his Wars be Thine
Flash on our fighting line
   Victory's Wing!

Thou in his suppliant hands
Hast placed such Mighty Lands:
   Save thou our King!
As once from Golden Skies
Rebels with flaming eyes,
So the King's Enemies
   Doom Thou and fling!

Mountains that break the night
Holds he by eagle right
   Stretching far Wing!
Dawn lands for Youth to reap,
Dim lands where Empires sleep,
His! And the Lion Deep
   Roars for the King.

But most these few dear miles
Of sweetly-meadowed Isles, —
   England all Spring;
Scotland that by the marge
Where the blank North doth charge
Hears Thy Voice loud and large,
   Save, and their King!

Grace on the golden Dales
Of Thine Old Christian Wales
   Shower till they sing,
Till Erin's Island lawn
Echoes the dulcet-drawn
Song with a cry of Dawn —
   God save the King!

JAMES ELROY FLECKER

The poem by Wilfred Owen reproduced below is both naive and sinister. Its overt homosexuality and playful coyness raise the issue of whether the poet's homosexuality — and that of Sassoon — has ever satisfactorily been dealt with by those who have written on them. To raise their sexuality into a critical issue is not to condemn or judge them. It is rather to recognise a central feature of their consciousness and awareness as human beings, and thus perhaps to increase our awareness and understanding of their poetry.

It Was a Navy Boy

It was a navy boy, so prim, so trim,
That boarded my compartment of the train.
   I shared my cigarettes and books to him.
   He shared his heart to me. (Who knows my gain!)

(His head was golden like the oranges
That catch their brightness from Las Palmas sun.)
   'O whence and whither bound, lad?' 'Home,' he says,
   'Home, from Hong Kong, sir, and a ten months' run.'

(His blouse was all as blue as morning sea,
His face was fresh like dawn above that blue.)
   'I got one letter, sir, just one,' says he,
   'And no shore-leave out there, sir, for the crew.'

(His look was noble as a good ship's prow
And all of him was clear as pure east wind.)
   'I am no "sir"', I said, 'but tell me now
   What carried you? Not tea, nor tamarind?'

Strong were his silken muscles hiddenly
As under currents where the waters smile.
   'Nitre* we carried. By next week maybe
   That should be winning France another mile.'

His words were shapely, even as his lips,
And courtesy he used like any lord.

* Nitrate – a major component of explosives.

'Was it through books that you first thought of ships?'
'Reading a book, sir, made me go abroad.

'Another hour and I'll be home,' he said.
(His eyes were happy even as his heart.)
    'Twenty-five pounds I'm taking home,' he said,
    'It's five miles there; and I shall run, best part.'

And as we talked, some things he said to me
Not knowing, cleansed me of a cowardice,
    As I had braced me in the dangerous sea.
    Yet I should scarce have told it but for this.

'Those pounds,' I said. 'You'll put some twenty by?'
'All for my mother, sir.' And turned his head.
    'Why all?' I asked, in pain that he should sigh:
    'Because I must. She needs it most,' he said.

                                    WILFRED OWEN+

The public-school ethos as created by Thomas Arnold at Rugby was based on religion and sport, hence the cruel but apt tag of 'muscular Christianity'which, although originally applied to Charles Kingsley's writings, came to symbolise the products of schools like Rugby. Given that the most prominent voice at the start of the war was that of the public-school man, it is hardly surprising that several poets tended to see the war as a crusade, and as a game. Bob Dylan put paid to the former line of thought with his song 'With God On Our Side'; someone still has to do a hatchet job on the latter. It is easy to patronise the poets who wrote about war as a game, harder to understand that they were after all only relating a future and unknown experience to one which was known and with them all the time.

Kipling's 'For All We Have and Are' utilises another common strand in English ideas, the hard-line Calvinistic approach that almost takes delight in sin, and sees pain as the only cure for it. Halliday's 'The Grave' and Pain's 'The Army of the Dead' are not untypical of many poems of their kind; woven into them is a reminder that even early in the war some poets remembered that the enemy were both human and equal.

The Cricketers of Flanders

The first to climb the parapet
With 'cricket-ball' in either hand;
The first to vanish into smoke
Of God-forsaken No-Man's-Land.
First at the wire and soonest through.
First at those red-mouthed hounds of hell
The Maxims*, and the first to fall, —
They do their bit, and do it well.

Full sixty yards I've seen them throw
With all that nicety of aim
They learned on British cricket fields.
Ah! Bombing is a Briton's game!
'Lobbing them over,' with an eye
As true as though it *were* a game,
And friends were having tea close by.

Pull down some art-offending thing
Of carven stone, and in its stead
Let splendid bronze commemorate
These men, the living and the dead.
No figure of heroic size
Towering skywards like a god;
But just a lad who might have stepped
From any British bombing squad.

His shrapnel helmet set a-tilt,
His bombing waistcoat sagging low,
His rifle slung across his back:
Poised in the very act to throw.
And let some graven legend tell
Of those weird battles in the West
Wherein he put old skill to use
And played old games with sterner zest.

* Belt-fed heavy machine-guns.

Thus should he stand, reminding those
In less believing days, perchance,
How Britain's fighting cricketers
Helped bomb the Germans out of France.
And other eyes than ours would see;
And other hearts than ours would thrill,
And others say, as we have said:
'A sportsman and a soldier still!'

ANONYMOUS

In Memoriam J.H.H.

Last year, scarce one short season back,
    They cheered your swift, triumphant pace,
And all along the Terrace track*
    Acclaimed you winner of the race.

To-day they shout another's name,
    O friend of mine so far away,
For you have played a greater game
    For sterner stakes than I or they.

Yes, you the hardest race have run,
    Where none might hope to cheer you on;
But now the agony is done
    And all the doubts and fears are gone.

Brave heart, as often in old days,
    You breast the tape before us all;
And down Death's unrelenting ways,
    Your feet have passed beyond recall.

We have no place for wrath or tears
    Where all around the thunders roll —
One friend the less for coming years,
    One friend the more beyond the goal.

C.J. RONALD

*The running track at Haileybury College, Hertford.

The Grave

They dug his grave by lantern light,
    A nameless German boy:
A remnant from that hurried flight,
Lost, wounded, left in hapless plight
    For carrion to destroy.
They thought him dead at first until
    They felt the heart's slow beat:
So calm he lay, serene and still,
It seemed a butchery to kill
    An innocence so sweet.

A movement of his lips maybe
    To call his mother there:
A tear, a smile of victory —
Then easeful death proclaimed him free,
    Free from a tyrant's care.

Somewhere a mother droops and sighs
    For tidings long delayed:
Somewhere a sister mourns and cries
For him who in that cold grave lies,
    Dug by the foeman's spade.

PRIVATE WILFRID J. HALLIDAY

For All We Have and Are

For all we have and are,
For all our children's fate,
Stand up and take the war,
The Hun is at the gate!
Our world has passed away,
In wantonness o'erthrown.
There is nothing left today
But steel and fire and stone!

Though all we knew depart,
The old Commandments stand:—
'In courage keep your heart,
In strength lift up your hand.'

Comfort, content, delight,
The ages' slow-bought gain,
They shrivelled in a night.
Only ourselves remain
To face the naked days
In silent fortitude,
Through perils and dismays
Renewed and re-newed.
   Though all we made depart,
   The old Commandments stand:—
   'In patience keep your heart,
   In strength lift up your hand.'

No easy hopes or lies
Shall bring us to our goal,
But iron sacrifice
Of body, will, and soul.
There is but one task for all —
One life for each to give.
Who stands if Freedom fall?
Who dies if England live?

RUDYARD KIPLING

The Dead Heroes

Flame out, you glorious skies,
Welcome our brave,
Kiss their exultant eyes;
Give what they gave.

Flash, mailèd seraphim,
Your burning spears;

60

New days to outflame their dim
Heroic years.

Thrills their baptismal tread
The bright proud air;
The embalmed plumes outspread
Burn upwards there.

Flame out, flame out, O Song!
Star ring to star,
Strong as our hurt is strong
Our children are.

Their blood is England's heart
By their dead hands
It is their noble part
That England stands.

England — Time gave them thee;
They gave back this
To win Eternity
And claim God's kiss.

ISAAC ROSENBERG
1914

'The Volunteer' introduces another style of poetry. One could be forgiven for thinking that Sassoon, Graves, and Owen pioneered the use of colloquial language in war poetry. Sassoon in particular claimed credit for using 'telephonic' language, and introducing the word 'frowst' to the English Muse. In fact the ground had been prepared long before by poets such as John Masefield, and right from the very early days of the war poetry that tried to catch the rhythms and diction of common speech was being written, with varying degrees of success. It is a limited form, and there are signs that both Owen and Sassoon became bored with it. It is interesting how much anguish and conflict can be expressed in this form. Service's 'The Volunteer' is melodramatic and perhaps too simple, but it goes some way to charting the path into uniform of many men whose instincts were not to fight; one only has to look at Isaac Rosenberg to see that something very strange and unlikely took many men into the recruiting offices. Blackall's 'From the Front' comes from what might be described as the official-colloquial style of poetry, allowed by authority and much loved of magazines, because by looking at the minutiae of army life (and human nature) it gave the impression of realism with a sturdy attitude to the horrors. For all that, a great many soldiers thought and behaved as the poem suggests.

The Volunteer

Sez I: My Country Calls? Well, let it call.
I grins perlitely and declines with thanks.
Go, let 'em plaster every blighted wall,
'Ere's *one* they don't stampede into the ranks.
Them politicians with their greasy ways;
Them empire-grabbers — fight for 'em? No fear!
I've seen this mess a-comin' from the days
Of Algyserious and Aggydear:*
 I've felt me passion rise and swell,
  But ... wot the 'ell, Bill? Wot the 'ell?

Sez I: If they would do the decent thing,
And shield the missis and the little 'uns,
Why, even *I* might shout God save the King,
And face the chances of them 'ungry guns.
But we've got three, another on the way;
It's that wot makes me snarl and set me jor:
The wife and nippers wot of 'em, I say,
If I gets knocked out in this blasted war?
 Gets proper busted by a shell,
  But ... wot the 'ell, Bill? Wot the 'ell?

Ay, wot the 'ell's the use of all this talk?
To-day some boys in blue† was passin' me,

---

* The Algéçiras Conference of 1906, and the Agadir Crisis of 1911. Both involved the ambitions and alliances of France, Germany and Great Britain, although ostensibly concerned with Morocco.

† British convalescents in the Great War wore a blue uniform – nothing to do with the police.

And some of 'em they 'ad no legs to walk,
And some of 'em they 'ad no eyes to see.
And — well, I couldn't look 'em in the face,
And so I'm goin', goin' to declare
I'm under forty-one and take me place
To face the music with the bunch out there.
 A fool, you say! Maybe you're right.
 I'll 'ave no peace unless I fight.
 I've ceased to think; I only know
 I've gotta go, Bill, gotta go.

ROBERT SERVICE

From the Front
The Song of the Trench, December, 1914

This is the song of the blooming trench:
It's sung by us and it's sung by the French;
It's probably sung by the German Huns;
But it isn't all beer, and skittles, and buns.
It's a song of water, and mud and slime,
And keeping your eyes skinned all the time.
Though the putrid 'bully' may kick up a stench,
Remember, you've got to stick to your trench —
Yes, stick like glue to your trench.

You dig while it's dark, and you work while it's light,
And then there's the 'listening post' at night.
Though you're soaked to the skin and chilled to the bone;
Though your hands are like ice, and your feet like stone;
Though your watch is long, and your rest is brief,
And you pray like hell for the next relief;
Though the wind may howl, and the rain may drench,
Remember, you've got to stick in your trench —
Yes, stick like mud to your trench.

Perhaps a bullet may find its mark,
And then there's a funeral after dark;

And you say, as you lay him beneath the sod,
A sportsman's soul has gone to God.
Behind the trench, in the open ground,
There's a little cross and a little mound;
And if at your heart-strings you feel a wrench,
Remember, he died for his blooming trench —
Yes, he died like a man for his trench.

There's a rush and a dash, and they're at your wire,
And you open the hell of a rapid fire;
The Maxims rattle, the rifles flash,
And the bombs explode with a sickening crash.
You give them lead, and you give them steel,
Till at last they waver, and turn, and reel.
You've done your job — there was never a blench
You've given them hell, and you've saved your trench;
By God, you've stuck to your trench!

The daylight breaks on the rain-soaked plain
(For some it will never break again),
And you thank your God, as you're 'standing to',
You'd your bayonet clean, and your bolt* worked true.
For your comrade's rifle had jammed and stuck,
And he's lying there, with his brains in the muck.
So love your gun — as you haven't a wench —
And she'll save your life in the blooming trench —
Yes, save your life in the trench.

CAPTAIN C.W. BLACKALL

The Soldier's Cigarette
(October, 1915)

I'm cheap and insignificant,
    I'm easy quite to get,
In every place I show my face
    They call me cigarette.

---

*Rifle bolts — which re-cock and reload the weapon — are easily jammed by mud, rust or other imperfections.

They buy me four a penny, throw
   Me down without regret,
The elegant, the nonchalant,
   The blasé cigarette.

I'm small and nothing much to see,
   But men won't soon forget
How unafraid my part I've played,
   The dauntless cigarette.

When trenches all are water-logged
   I'm thereabouts, you bet,
With cheery smile the hours I while,
   The patient cigarette.

I sit within the trenches and
   Upon the parapet
Jack Johnson's* shock with scorn I mock,
   The careless cigarette.

If bullets whiz and Bill gets hit,
   Don't hurry for the 'vet.',
It's 'I'm alright, give us a light,'
   And 'Where's my cigarette?'

Ubiquitous and agile too,
   I'm but a youngster yet,
The debonaire, the savoir faire
   Abandoned cigarette.

When meals are few and far between,
   When spirit's ebb has set,
When comrades fall, and Death's gates call,
   Who's there but cigarette?

*Type of German shell, named after the first black world professional heavyweight boxing champion.

I cool the mind and quiet the brain
When danger's to be met;
When more is vain I ease the pain,
Immortal cigarette!

HAROLD BECKH+

A Pot of Tea

You make it in your mess-tin by the brazier's rosy gleam;
You watch it cloud, then settle amber clear;
You lift it with your bay'nit and you sniff the fragrant steam;
The very breath of it is ripe with cheer.
You're awful cold and dirty, and a-cursin' of your lot;
You scoff the blushin' 'alf of it, so rich and rippin' 'ot;
It bucks you up like anythink, just seems to touch the spot:
God bless the man that first discovered Tea!

Since I came out to fight in France, which ain't the other day,
I think I've drunk enough to float a barge;
All kinds of fancy foreign dope, from caffy and doo lay,*
To rum they serves you out before a charge.
In back rooms of estaminays I've gurgled pints of cham;†
I've swilled down mugs of cider till I've felt a bloomin' dam;
But 'struth! they all ain't in it with the vintage of Assam:
God bless the man that first invented Tea!

I think them lazy lumps o' gods wot kips on asphodel
Swigs nectar that's a flavour of Oolong;
I only wish them sons o' guns a-grillin' down in 'ell,
Could 'ave their daily ration of Suchong.
Hurrah! I'm off to battle, which is 'ell and 'eaven too;
And if I don't give some poor bloke a sexton's job to do,
To-night, by Fritz's camp fire, won't I 'ave a gorgeous brew
(For fightin' mustn't interfere with Tea).

* *Café [avec] du lait* — coffee with milk.

† Champagne.

To-night we'll all be tellin' of the Boches that we slew,
　　As we drink the giddy victory in Tea.

ROBERT SERVICE

The Soldier's Letter

I've lost my rifle and bayonet,
I've lost my pull-through too,
I've lost the socks that you sent me
That lasted the whole winter through,
I've lost the razor that shaved me,
I've lost my four-by-two*,
I've lost my hold-all and now I've got damn all
Since I've lost you.

ANONYMOUS

Many Sisters to Many Brothers

When we fought campaigns (in the long Christmas rains)
　　With soldiers spread in troops on the floor,
I shot as straight as you, my losses were as few,
　　My victories as many, or more.
And when in naval battle, amid cannon's rattle,
　　Fleet met fleet in the bath,
My cruisers were as trim, my battleships as grim,
　　My submarines cut as swift a path.
Or, when it rained too long, and the strength of the strong
　　Surged up and broke a way with blows,
I was as fit and keen, my fists hit as clean,
　　Your black eye matched my bleeding nose.
Was there a scrap or ploy in which you, the boy,
　　Could better me? You could not climb higher,
Ride straighter, run as quick (and to smoke made you sick)
　　… But I sit here, and you're under fire.

---

* Flannelette cloth which, attached to the pull-through (line 2), was used to clean a rifle's barrel.

Oh, it's you that have the luck, out there in the blood and muck:
    You were born beneath a kindly star;
All we dreamt, I and you, you can really go and do,
    And I can't, the way things are.
In a trench you are sitting, while I am knitting
    A hopeless sock that never gets done.
Well, here's luck, my dear — and you've got it, no fear;
    But for me . . . a war is poor fun.

ROSE MACAULAY

Brooke's sonnet 'The Soldier' is sometimes seen as having unleashed a whole pack of imitators. It certainly did that, as Rifleman Cox's poem 'To My Mother — 1916' shows, but much of that style was not *caused* by Brooke so much as symbolised by him. The wolves have been baying at the door of patriotic war poets for many a year now, sometimes in a way that is more sickening than the poems they decry. Brooke wrote what he felt, and wrote it well: criticism has sometimes blamed him and his imitators and fellows for failing to know what very few people knew in 1914. Sorley seemed to know what the war would bring; so, perhaps surprisingly, did Lord Kitchener, at least in the occasional flash of insight. Sorley's 'Sonnet' seems to me to be a clear rebuttal of Brooke's, written in sadness more than anger; that might not be a bad line for later generations to imitate. Brooke's poetry seems to me to be infinitely preferable to one of the cruellest poems of the whole war, Harold Begbie's 'Fall In'. In Begbie's world we fight not because we wish to defend ourselves, and not because we believe in what we are fighting for, and not even for the simplest of reasons, which is that to a young man war is exciting. If we are in Begbie's world we fight because people will laugh at us if we do not.

The Soldier

If I should die, think only this of me:
    That there's some corner of a foreign field
That is for ever England. There shall be
    In that rich earth a richer dust concealed;
A dust whom England bore, shaped, made aware,
    Gave, once, her flowers to love, her ways to roam.

A body of England's, breathing English air,
   Washed by the rivers, blest by the suns of home.

And think, this heart, all evil shed away,
  - A pulse in the eternal mind, no less
     Gives somewhere back the thoughts by England given;
Her sights and sounds; dreams happy as her day;
   And laughter, learnt of friends; and gentleness,
     In hearts at peace, under an English heaven.

RUPERT BROOKE+

Sonnet

When you see millions of the mouthless dead
Across your dreams in pale battalions go,
Say not soft things, as other men have said,
That you'll remember. For you need not so.
Give them not praise. For, deaf, how should they know
It is not curses heaped on each gashed head?
Nor tears. Their blind eyes see not your tears flow.
Nor honour. It is easy to be dead.
Say only this, 'They are dead'. Then add thereto,
'Yet many a better one has died before'.
Then, scanning all the o'ercrowded mass, should you
Perceive one face that you loved heretofore,
It is a spook. None wears the face you knew.
Great death has made all his for evermore.

CHARLES HAMILTON SORLEY+

To My Mother — 1916

If I should fall, grieve not that one so weak
    And poor as I
    Should die.
Nay! Though thy heart should break
Think only this: that when at dusk they speak

Of sons and brothers of another one,
Then thou canst say — 'I too had a son;
He died for England's sake!'

RIFLEMAN DONALD S. COX

The Song of the Happy Warrior*

The song of the boy who was brave and fair,
He was young and his eyes were grey,
He was swift to run and strong to strive
    And ready for any play.
He climbed to the top of the apple tree
    When nobody else would dare;
He couldn't get down and he feared he'd fall
    As the branch swayed in the air.
O! the ground seemed such a way below,
    But he smiled a doubtful smile-a,
And he grit his teeth and sang 'Cheer-o!'
    Though the drop to the ground seemed a mile-a.

The song of the man in the khaki coat
    As he stands in the wet and snow,
A smoking rifle in his hands
    And his feet in the mud below.
The tale of the charge and the man that fell,
    Of the tunic dyed with red,
The tight-clenched teeth and the clammy brow
    And the stain where the wound had bled.
Oh! he groaned as he jolted to and fro
    And wan, wan was his smile-a,
But he grit his teeth and he hummed 'Cheer-o!'
    And he died at the end of a mile-a.

RIFLEMAN DONALD S. COX

* See also p. 128.

Fall In

What will you lack, sonny, what will you lack
When the girls line up the street,
Shouting their love to the lads come back
From the foe they rushed to beat?
Will you send a strangled cheer to the sky
And grin till your cheeks are red?
But what will you lack when your mate goes by
With a girl who cuts you dead?

Where will you look, sonny, where will you look
When your children yet to be
Clamour to learn of the part you took
In the war that kept men free?
Will you say it was naught to you if France
Stood up for her foe or bunked?
But where will you look when they give the glance
That tells you they know you funked?

How will you fare, sonny, how will you fare
In the far-off winter night,
When you sit by the fire in an old man's chair
And your neighbours talk of the fight?
Will you slink away, as it were from a blow,
Your old head shamed and bent?
Or — say I was not with the first to go,
But I went, thank God, I went?

Why do they call, sonny, why do they call
For men who are brave and strong?
Is it naught to you if your country fall,
And Right is smashed by Wrong?
Is it football still and the picture show,
The pub and betting odds,
When your brothers stand to the tyrant's blow
And England's call is God's?

HAROLD BEGBIE

Troops ships were a common source of poetic inspiration at the start of the war, until superseded by combat. They were a common experience — it was after all the only way to get to France — and came at the time in a soldier's service career when he was most highly charged, training and excitement running side by side with trepidation and fear.

The Troop Ship

Grotesque and queerly huddled
Contortionists to twist
The sleepy soul to a sleep,
We lie all sorts of ways
And cannot sleep.
The wet wind is so cold,
And the lurching men so careless,
That, should you drop to a doze,
Winds' fumble or men's feet
Are on your face.

ISAAC ROSENBERG+

Troopship: mid-Atlantic

Dark waters into crystalline brilliance break
About the keel as, through the moonless night,
The dark ship moves in its own moving lake
Of phosphorescent cold moon-coloured light;
And to the clear horizon all around
Drift pools of fiery beryl flashing bright,
As though unquenchably burning cold and white
A million moons in the night of waters drowned.

And staring at the magic with eyes adream
That never till now have looked upon the sea,
Boys from the Middle West lounge listlessly
In the unlanthorned darkness, boys who go,

Beckoned by some unchallengeable dream,
To unknown lands to fight an unknown foe.

WILFRID WILSON GIBSON
on the SS Baltic, July 1917

Night on the Convoy
(Alexandria-Marseilles)

Out in the blustering darkness, on the deck
A gleam of stars look down. Long blurs of black,
The lean Destroyers, level with our track,
Plunging and stealing, watch the perilous way
Through backward racing seas and caverns of chill spray.
One sentry by the davits, in the gloom
Stands mute: the boat heaves onward through the night.
Shrouded is every chink of cabined light:
And sluiced by floundering waves that hiss and boom
And crash like guns, the troop-ship shudders ... doom.

Now something at my feet stirs with a sigh;
And slowly growing used to groping dark,
I know that the hurricane-deck, down all its length,
Is heaped and spread with lads in sprawling strength —
Blanketed soldiers sleeping. In the stark
Danger of life at war, they lie so still,
All prostrate and defenceless, head by head ...
And I remember Arras, and that hill
Where dumb with pain I stumbled among the dead.

We are going home. The troop-ship, in a thrill
Of fiery-chamber'd anguish, throbs and rolls.
We are going home ... victims ... three thousand souls.

SIEGFRIED SASSOON
May 1918

73

The remaining poems in this section have been chosen to display the remarkable variety of writing that existed before 1916. The dissenting voices were there in plenty in the early years of the war, the most moving often being the most simple, as in 'Farewell' and 'Matey'. Owen's panoramic view of the battlefield, 'A Terre', seems strangely clumsy and egocentric by the side of Sorley's marvellously dignified, rhythmically disturbing 'A Hundred Thousand Million Mites We Go'.

The Army of the Dead

I dreamed that overhead
I saw in twilight grey
The Army of the Dead
Marching upon its way,
So still and passionless,
With faces so serene,
That scarcely could one guess
Such men in war had been.

No mark of hurt they bore,
Nor smoke, nor bloody stain,
Nor suffered any more
Famine, fatigue or pain;
Nor any lust of hate
Now lingered in their eyes —
Who have fulfilled their Fate
Have lost all emnities.

A new and greater pride
So quenched the pride of race
That foes marched side by side
Who once fought face to face.
That ghostly army's plan
Knows but one race, one rod —
All nations there are Men
And the one King is God.

No longer on their ears
The bugle's summons falls;

Beyond these tangled spheres
The Archangel's trumpet calls;
And by that trumpet led
Far up the exalted sky
The Army of the Dead
Goes by, and still goes by.

Look upward, standing mute;
   Salute!

BARRY PAIN

What is War?

What is war?
Ask the young men who fight,
Men who defend the right,
Ask *them* — what is war?
'Honour — or death — that is war,'
   Say the young men.

   What is war?
Ask of the women who weep,
Mourning for those who sleep,
Ask *them* — what is war?
'Sorrow and grief — that is war,'
   Say the women.

   What is war?
By ways beyond our ken,
God tries the souls of men,
Sends retribution just,
Punishing vice and lust,
God's wrath for sin — that is war.

J.M. ROSE-TROUP

Farewell

(To Sergeant H. Fraser and Lance-Sergeant G.M'Kay)

Well, you have gone now, comrades,
And I shall see no more
The gallant friendly faces
    Framed in my dug-out door.
I have no words to tell you
    The things I longed to say,
But the company is empty
    Since you have gone away.

The company is filled now
    With faces strange to see,
And scarce a man of the old men
    That lived and fought with me.
I know the drafts are good men,
    I know they're doing well,
But they're not the men I slept with
    Those nights at La Boisselle.

Oh, the days of friendship
    We shall not see again,
The little winter trenches
    And the marches in the rain.
Becourt, Authuille, Thiepval,
    Herancourt, Avelay,
These names are keys that open
    Remembered doors to me.

Doors that will open never,
    Upon this tortured land.
I shall not see you ever,
    Or take you by the hand.
Only for ancient friendship,
    For all the times we knew,
Maybe you will remember
    As I remember you.

EWART ALAN MACKINTOSH+

Matey
(*Cambrin, May 1915*)

Not comin' back tonight, matey,
And reliefs are coming through,
We're all goin' out all right, matey,
Only we're leaving you.
Gawd! it's a bloody sin, matey,
Now that we've finished the fight,
We go when reliefs come in, matey,
But you're stayin' 'ere tonight.

Over the top is cold, matey —
You lie on the field alone,
Didn't I love you of old, matey,
Dearer than the blood of my own?
You were my dearest chum, matey —
(Gawd! but your face is white)
But now, though reliefs 'ave come, matey,
I'm goin' alone tonight.

I'd sooner the bullet was mine, matey —
Goin' out on my own,
Leavin' you 'ere in the line, matey,
All by yourself, alone,
Chum o' mine and you're dead, matey,
And this is the way we part,
The bullet went through your head, matey,
But Gawd! it went through my 'eart.

PATRICK MACGILL

Christ in Flanders

We had forgotten You, or very nearly —
You did not seem to touch us very nearly —
    Of course we thought about You now and then;
Especially in any time of trouble —
We knew that You were good in time of trouble —
    But we are very ordinary men.

77

And there were always other things to think of —
There's lots of things a man has got to think of —
    His work, his home, his pleasure, and his wife;
And so we only thought of You on Sunday —
Sometimes, perhaps, not even on a Sunday —
    Because there's always lots to fill one's life.

And, all the while, in street or lane or byway —
In country lane, or city street, or byway —
    You walked among us, and we did not see.
Your feet were bleeding as You walked our pavements —
How *did* we miss Your footprints on our pavements? —
    Can there be other folk as blind as we?

Now we remember; over here in Flanders —
(It isn't strange to think of You in Flanders) —
    This hideous warfare seems to make things clear.
We never thought about You much in England —
But now that we are far away from England,
    We have no doubts, we know that You are here.

You helped us pass the jest along the trenches —
Where, in cold blood, we waited in the trenches —
    You touched its ribaldry and made it fine.
You stood beside us in our pain and weakness —
We're glad to think You understand our weakness —
    Somehow it seems to help us not to whine.

We think about you kneeling in the Garden —
Ah! God! the agony of that dread Garden —
    We know you prayed for us upon the cross.
If anything could make us glad to bear it —
'Twould be the knowledge that You willed to bear it —
    Pain — death — the uttermost of human loss.

Though we forgot You — You will not forget us —
We feel so sure that You will not forget us —
    But stay with us until this dream is past.

And so we ask for courage, strength, and pardon —
Especially, I think, we ask for pardon —
   And that You'll stand beside us to the last.

LUCY WHITMELL

Headquarters

A league and a league from the trenches — from the traversed* maze of
   the lines,
Where daylong the sniper watches and daylong the bullet whines,
And the cratered earth is in travail with mines and with countermines —

Here, where haply some woman dreamed (are those her roses that
   bloom
In the garden beyond the windows of my littered working-room?),
We have decked the map for our masters as a bride is decked for the
   groom.

Fair, on each lettered numbered square — cross-road and mound and
   wire,
Loophole, redoubt and emplacement — lie the targets their mouths
   desire;
Gay with purples and browns and blues, have we traced them their
   arcs of fire.

And ever the type-keys chatter; and ever our keen wires bring
Word from the watchers a-crouch below, word from the watchers
   a-wing:
And ever we hear the distant growl of our hid guns thundering;

Hear it hardly, and turn again to our maps, where the trench lines
   crawl,
Red on the grey and each with a sign for the ranging shrapnel's fall —
Snakes that our masters shall scotch at dawn, as is written here on the
   wall.

---

* Traverses — right-angles in trench-works to prevent enfilading fire.

For the weeks of our waiting draw to a close ... There is scarcely a leaf
    astir
In the garden beyond my windows, where the twilight shadows blur
The blaze of some woman's roses ... 'Bombardment orders, sir.'

GILBERT FRANKAU

Where Are Our Uniforms?

Where are our uniforms?
    Far, far away,
When will our rifles come?
P'r'aps, p'r'aps some day.
And you bet we shan't be long
Before we're fit and strong;
You'll hear us say 'Oui, oui, tray bong'
    When we're far away.

SOLDIER'S SONG

Kaiser Bill

Kaiser Bill went up the hill
To see the British Army,
General French jumped out of a trench
And made the cows go barmy.

CHILDREN'S SONG

All the Hills and Vales Along

All the hills and vales along
Earth is bursting into song,
And the singers are the chaps
Who are going to die perhaps.
    O sing, marching men,
    Till the valleys ring again.
    Give your gladness to earth's keeping,
    So be glad, when you are sleeping.

Cast away regret and rue,
Think what you are marching to.
Little live, great pass.
Jesus Christ and Barabbas
Were found the same day.
This died, that went his way.
　So sing with joyful breath,
　For why, you are going to death.
　Teeming earth will surely store
　All the gladness that you pour.

Earth that never doubts nor fears.
Earth that knows of death, not tears,
Earth that bore with joyful ease
Hemlock for Socrates,
Earth that blossomed and was glad
'Neath the cross that Christ had,
Shall rejoice and blossom too
When the bullet reaches you.
　Wherefore, men marching
　On the road to death, sing!
　Pour your gladness on earth's head,
　So be merry, so be dead.

From the hills and valleys earth
Shouts back the sound of mirth,
Tramp of feet and lilt of song
Ringing all the road along.
All the music of their going,
Ringing swinging glad song-throwing,
Earth will echo still, when foot
Lies numb and voice mute.
　On, marching men, on
　To the gates of death with song.
　Sow your gladness for earth's reaping,
　So you may be glad, though sleeping.
　Strew your gladness on earth's bed,
　So be merry, so be dead.

CHARLES HAMILTON SORLEY+

A Hundred Thousand Million Mites

A hundred thousand million mites we go
Wheeling and tacking o'er the endless plain,
Some black with death — and some are white with woe.
Who sent us forth? Who takes us home again?

And there is sound of hymns of praise — to whom?
And curses — on whom curses? — snap the air.
And there is hope goes hand in hand with gloom,
And blood and indignation and despair.

And there is murmuring of the multitude
And blindness, and great blindness, until some
Step forth and challenge blind Vicissitude
Who tramples on them: so that fewer come.

And nations, ankle-deep in love or hate,
Throw darts or kisses all the unwitting hour
Beside the ominous unseen tide of fate;
And there is emptiness and drink and power.

And some are mounted on swift steeds of thought
And some drag sluggish feet of stable toil.
Yet all, as though they furiously sought,
Twist turn and tussle, close and cling and coil.

A hundred thousand million mites we sway
Writhing and tossing on the eternal plain,
Some black with death — but most are bright with Day!
Who sent us forth? Who brings us home again?

CHARLES HAMILTON SORLEY+

The Show

We have fallen in the dreams the ever-living
Breathe on the tarnished mirror of the world,
And then smooth out with ivory hands and sigh.

W.B. YEATS

My soul looked down from a vague height, with Death,
As unremembering how I rose or why,
And saw a sad land, weak with sweats of dearth,
Grey, cratered like the moon with hollow woe,
And pitted with great pocks and scabs of plagues.

Across its beard, that horror of harsh wire,
There moved thin caterpillars, slowly uncoiled.
It seemed they pushed themselves to be as plugs
Of ditches, where they writhed and shrivelled, killed.

By them, had slimy paths been trailed and scraped
Round myriad warts that might be little hills.

From gloom's last dregs these long-strung creatures crept,
And vanished out of dawn down hidden holes.

(And smell came up from those foul openings
As out of mouths, or deep wounds deepening.)

On dithering feet upgathered, more and more,
Brown strings, towards strings of grey, with bristling spines,
All migrants from green fields, intent on mire.

Those that were grey, of more abundant spawns,
Ramped on the rest and ate them and were eaten.

I saw their bitten backs curve, loop, and straighten.
I watched those agonies curl, lift, and flatten.

Whereat, in terror what that sight might mean,
I reeled and shivered earthward like a feather.

And Death fell with me, like a deepening moan.
And He, picking a manner of worm, which half had hid
Its bruises in the earth, but crawled no further,
Showed me its feet, the feet of many men,
And the fresh-severed head of it, my head.

WILFRED OWEN+

To Germany

You are blind like us. Your hurt no man designed,
And no man claimed the conquest of your land.
But gropers both through fields of thought confined
We stumble and we do not understand.
You only saw your future bigly planned,
And we, the tapering paths of our own mind,
And in each other's dearest ways we stand,
And hiss and hate. And the blind fight the blind.

When it is peace, then we may view again
With new-won eyes each other's truer form
And wonder. Grown more loving-kind and warm
We'll grasp firm hands and laugh at the old pain,
When it is peace. But until peace, the storm
The darkness and the thunder and the rain.

CHARLES HAMILTON SORLEY+

This Is No Case of Petty Right or Wrong

This is no case of petty right or wrong
That politicians or philosophers
Can judge. I hate not Germans, nor grow hot
With love of Englishmen, to please newspapers.
Beside my hate for one fat patriot

My hatred of the Kaiser is love true:—
A kind of god he is, banging a gong.
But I have not to choose between the two,
Or between justice and injustice. Dinned
With war and argument I read no more
Than in the storm smoking along the wind
Athwart the wood. Two witches' cauldrons roar.
From one the weather shall rise clear and gay;
Out of the other an England beautiful
And like her mother that died yesterday.
Little I know or care if, being dull,
I shall miss something that historians
Can rake out of the ashes when perchance
The phoenix broods serene above their ken.
But with the best and meanest Englishmen
I am one in crying, God save England, lest
We lose what never slaves and cattle blessed.
The ages made her that made us from dust:
She is all we know and live by, and we trust
She is good and must endure, loving her so:
And as we love ourselves we hate our foe.

EDWARD THOMAS+

The Star-shell*
(Loos)

A star-shell holds the sky beyond
Shell-shivered Loos, and drops
In million sparkles on a pond
That lies by Hulluch copse.

A moment's brightness in the sky,
To vanish at a breath,
And die away, as soldiers die
Upon the wastes of death.

PATRICK MACGILL

* Type of flare, generally fired from an artillery piece.

Marching
(*La Bassée Road, June, 1915*)

Four by four, in column of route,
By roads that the poplars sentinel,
Clank of rifle and crunch of boot —
All are marching and all is well.
White, so white is the distant moon,
Salmon-pink is the furnace glare
And we hum, as we march, a ragtime tune,
Khaki boys in the long platoon,
Ready for anything — anywhere.

Lonely and still the village lies,
The houses sleep and the blinds are drawn,
The road is straight as the bullet flies,
And we go marching into the dawn;
Salmon-pink is the furnace sheen
Where the coal stacks bulk in the ghostly air
The long platoons on the move are seen,
Little connecting files between,
Moving and moving, anywhere.

PATRICK MACGILL

Marching
(*As seen from the left file*)

My eyes catch ruddy necks
Sturdily pressed back —
All flaming pendulums*, hands
Swing across the Khaki —
Mustard-coloured Khaki —
To the automatic feet

---

* Ian Parsons (see Bibliography) has 'All a red brick moving glint./Like flaming pendulums ...'
at lines 3-4.

We husband the ancient glory
In these bared necks and hands.
Not broke in the forge of Mars;
But a subtler brain beats iron
To shoe the hoofs of death
(Who paws dynamic air now).
Blind fingers loose an iron cloud
To rain immortal darkness
On strong eyes.

ISAAC ROSENBERG+

Two Sonnets

I

Saints have adored the loftly soul of you.
Poets have whitened at your high renown.
We stand among the many millions who
Do hourly wait to pass your pathway down.
You, so familiar, once were strange: we tried
To live as of your presence unaware.
But now in every road on every side
We see your straight and steadfast signpost there.

I think it like that signpost in my land,
Hoary and tall, which pointed me to go
Upward, into the hills, on the right hand,
Where the mists swim and the winds shriek and blow,
A homeless land and friendless, but a land
I did not know and that I wished to know.

II

Such, such is Death: no triumph: no defeat:
Only an empty pail, a slate rubbed clean,
A merciful putting away of what has been.

And this we know: Death is not Life effete,
Life crushed, the broken pail. We who have seen
So marvellous things know well the end not yet.

Victor and vanquished are a-one in death:
Coward and brave: friend, foe. Ghosts do not say
'Come, what was your record when you drew breath?'
But a big blot has hid each yesterday
So poor, so manifestly incomplete.
And your bright Promise, withered long and sped,
Is touched, stirs, rises, opens and grows sweet
And blossoms and is you, when you are dead.

CHARLES HAMILTON SORLEY+
12 June 1915

New Army Education

I learned to wash in shell-holes, and to shave myself in tea,
While the fragments of a mirror did a balance on my knee.
I learned to dodge the whizzbangs* and the flying lumps of lead,
And to keep a foot of earth between the snipers and my head.
I learned to keep my haversack well-filled with buckshee food,
To take my army issue and to pinch what else I could.
I learned to cook maconachie* with candle-ends and string,
With four-by-two and sardine oil, and any old darn thing.
I learned to use my bayonet according as you please,
For a bread-knife or a chopper, or a prong for toasting cheese.
I learned to gather souvenirs that home I hoped to send,
And hump them round for months and months, and dump them in
    the end.
I never used to grumble after breakfast in the line
That the eggs were cooked too lightly or the bacon cut too fine.
I never told a sergeant just exactly what I thought,
I never did a pack drill, for I never quite got caught.
I never stopped a whizzbang, though I've stopped a lot of mud;
But the one that Fritz sent over with my name on was a dud.

ANONYMOUS

*Whizzbang — a type of German shell. Maconachie — tinned stew named after its manufacturers. Also known as 'conner'.

III

'Hell's mouth'

COMBAT

Rupert Brooke had symbolised the British soldier at the beginning of the war. Now his place was taken by Old Bill*, a veteran of 1915, who crouched in a shell crater for want of 'a better 'ole to go to'. The Somme set the picture by which future generations saw the First World War: brave, helpless soldiers; blundering obstinate generals; nothing achieved. After the Somme men decided that the war would go on for ever.

A.J.P. TAYLOR

5 June 1916:	Field-Marshal Lord Kitchener, Minister of War, drowned while *en route* to Russia when the cruiser HMS *Hampshire* strikes a mine off the Orkneys.
13 November 1916:	Battle of the Somme ends.
December 1916:	Germans issue first, vaguely worded 'peace note' to the Allies, which is rejected out of hand.
8 March 1917:	Revolution breaks out in Russia.
15 March 1917:	Tsar Nicholas II abdicates. A provisional government is set up.
6 April 1917:	United States of America declares war on Germany. American troops will not go into action until early in 1918, however.
9 April-16 May 1917:	Battle of Arras; Canadian troops take Vimy Ridge, among other gains. 150,000 British casualties, 100,000 German. The offensive is kept up while Haig prepares for his attack at Ypres, but there are no further significant gains.

*'Old Bill' was the cartoon creation of Captain Bruce Bairnsfather, an artist and playwright. The wily, scruffy, humorous 'old soldier', with his great moustache and his line in grousing wit, proved immensely popular with the troops, and indeed at home.

16 April-15 May 1917: French launch great offensive, called the Second Battle of the Aisne. Gains are in the region of 600 yards. Elements of the French army in Champagne mutiny; 100,000 French soldiers are court-martialled, and many shot.

7-14 June 1917: Battle of Messines. The Messines Ridge, occupied by the Germans since early in the war, dominates the Ypres Salient. General Plumer's Second Army assaults the ridge after the explosion of nineteen huge mines under the German positions. The attack is a triumphant success and the British take and hold the ridge until the German assault during the Battle of the Lys, 9-29 April 1918. For the first time, British losses while attacking are less than the Germans'.

31 July-6 November 1917: Third Battle of Ypres (Passchendaele). British casualties over 300,000; German casualties under 200,000. The village of Passchendaele and the remaining initial objectives are eventually taken by the Canadians on 6 November. The damage to the morale of British troops is considerable, however, as is their loss of confidence in their leaders. This is one of the costliest advances in the history of British and Commonwealth arms.

6-7 November 1917: The 'October Revolution' (Russia still uses the Julian Calendar, which in 1917 is thirteen days behind the western calendar). Lenin, driven into hiding in July after an abortive Bolshevik attempt to seize power, leads a revolt against the Provisional Government. By the eighth the Bolsheviks are in power.

8 November 1917: Lenin reads his Decree on Peace to the Soviet Congress; by now Russian armies have collapsed on the Eastern Front. Peace, on ruinous terms for the new-born Soviet Union, signed between Russia and Germany on 15 December 1917 at Brest-Litovsk. With Russia out of the way, large numbers of German and Austro-Hungarian troops are released to fight on other fronts — especially the Western Front. Civil war breaks out in Russia, which will continue until 1920.

28 November 1917: Battle of Cambrai. 381 British tanks advance five miles into German-held territory. British casualties 1,500; 10,000 German prisoners. Most of the captured territory is retaken shortly afterwards by the German Army, because of failures to exploit the break-through.

21 March-5 April 1918: Massive German attack against British Fifth and Third Armies (part of the 'Ludendorff offensive', also known as the Second Battle of the Somme). British armies, pierced in several places, fall back, and French forces fall back to conform. Exhaustion eventually stops the Germans after an advance of forty miles, unheard of before on the Western Front. But their casualties are almost as great as the Allies', and the attack has been a last-ditch effort to win before the growing American forces are pitched into battle.

1 April 1918: Isaac Rosenberg killed.

9-29 April 1918: Battle of the Lys. Ludendorff switches his attack to the thinly-defended northern sector near Ypres. Germans recapture Messines Ridge, but on 21 April French reinforcements arrive and save the line, while other actions by Belgian, British and Canadian troops defeat German attacks.

12 April 1918: As the German attack on the Somme continues, Haig issues his most famous Order of the Day: 'With our backs to the wall, and believing in the justice of our cause, each one of us must fight on to the end'. The Allies continue to retire, sometimes in disarray.

27 May-2 June 1918: Third Battle of the Aisne. This is the third of Ludendorff's great 1918 attacks, made against the French positions on the Chemin des Dames. Initially the French lines are penetrated up to a distance of thirteen miles, the greatest advance in one day since 1914. After further German advances the Americans hold the Marne crossings, however, capture Cantigny, and go on to clear the Germans out of Belleau Wood. Their pressure brings considerable psychological gains to the Allies. The British line also holds, and by the end of the battle Ludendorff holds a thirty-five-mile deep salient aimed at Paris, but lacks the power to continue his attack.

3 June 1918: German forces reach the River Marne, but the impetus has gone from their attacks and the Allies, with fresh American troops on hand, begin to push back.

9-13 June 1918: Battle of Noyon-Montdidier. Ludendorff launches another attack, threatening Paris and aiming to link his Somme gains with those on the Aisne-Marne fronts to the south-east. The French defence in depth halts the attack after some early gains, and inflicts heavy losses on the Germans.

15 July-5 August 1918: Second Battle of the Marne. The fifth and last of the major German offensives was aimed at securing the Marne river crossings, crushing a French army between two German. One German attack is held by the French, but another breaks the line until held by French and American troops, with British and Italian forces in support. Thus ends the last major German offensive on the Western Front.

18 July-3 August 1918: Foch goes back on to the attack in the Marne sector, the British, French, American and Italian troops forcing Ludendorff's armies back and retaking the salient won by the Germans early in June.

8 August-3 September 1918: Battle of Amiens. Foch launches a fresh attack, aimed at driving the Germans out of the salient won by their gains on the Somme since March. Ludendorff calls this 'the Black Day of the German Army' as entire units collapse under the onslaught. By the end of the battle all the German gains on the Somme have been retaken. This is the turning point of the war on the Western Front.

12 September 1918: Battle of St Mihiel. As the Germans in this sector begin to fall back to conform with German losses on the Marne and the Somme, they are attacked by sixteen American divisions, supported by the French, and are driven from the salient within thirty-six hours, losing many men as prisoners and 250 guns. This is the first great American triumph of the war.

26 September-11 November 1918:	Battle of the River Meuse-Argonne Forest. In the south-east, the Americans attack on a wide front to coincide with other Allied attacks along the length of the Western Front. The Germans are gradually forced back, faster and farther as French forces join in.
27 September-11 November 1918:	Battle of Cambrai-St Quentin. The western half of the great attack, designed to trap the Germans in a pincer. By 4 October British, Canadian and French forces hold the entire German defensive position, and by the end of the month the Germans have been driven back behind the Scheldt river. The Allies prevent the Germans from reinforcing against the French-American attack in the south-east, and early in November the Scheldt position is turned. Further north, the Belgians force the Germans out of Ostend, Zeebrugge and Bruges. By 11 November British and Canadian forces are at Mons; one battalion occupying a position some 100 yards nearer Germany than it had in 1914.
4 November 1918:	Wilfred Owen killed during the crossing of the Sambre Canal.
10 November 1918:	Kaiser Wilhelm II abdicates and flees to exile in neutral Holland, where he dies in 1941.
11 November 1918:	Germany seeks, and is granted, an armistice, with effect from 'the eleventh hour of the eleventh day of the eleventh month'.
18 January 1919-20 January 1920:	Paris Peace Conference. The Treaty of Versailles, signed 28 June 1919, finally ends the war with Germany. Other treaties deal with the remaining enemy nations: St Germain, 10 September 1919, Austria; Neuilly, 27 November 1919, Bulgaria; Trianon, 4 June 1920, Hungary; and Sèvres, 10 August 1920, Turkey. The First World War is at last over. Of more than 65 million men mobilised by all the combatants, 37½ million have become casualties — killed or died, missing, wounded or prisoner.

The poems given below cover roughly the period from mid-1916 to the end of the war in 1918 although, as with the previous section, this chronological division has been loosely interpreted where an interesting point of comparison or contrast can be made.

One can very often date war poetry by its use of the words 'Hun' or 'Boche'. These were quite popular in all areas of poetry before 1916. After that, they tend more often than not to mark out poetry either by those who stayed at home, or by those not involved in the actual fighting. Fighting soldiers rarely talked about the enemy in personal terms. If they did so, the most common term was 'Fritz'. The poets were concerned mainly with their own experience, their own landscape, and their own suffering. If they thought about the enemy, it was often in terms of someone sharing the same mess as they were in.

The poems from *Punch* are noteworthy. A number are reproduced here from 1917 and 1918, and a metaphorical 'Old Bill' features largely in them. Poems in *Punch* from the earlier years of the war tended to strive for humour in a rather patronising way, both about the soldiers and about German '*Kultur*' and individuals. In the post-1916 issues, however, the poems about soldiers tend to be more gritty, and much more in line with what we now know about conditions at the front. Attacks on German institutions become rather more subtle, and sometimes even tired, as if it were a routine to be gone through. Despite all this, *Punch* never lost its sense of humour. It is possible that the change in tone after 1916 noted by many commentators was actually much more marked in the officer class than in the rank and file. Soldiers' songs seemed to change less in tone than did pure poetry. Apart from the early optimism of the British Expeditionary Force, the plain footslogger had looked at the war with a shrewd eye from early in 1915. Knowing what we know about the horrors of the First World War, the application of any form of humour to it can appear grossly distasteful.* For the soldiers who fought in it, however, humour was sometimes as much a means of survival as rum or tobacco.

Poems by the famous authors of the war achieve a grandeur and poignancy that is extraordinary. Sassoon's 'To Any Dead Officer', Owen's 'Spring Offensive' and 'Futility', and Rosenberg's 'Dead Man's Dump' speak for themselves. What is surprising is the wealth of

---

* One very popular soldiers' adaptation ran:
  'If you want to find the old battalion,
  I know where they are …
  They're hanging on the old barbed wire.
  I've seen 'em, I've *seen* 'em,
  Hanging on the old barbed wire (etc.)'
Such songs were far more a form of exorcism than they were a demonstration of callousness or brutalised natures. See page 98.

poetry by virtually unknown authors, verse which cannot equal the work of the better-known poets but which can still achieve a remarkable poignancy and accuracy. It would be too easy to make the point that three standard literary reference works make no reference to Major 'H.D.'A.B.' Arthur Graeme West, Sergeant Frank Brown, F.W. Harvey, Margaret Postgate, or H. Smalley Sarson; their poetry is not 'great' in the sense that Owen's is. It is nevertheless sad that so much poetry of real merit lies neglected just underneath the famous works. That situation is even more marked in some of the sections which follow. Active service stimulated poets such as Owen and Rosenberg into high achievement; the war did the same for many authors who did not see active service, but went through their own form of hell in observing others fighting for them. This being said, the section which follows is perhaps the most conventional selection of any in this book. No one could or should try to unseat the famous trench poets from the position of power which they have long occupied. All that is necessary is to point out that they did not stand alone.

Soldiers' songs do not quite fit into any of the conventional categories for poetry, and for most editors their natural home is at the start of a selection, as a warm-up to the proper poetry which is to come. The songs are interesting for a variety of reasons. Attempts to write songs for the soldiers often failed, though the influence of music hall on what the soldiers sang is considerable. To be successful a song needed a number of features. It had to be strongly rhythmic and simple, because the songs were sung most often when, and were most useful for, marching. A good song was either thoroughly obscene or grossly sentimental, wholly unconcerned with the wider issues of life and the war, and frequently mocking about the army and its personalities. Above all the songs were basic — basic about life, about sexuality, and about death. They illustrate how very much poets such as Owen and Sassoon were writing as poets, rather than as spokesmen for the soldiers they led and fought with. As poets they may say things that the troops were too inarticulate to express, but the soldiers in their songs are in their own way expressing something so basic and simple that it slips through the fingers of the great poets.

Tiddleywinks, Old Man
Air: Hornpipe

Tiddleywinks, old man,
Find a woman if you can.
If you can't find a woman,
Do without, old man.
When the Rock of Gibraltar
Takes a flying leap at Malta,
You'll never get your ballocks in a corn-beef can.

ANONYMOUS SONG

When This Blasted War Is Over
Air: Hymn, 'Take It to the Lord in Prayer' ('What a Friend I have in Jesus')

When this blasted war is over,
Oh, how happy I shall be!
When I get my civvy clothes on
No more soldiering for me.
No more church parades on Sunday,
No more asking for a pass.
I shall tell the Sergeant-Major
To stick his passes up his arse.

When this blasted war is over,
Oh, how happy I shall be.
When I get my civvy clothes on,
No more soldiering for me.
I shall sound my own revally,
I shall make my own tattoo.*
No more N.C.O.'s to curse me,
No more bleeding Army stew.

N.C.O.'s will all be navvies,
Privates ride in motor cars.

*Reveille — the morning signal for soldiers to wake and get up.
Tattoo — the signal for soldiers to return to quarters, usually at 10pm.

N.C.O.'s will smoke their Woodbines,
Privates puff their big cigars.
No more standing-to in trenches,
Only one more church parade.
No more shivering on the firestep,*
No more Tickler's marmalade.

ANONYMOUS SONG

I Don't Want to be a Soldier
Air: 'On Sunday I Walk Out With a Soldier'

I don't want to be a soldier,
I don't want to go to war.
I'd rather stay at home,
Around the streets to roam,
And live on the earnings of a well-paid whore.
I don't want a bayonet up my arse-hole,
I don't want my ballocks shot away.
I'd rather stay in England,
In merry merry England,
And fuck my bloody life away.

ANONYMOUS SONG

Good-bye Nellie

Good-bye Nellie,
I'm going across the main,
Farewell, Nellie,
This parting gives me pain.
I shall always love you
As true as the stars above.
I'm going to do my duty
For the girl I love.

ANONYMOUS SONG

*Formed part of the front wall of a trench. Standing on it, a soldier was able to see over the parapet or through firing-slits.

If You Want to Find the Sergeant

If you want to find the Sergeant,
I know where he is, I know where he is,
   I know where *he* is
If you want to find the Sergeant
   I know where he is —
He's lying on the Canteen floor.
I've seen him, I've *seen* him,
Lying on the Canteen floor.

*

If you want to find the old battalion,
I know where they are, I know where they are,
   I know where *they* are,
If you want to find the old battalion,
   I know where they are —
They're hanging on the old barbed wire.
I've seen 'em, I've *seen* 'em,
Hanging on the old barbed wire.

ANONYMOUS SONG

The poems that follow could be described as simple views of trench warfare, for the most part by unknown or relatively unknown poets. 'No Man's Land' by 'H.D'A.B.' is a good example of many hundreds of poems written in the war. The author's inexperience shows through in some clumsy rhyming ('fell' and 'invisible'), and the poem has no overview, relying simply on a description of events. Yet the description is vivid, and the poem blends the excitement of battle-lust with the feeling of tragic loss that is typical of many poems and many poets. Comradeship is clearly starting to loom as a major element of front-line experience in such poems, the soldier's allegiance being to his fellow soldiers, not to any abstract concept of nation or state. That feeling is carried on in Robert Nichols's 'Comrades'. Nichols had some front-line experience, but was then invalided out of the Army and made his name with *action vérité* poetry which he read out with great gusto to audiences, going on extended speaking tours in England

and abroad to do so. His reputation has suffered from this, since he has been seen as a propagandist for the war and a poetic profiteer, but there is a vividness and immediacy in his poetry that makes it memorable.

The Face (Guillemont)

Out of the smoke of men's wrath,
The red mist of anger,
Suddenly,
As a wraith of sleep,
A boy's face, white and tense,
Convulsed with terror and hate,
The lips trembling ...

Then a red smear, falling ...
I thrust aside the cloud, as if it were tangible,
Blinded with a mist of blood.
The face cometh again
As a wraith of sleep:
A boy's face, delicate and blond,
The very mask of God,
Broken.

FREDERIC MANNING

The Trenches

Endless lanes sunken in the clay,
Bays, and traverses, fringed with wasted herbage,
Seed-pods of blue scabious, and some lingering blooms;
And the sky, seen as from a well,
Brilliant with frosty stars.
We stumble, cursing on the slippery duck-boards.*
Goaded like the damned by some invisible wrath,
A will stronger than weariness, stronger than animal fear,
Implacable and monotonous.

* Constructions of wooden slats, laid down on muddy tracks and in trenches.

Here a shaft, slanting, and below
A dusty and flickering light from one feeble candle
And prone figures sleeping uneasily,
Murmuring,
And men who cannot sleep,
With faces impassive as masks,
Bright, feverish eyes, and drawn lips,
Sad, pitiless, terrible faces,
Each an incarnate curse.

Here in a bay, a helmeted sentry
Silent and motionless, watching while two sleep,
And he sees before him
With indifferent eyes the blasted and torn land
Peopled with stiff prone forms, stupidly rigid,
As tho' they had not been men.

Dead are the lips where love laughed or sang,
The hands of youth eager to lay hold of life,
Eyes that have laughed to eyes,
And these were begotten,
O Love, and lived lightly, and burnt
With the lust of a man's first strength: ere they were rent,
Almost at unawares, savagely; and strewn
In bloody fragments, to be the carrion
Of rats and crows.

And the sentry moves not, searching
Night for menace with weary eyes.

FREDERIC MANNING

Givenchy Field

The dead lie on Givenchy field
    As lie the sodden Autumn leaves,
The dead lie on Givenchy field,
    The trailing mist a cerement weaves.

Abandoned, save for murder's work,
　　A mine-shaft bulks against the stars,
And fast receding in the mirk
　　The trenches show like umber scars.

'All's quiet,' the sentry's message runs.
　　Outwearied men to slumber yield;
The rain drips down the hooded guns,
　　All's quiet upon Givenchy field.

MAJOR 'H.D'A.B.'

Trenches
From '*The Song of Tiadatha*'

On the day that Tiadatha
Sallied forth into the trenches,
Wondrously was he accoutred.
On his head a cap with ear-flaps
(Very like a third-rate footpad's),
On his feet a pair of waders,
Reaching upwards to his tummy.
Many bags of tricks he carried,
Compass, map case and revolver,
Respirator, two trench daggers,
And his pack was great with torches,
Tommy's cookers,* iron rations,
And a box of ear defenders,
Present from his Aunt Matilda.

As they saw him in the distance,
Bearing down upon their billets,
His platoon turned out in wonder,
Watched the apparition coming,
Speculated who it might be,
Freely making bets about it,
Till they found it was none other
Than their own platoon commander

*Small methylated spirit or solid fuel stove.

101

Then he trudged off to the trenches,
Followed many muddy C.T.s,*
Till at last he reached a dug-out,
And 'reported for instruction'
To the hero who commanded
That small sector of the trenches.
This stout hero and his fellows
Made my Tiadatha welcome
Straightaway plying him with whisky,
Saying, 'Won't you take your kit off?
All you'll need up here's a Sam Browne.'

Then his host expounded to him
Many mysteries of warfare,
And the routine of the trenches,
All the habits of the Boche cove.
All the Boche's beastly habits,
When he crumped,† and when he didn't.
How you got retaliation;
Spoke of Very‡ lights and whizzbangs,
Lewis guns§ and working parties.
Of his leave, due Friday fortnight,
Of the foibles of his Colonel,
Of the rats that he had captured
With some cheese upon a bayonet.

Then they took him round their trenches,
Round their muddy maze of trenches,
Rather like an aggravated
Rabbit warren with the roof off,
Worse to find one's way about in
Than the dark and windy subways
Of the Piccadilly tube are.

*Communication trenches, used to link main trenches one to another.
† Generally used of a bombardment by trench mortars.
‡ Flares fired from a pistol.
§ Light machine-guns, drum-fed.

In the day and night that followed
Many things learnt Tiadatha
Of the subtleties of trench-craft.

MAJOR OWEN RUTTER

The Night Patrol

Over the top! The wire's thin here, unbarbed
Plain rusty coils, not staked, and low enough:
Full of old tins,* though — 'When you're through, all three,
Aim quarter left for fifty yards or so,
Then straight for that new piece of German wire;
See if it's thick, and listen for a while
For sounds of working; don't run any risks;
About an hour; now, over!' And we placed
Our hands on the topmost sand-bags, leapt, and stood
A second with curved backs, then crept to the wire,
Wormed ourselves tinkling through, glanced back, and dropped.
The sodden ground was splashed with shallow pools,
And tufts of crackling cornstalks, two years old,
No man had reaped, and patches of spring grass,
Half-seen, as rose and sank the flares, were strewn
With the wrecks of our attack: the bandoliers,
Packs, rifles, bayonets, belts, and haversacks,
Shell fragments, and the huge whole forms of shells
Shot fruitlessly — and everywhere the dead.
Only the dead were always present — present
As a vile sickly smell of rottenness;
The rustling stubble and the early grass,
The slimy pools — the dead men stank through all,
Pungent and sharp; as bodies loomed before,
And as we passed, they stank; then dulled away
To that vague factor, all encompassing,
Infecting earth and air. They lay, all clothed,
Each in some new and piteous attitude

*Soldiers hung empty tin cans on the wire outside their trenches. If a German working- or raiding-party disturbed the British wire, the tins would clank, making an effective alarm.

That we well marked to guide us back; as he,
Outside our wire, that lay on his back and crossed
His legs Crusader-wise; I smiled at that,
And thought of Elia and his Temple Church.
From him, a quarter left, lay a small corpse,
Down in a hollow, huddled as in bed,
That one of us put his hand on unawares.
Next was a bunch of half a dozen men
All blown to bits, an archipelago
Of corrupt fragments, vexing to us three,
Who had no light to see by, save the flares.
On such a trail, so lit, for ninety yards
We crawled on belly and elbows, till we saw,
Instead of lumpish dead before our eyes,
The stakes and crosslines of the German wire.
We lay in shelter of the last dead man,
Ourselves as dead, and heard their shovels ring
Turning the earth, their talk and cough at times.
A sentry fired and a machine-gun spat;
They shot a flare above us, when it fell
And spluttered out in the pools of No Man's Land,
We turned and crawled past the remembered dead:
Past him and him, and them and him, until,
For he lay some way apart, we caught the scent
Of the Crusader and slid past his legs,
And through the wire and home, and got our rum.

ARTHUR GRAEME WEST+

No-Man's-Land

There's a zone
Wild and lone
None claim, none own,
That goes by the name of No-Man's-Land;
Its frontiers are bastioned, and wired, and mined,
The rank grass shudders and shakes in the wind,
And never a roof nor a tree you find
In No-Man's-Land.

Sprung from hell
Monsters fell
Invisible
Await who venture through No-Man's-Land,
Like a stab in the dark is the death they deal
From an eye of fire in a skull of steel
When the echoes wake to their thunder-peal
In No-Man's-Land.

They that gave
Lives so brave
Have found a grave.
In the haggard fields of No-Man's-Land,
By the foeman's reddened parapet,
They lie with never a head-stone set,
But their dauntless souls march forward yet
In No-Man's-Land.

MAJOR 'H.D'A.B.'

Comrades: An Episode

Before, before he was aware
The 'Verey' light had risen ... on the air
It hung glistering ...
    And he could not stay his hand
From moving to the barbed wire's broken strand.
A rifle cracked.
    He fell.
Night waned. He was alone. A heavy shell
Whispered itself passing high, high overhead,
His wound was wet to his hand; for still it bled
On to the glimmering ground.
Then with a slow, vain smile his wound be bound,
Knowing, of course, he'd not see home again —
Home whose thoughts he'd put away.

    His men
Whispered: 'Where's Mister Gates?' 'Out on the wire.'

'I'll get him,' said one …
  Dawn blinked, and the fire
Of the Germans heaved up and down the line.
  'Stand to!'
Too late! 'I'll get him .' 'O the swine!
When we might have got him in safe and whole!'
'Corporal didn't see 'un fall out on patrol,
Or he'd a got 'un.' 'Sssh!'
  'No talking there.'
A whisper: ''A went down at the last flare.'
Meanwhile the Maxims toc-toc-tocked; their swish
Of bullets told death lurked against the wish.
No hope for him!
  His corporal, as one shamed,
Vainly and helplessly his ill-luck blamed.

                    *

Then Gates slowly saw the morn
Break in a rosy peace through the lone thorn
By which he lay, and felt the dawn-wind pass
Whispering through the pallid, stalky grass
Of No-Man's-Land …
  And the tears came
Scaldingly sweet, more lovely than a flame.
He closed his eyes: he thought of home.
He grit his teeth. He knew no help could come …

                    *

The silent sun over the earth held sway,
Occasional rifles cracked and far away
A heedless speck, a 'plane, slid on alone,
Like a fly travelling a cliff of stone.

'I must get back,' said Gates aloud, and heaved
At his body. But it lay bereaved
Of any power. He could not wait till night …
And he lay still. Blood swam across his sight.
Then with a groan:
'No luck ever! Well, I must die alone.'

Occasional rifles cracked. A cloud that shone,
Gold-rimmed, blackened the sun and then was gone ...
The sun still smiled. The grass sang in its play.
Some one whistled: 'Over the hills and far away',
Gates watched silently the swift, swift sun
Burning his life before it was begun ...
Suddenly he heard Corporal Timmins' voice:
    'Now then,
'Urry up with that tea.'
    'Hi Ginger!' 'Bill!' His men!
Timmins and Jones and Wilkinson (the 'bard')
And Hughes and Simpson. It was hard
Not to see them: Wilkinson, stubby, grim,
With his 'No, sir,' "Yes, sir,' and the slim Simpson: 'Indeed, sir?'
    (while it seemed he winked
Because his smiling left eye always blinked),
And Corporal Timmins, straight and blonde and wise,
With his quiet-scanning, level hazel eyes;
And all the others ... tunics that didn't fit ...
A dozen different sorts of eyes. O it
Was hard to lie there! Yet he must. But no:
'I've got to die. I'll get to them. I'll go.'

Inch by inch he fought, breathless and mute,
Dragging his carcase like a famished brute ...
His head was hammering, and his eyes were dim;
A bloody sweat seemed to ooze out of him
And freeze along his spine ... Then he'd lie still
Before another effort of his will
Took him one nearer yard.

*

    The parapet was reached.
He could not rise to it. A look-out screeched:
'Mr. Gates!'
    Three figures in one breath
Leaped up. Two figures fell in toppling death;
And Gates was lifted in. 'Who's hit?' said he.
'Timmins and Jones.' 'Why did they that for me? —

I'm gone already!' Gently they laid him prone
And silently watched.
    He twitched. They heard him moan,
'Why for me?' His eyes roamed round, and none replied.
'I see it was alone I should have died.'
They shook their heads. Then, 'Is the doctor here?'
'He's coming, sir, he's hurryin', no fear.'
'No good ...
    Lift me.' They lifted him.
He smiled and held his arms out to the dim.
And in a moment passed beyond their ken,
Hearing him whisper, 'O my men, my men!'

ROBERT NICHOLS

Harrow and Flanders

Here in the marshland, past the battered bridge,
    One of a hundred grains untimely sown,
Here, with his comrades of the hard-won ridge,
    He rests, unknown.

His horoscope had seemed so plainly drawn —
    School triumphs earned apace in work and play;
Friendships at will; then love's delightful dawn
    And mellowing day;

Home fostering hope; some service to the State;
    Benignant age; then the long tryst to keep
Where in the yew-tree shadow congregate
    His fathers sleep.

Was here the one thing needful to distill
    From life's alembic, through this holier fate,
The man's essential soul, the hero will?
    We ask; and wait.

LORD CREWE

Frank Brown's 'The Veteran' makes an interesting comparison with Owen's far more famous 'A Terre'. It is difficult to know precisely what reaction we are meant to have to the speaker in Brown's poem. At one and the same time he appears to be justifying the war, yet also to be giving full rein to its horrors. It may be that we should read the speaker's words as being heavily ironic. It may also be that in showing what is in effect a schizophrenic attitude to the war Brown sums up the confusion felt by many of those who fought. Owen's poem can appear clumsy and 'poetic' in comparison. His wounded soldier keeps forgetting that he is a wounded soldier and not Wilfred Owen the poet, and Shelley keeps popping his head out of the hospital bed. Owen is writing a poem to prove a point; Brown is writing a poem and letting the speaker make his own point.

The Veteran

Well, boy, you're off to war.
I'd go again myself
If I was fit. Just reach my sword
From off that dusty shelf.
Ah, thanks! The thrill it carries!
This battered hilt to hold.
I'm mutilated, boy, but still
I'm far from being old.

Just think, a scant eight months ago
I left here strong and tall,
And with my Briton brothers
Threw in my lot, my all.
Just eight short months, but in that time
I've lived a tragic life,
And seen my fill of hate and flame
And death in callous strife.

Eight months ago I used to dream
Of glory's honoured crown;
Eight months, and in that hasting time
My idols tumbled down.
I dreamt the thrill of battle;

The roaring charge; the check;
I never thought that I'd return
A battered, useless wreck.

Oh, I was but driftwood in
The backwash of a corps.
I've suffered and I've risked my life, —
That's what I 'nlisted for.
And were I hale and hearty
I'd do the same again,
And take my place among the ranks
Of Britain's fighting men.

What, youngster? Tell about my wounds?
There's nothing much to say.
The first was in the village —
We captured it that day —
I got a bullet in the breast.
Unconsciously for hours
I just lay where I tumbled
Drenched thro' with chilling showers.

To get me to the ambulance
The bearer's had to creep.
A doctor tended me who looked
Half dead for want of sleep.
They'd run quite out of medicine;
Few orderlies beside,
And those of us who wanted to
Might live — the others died.

I needed life so much, I guess
I fought the angel back.
It's funny how you hate to die,
When lying on your back.
They patched me up, eventually;
Back to the lines I went, —
Back to the freezing trench; 'twas then
I knew what suff'ring meant.

The cutting wind nipped to the bone,
The rifle froze the hand,
And all day long the shrapnel searched
The frost-encrusted land.
To face a madly charging foe
Demands a courage bold,
But more than that is needed to
Combat insistent cold.

One day we found a French platoon;
No wound — no blood was shed;
The poison-gas* had done its work;
The whole platoon was dead.
I remember cogitating
As among that group I stood,
'If hell is anything like war,
Thank God! my life's been good.'

But go, my boy! Off to the front,
And let no tongue dissuade.
Go, for war's proficiency,
With rifle and with spade.
God speed you, boy! I envy you,
As chained to a wooden peg,
I, crippled, sit with a broken life,
One hand, and half a leg.

SERGEANT FRANK S. BROWN

A Terre
(being the philosophy of many soldiers)

Sit on the bed. I'm blind, and three parts shell.
Be careful; can't shake hands now; never shall.

* Poison gas was first used by the Germans during the Second Battle of Ypres, April 1915, and was adopted by all the major combatants. Of all the many horrors of the Great War, gas was perhaps the most awful and one of the most feared. Luckily it was rarely very effective, being dependent on the wind, and quite frequently blew back on to whichever side was trying to use it.

Both arms have mutinied against me, — brutes.
My fingers fidget like ten idle brats.

I tried to peg out soldierly, — no use!
One dies of war like any old disease.
This bandage feels like pennies on my eyes.*
I have my medals? — Discs to make eyes close.
My glorious ribbons? Ripped from my own back
In scarlet shreds. (That's for your poetry book.)

A short life and a merry one, my buck!
We used to say we'd hate to live dead-old, —
Yet now ... I'd willingly be puffy, bald,
And patriotic. Buffers catch from boys
At least the jokes hurled at them. I suppose
Little I'd ever teach a son, but hitting,
Shooting, war, hunting, all the arts of hurting.
Well, that's what I learnt, — that, and making money.

Your fifty years ahead seem none too many?
Tell me how long I've got? God! For one year
To help myself to nothing more than air!
One Spring! Is one too good to spare, too long?
Spring wind would work its own way to my lung,
And grow me legs as quick as lilac-shoots.

My servant's lamed, but listen how he shouts!
When I'm lugged out, he'll still be good for that.
Here in this mummy-case, you know, I've thought
How well I might have swept his floors for ever.
I'd ask no nights off when the bustle's over,
Enjoying so the dirt. Who's prejudiced
Against a grimed hand when his own's quite dust,
Less live than specks that in the sun-shafts turn,
Less warm than dust that mixes with arms' tan?
I'd love to be a sweep, now, black as Town,
Yes, or a muckman. Must I be his load?

---

* Refers to the ancient custom of placing coins on a corpse's eyes when the body is laid out.

O Life, Life, let me breathe, — a dug-out rat!
Not worse than ours the lives rats lead —
Nosing along at night down some safe rut,
They find a shell-proof home before they rot.
Dead men may envy living mites in cheese,
Or good germs even. Microbes have their joys,
And subdivide, and never come to death.
Certainly flowers have the easiest time on earth.
'I shall be one with nature, herb, and stone,'
Shelley would tell me. Shelley would be stunned:
The dullest Tommy hugs that fancy now.
'Pushing up daisies' is their creed, you know.

To grain, then, go my fat, to buds my sap,
For all the usefulness there is in soap.
D'you think the Boche will ever stew man-soup?
Some day, no doubt, if . . .
    Friend, be very sure
I shall be better off with plants that share
More peaceably the meadow and the shower.
Soft rains will touch me, — as they could touch once,
And nothing but the sun shall make me ware.
Your guns may crash around me. I'll not hear;
Or, if I wince, I shall not know I wince.

Don't take my soul's poor comfort for your jest.
Soldiers may grow a soul when turned to fronds,
But here the thing's best left at home with friends.

My soul's a little grief, grappling your chest,
To climb your throat on sobs; easily chased
On other sighs and wiped by fresher winds.

Carry my crying spirit till it's weaned
To do without what blood remained these wounds.

WILFRED OWEN+

To Any Dead Officer

Well, how are things in Heaven? I wish you'd say,
    Because I'd like to know that you're all right.
Tell me, have you found everlasting day,
    Or been sucked in by everlasting night?
For when I shut my eyes your face shows plain;
    I hear you make some cheery old remark —
I can rebuild you in my brain,
    Though you've gone out patrolling in the dark.

You hated tours of trenches; you were proud
    Of nothing more than having good years to spend;
Longed to get home and join the careless crowd
    Of chaps who work for peace with Time for friend.
That's all washed out now. You're beyond the wire:
    No earthly chance can send you crawling back;
You're finished with machine-gun fire —
    Knocked over in a hopeless dud-attack.

Somehow I always thought you'd get done in,
    Because you were so desperate keen to live:
You were all out to try and save your skin,
    Well knowing how much the world had got to give.
You joked at shells and talked the usual 'shop',
    Stuck to your dirty job and did it fine:
With 'Jesus Christ! when *will* it stop?
    Three years … It's hell unless we break their line.'

So when they told me you'd been left for dead
    I wouldn't believe them, feeling it *must* be true.
Next week the bloody Roll of Honour said
    'Wounded and missing' — (That's the thing to do
When lads are left in shell-holes dying slow,
    With nothing but blank sky and wounds that ache,
Moaning for water till they know
    It's night, and then it's not worth while to wake!)

*

Good–bye, old lad! Remember me to God,
  And tell Him that our Politicians swear
They won't give in till Prussian Rule's been trod
  Under the Heel of England ... Are you there? ...
Yes ... and the War won't end for at least two years;
But we've got stacks of men ... I'm blind with tears,
  Staring into the dark. Cheero!
I wish they'd killed you in a decent show.

SIEGFRIED SASSOON

Song

Do your balls hang low?
Do they dangle to and fro?
Can you tie them in a knot?
Can you tie them in a bow?

Do they rattle when you walk?
Do they jingle when you talk?

Do they itch when it's hot?
Do you rest them in a pot?

Can you sling them on your shoulder
Like a lousy fucking soldier?
DO YOUR BALLS HANG LOW?

ANONYMOUS

Untitled

I shouted for blood as I ran, brother,
  Till my bayonet pierced your breast;
I lunged thro' the heart of a man, brother,
  That the sons of men might rest.

I swung up my rifle apace, brother.
  Gasping with wrath awhile,

115

And I smote at your writhing face, brother,
    That the face of peace might smile.

Your eyes are beginning to glaze, brother,
    Your wounds are ceasing to bleed.
God's ways are wonderful ways, brother,
    And hard for your wife to read.

                      JANET BEGBIE

Youth's Own

Out of the fields I see them pass,
    Youth's own battalion —
Like moonlight ghosting over grass —
    To dark oblivion.

They have a wintry march to go —
    Bugle and fife and drum!
With music, softer than the snow
    All flurrying, they come!

They have a bivouac to keep
    Out on a starry heath;
To fling them down, and sleep and sleep
    Beyond reveilly — Death!

Since Youth has vanished from our eyes,
    Who, living, glad can be?
Who will be grieving, when he dies
    And leaves this Calvary?

                  JOHN GALSWORTHY

Canadian Song

There's a little wet home in the trench,
That the rain storms continually drench,
A dead cow close by, with her hooves in the sky,
And she gives off a beautiful stench.

Underneath us, in place of a floor
Is a mess of cold mud and some straw,
And the Jack Johnsons roar as they speed through the air
O'er my little wet home in the trench.

ANONYMOUS

Sentry! What of the Night?

Sentry! What of the night?
The sentry's answer I will not repeat,
Though short in words 'twas with feeling replete.
It covered all he thought and more,
It covered all he'd thought before,
It covered all he might think yet
In years to come,
For he was wet and had no rum.

ANONYMOUS

Carol

While shepherds watched their flocks by night
  All seated on the ground,
A high-explosive shell came down
  And mutton rained around.

SAKI (HECTOR HUGH MONRO)+

Concert Party: Busseboom

The stage was set, the house was packed,
  The famous troop began;
Our laughter thundered, act by act;
  Time light as sunbeams ran.

Dance sprang and spun and neared and fled,
  Jest chirped at gayest pitch,

Rhythm dazzled, action sped
  Most comically rich.

With generals and lame privates both
  Such charms worked wonders, till
The show was over: lagging loth
  We faced the sunset chill;

And standing on the sandy way,
  With the cracked church peering past,
We heard another matinée,
  We heard the maniac blast

Of barrage south by Saint Eloi,
  And the red lights flaming there
Called madness: Come, my bonny boy,
  And dance to the latest air.

To this new concert, white we stood;
  Cold certainty held our breath;
While men in the tunnels below Larch Wood
Were kicking men to death.

EDMUND BLUNDEN

Escape

A Colonel —
  There are four officers, this message says,
  Lying all dead at Mesnil.
  One shell pitched clean amongst 'em at the foot
  Of Jacob's Ladder. They're all Sussex* men.
  I fear poor Flood and Warne were of that party.
  And the Brigade wants them identified. . . .

A Mind —
  Now God befriend me,

---

* i.e. from the Royal Sussex Regiment, in which Blunden served.

The next word not send me
To view those ravished trunks
And hips and blackened hunks.

A Colonel —
No, not you, Bunny, you've just now come down.
I've something else for you.

Orderly!

(*Sir!*)

Find Mr. Wrestman.

EDMUND BLUNDEN

Louse Hunting

Nudes — stark and glistening,
Yelling in lurid glee. Grinning faces
And raging limbs
Whirl over the floor one fire.
For a shirt verminously busy
Yon soldier tore from his throat, with oaths
Godhead might shrink at, but not the lice.
And soon the shirt was aflare
Over the candle he'd lit while we lay.

Then we all sprang up and stript
To hunt the verminous brood.
Soon like a demons' pantomime
The place was raging.
See the silhouettes agape,
See the gibbering shadows
Mixed with the battled arms on the wall.
See gargantuan hooked fingers
Pluck in supreme flesh
To smutch supreme littleness.
See the merry limbs in hot Highland fling
Because some wizard vermin
Charmed from the quiet this revel
When our ears were half lulled

By the dark music
Blown from Sleep's trumpet.

ISAAC ROSENBERG+

The Immortals

I killed them, but they would not die.
Yea! all the day and all the night
For them I could not rest nor sleep,
Nor guard from them nor hide in flight.

Then in my agony I turned
And made my hands red in their gore.
In vain — for faster than I slew
They rose more cruel than before.

I killed and killed with slaughter mad;
I killed till all my strength was gone.
And still they rose to torture me,
For Devils only die in fun.

I used to think the Devil hid
In women's smiles and wine's carouse.
I called him Satan, Balzebub.
But now I call him, dirty louse.

ISAAC ROSENBERG+

To the Rats

O loathsome rodent with your endless squeaking
You hurry to and fro and give no peace,
Above the noise of Hun projectiles' shrieking
The sound of scratching footfalls never cease.

There is a thing which I could never pen,
The horror with which I regard your race,
For how can I describe my feelings when
I wake and find you sitting on my face.

Oh, how shall I portray the depths I plumb
When, stretched upon this bed, my body numb,
I see you, agile, helter-skelter fly.

Oh, Ignominy! while I sleepless lie,
You play your foolish games with eager zest
And sport and gambol freely on my chest.

E.J.L. GARSTON

Chloe
(*The awful effect of four years' active service on a Poet*)

Accept this indent, Sweet, from me —
    That all the blessings thou hast earned
The gods may give (addressed to thee,
    Repeated unto all concerned).

Soft as the violet new-unfurled
    Thine eyes with gentle kindness speak,
And all the roses of the world
    Report for duty on thy cheek.

At eventime, when lights are low,
    I dream I press with lips that burn
A thousand kisses on thy brow
    (For information, and return).
And in the morning e'er I rise
    The image of my Best Beloved
That floats before my waking eyes
    Is duly noted and approved.

These lines, which tell in accents true
    The hopes that warm, the fears that freeze,
My love-lorn heart, are passed to you
    For necessary action, please.

MAJOR E. DE STEIN

One of the great delights of preparing this anthology was the discovery of A.P. (Sir Alan) Herbert as a poet of the war. His work is rarely strident, but it seems, to this reader at least, that it strikes a tone no other poet quite achieves, and has a remarkable humanity and sense of humour.

The German Graves

I wonder are there roses still
    In Ablain St. Nazaire,
And crosses girt with daffodil
    In that old garden there.
I wonder if the long grass waves
    With wild–flowers just the same
Where the Germans made their soldiers' graves
    Before the English came?

The English set those crosses straight
    And kept the legends clean;
The English made the wicket–gate
    And left the garden green;
And now who knows what regiments dwell
    In Ablain St. Nazaire?
But I would have them guard as well
    The graves we guarded there.

So do not tear those fences up
    And drive your waggons through,
Or trample rose and buttercup
    As careless feet may do;
For I have friends where Germans tread
    In graves across the line,
And as I do towards their dead
    So may they do to mine.

And when at last the Prussians pass
    Among those mounds and see
The reverent cornflowers crowd the grass
    Because of you and me,

They'll give perhaps one humble thought
    To all the 'English fools'
Who fought as never men have fought
    But somehow kept the rules.

                A.P. HERBERT

The Cookers
A Song of the Transport

The Officers' kit and the long low limbers,
    The Maltese cart and the mules go by
With a sparkle of paint and speckless timbers,
    With a glitter of steel to catch the eye;
But the things I like are the four black chimneys
    And the smoke-tails scattering down the wind,
For these are the Cookers, the Company Cookers,
    The cosy old Cookers that crawl behind.

The Company Cooks are mired and messy,
    Their cheeks are black but their boots are not;
The Colonel says they must be more dressy,
    And the General says he'll have them shot;
They hang their packs on the four black chimneys,
    They're a grubby disgrace, but *we* don't mind
As long as the Cookers, the jolly black Cookers,
    The filthy old Cookers are close behind.

For it's only the Cooks can make us perky
    When the road is rainy and cold and steep,
When the songs die down and the step gets jerky,
    And the Adjutant's horse is fast asleep;
And it's bad to look back for the four black chimneys
    But never a feather of smoke to find,
For it means that the Cookers, the crazy old Cookers,
    The rickety Cookers are *ditched* behind.

The Company Cook is no great fighter
    And there's never a medal for *him* to wear,
Though he camps in the shell-swept waste, poor blighter,
    And many a cook has 'copped it' there;
But the boys go over on beans and bacon,
    And Tommy is best when Tommy has dined,
So here's to the Cookers, the plucky old Cookers,
    And the sooty old Cooks that waddle behind.

A.P. HERBERT

Dead–Mule Tree
A Song of Wisdom

It's a long step round by the Crucifix for a man with a mighty load,
But there's hell to pay where the dead mule lies if you go by the
    Bailleul road,
Where the great shells sport like an angry child with a litter of broken
    bricks,
So we don't go down by the Dead–Mule Tree, but round by the Crucifix.

But the wild young men come bubbling out and look for an early
    grave;
They light their pipes on the parapet edge and think they're being
    brave;
They take no heed of the golden rules that the long, long years have
    taught,
*And they WILL go down by the Dead–Mule Tree when they know that nobody
ought.*

And some of us old ones feel some days that life is a tiring thing,
And we show our heads in the same place twice, we stand in a trench
    and sing;
We lark about like a kid just out and shatter a hundred rules,
But we never go down by the Dead–Mule Tree, we aren't such perfect fools.

And the War goes on and the men go down, and, be he young or old,
An English man with an English gun is worth his weight in gold,
And I hate to think of the fine young lads who laughed at you
   and me —
Who wouldn't go round by the Crucifix but died at the Dead-Mule Tree.

A.P. HERBERT

The Vision

An average man was Private Flynn,
   Good stuff for soldiering, no doubt;
Troublesome when the drink was in,
   A quiet lad when it was out.

Too fond of gaming and the girls,
   And given to 'language' that would fright
His mother dreaming of his curls
   And his soft boyish ways at night.

He had forgotten how to pray
   The way she taught him at her knees.
Her prayers ran like a river all day,
   And while she slept gave little ease.

The Calvary, by Souchez, holds
   Wide arms to clasp the new-made bed,
Where lies, nor toss their browns and golds,
   The precious, the beloved heads.

Flynn's Captain, who had proved a friend —
   At times a friend is needed most —
Slept there, and comfort was at end
   Because Flynn's faithful friend was lost.

'Gassed.' O'er that twisted grave and dumb,
    Flynn swore a choking oath to give
No quarter when the day should come
    And fed his hate to thrive and live.

Lest that his Captain feel forgot
    At night when all the trenches slept,
Flynn tended like a garden plot
    The graves o'er which the night-dews wept.

He raised a little cross of sticks,
    Pansies, forget-me-nots, amid,
Over him the gaunt Crucifix
    Shed comfort — or he thought it did.

Rank disobedience! No one knew
    How Flynn, so devil-may-care and brave,
Courted destruction just to do
    A little gardening on a grave.

One night the shells lit all the dark,
    Burst in a million splinters of flame;
At morn, before the singing lark,
    Flynn to his tender office came.

He smoothed the clay where it was rough,
    With his rough tender hand he drew
As 'twere a quilt of silken stuff
    Between the sleeper and the dew.

All done, he stretched his six foot four,
    And yawning, in the dawn's pale glow,
Bent to the Crucifix once more,
    Saluted ere he turned to go.

Then here's the marvel — the dead Christ
    Opened His Eyes, the very Eyes
That Mary loved, which through a mist
    The saved souls see in Paradise.

Flynn, like Elijah, caught to Heaven!
  Plain Private Flynn — saw God revealed!
Unto a simple soldier given,
  The secret heart of Heaven unsealed.

Could he go back to common joys
  After the joys of Heaven were won?
The quietness was rent with noise,
  And death sprang from the hidden gun.

They shot Flynn's eyes out. That was good.
  Eyes that saw God are better blind.
Flynn muses on beatitude,
  His empty eye-sockets behind.

In a bare London hospital ward
  He smiles and prays the live-long day.
He who has seen the living Lord
  Has found the Light, the Truth, the Way.

KATHERINE TYNAN

Ambulance Train

Red rowans in the rain
Above the rain-wet rock —
All night the lumbering train
With jolt and jar and shock,
And moan of men in pain,
Beats rumbling in my brain —
Red rowans in the rain
Above the rain-wet rock —
Again and yet again,
Red rowans in the rain.

WILFRID WILSON GIBSON

The Happy Warrior*

His wild heart beats with painful sobs,
His strain'd hands clench at ice-cold rifle,
His aching jaws grip a hot parch'd tongue,
His wide eyes search unconsciously.

He cannot shriek.

Bloody saliva
Dribbles down his shapeless jacket.

I saw him stab
And stab again
A well-killed Boche.

This is the happy warrior,
This is he ...

HERBERT READ

Crucifix Corner

There was a water dump there and regimental
Carts came every day to line up and fill full
Those rolling tanks with chlorinated clay mixture
And curse the mud with vain veritable vexture.
Aveluy across the valley, billets, shacks, ruins.
With time and time a crump there to mark doings.
On New Year's Eve the marsh gloomed tremulous
With rosy mist still holding so marvellous
Sunglow; the air smelt home; the time breathed home —
Noel not put away; New Year's Eve not yet come.
All things said 'Severn', the air was of those dusk meadows —
Transport rattled somewhere in southern shadows,
Stars that were not strange ruled the lit tranquil sky,
Arched far and high.

What should break that but gun-noise or last Trump?
Neither broke it. Suddenly at a light jump

* 'Who is the Happy Warrior? Who is he/That every man in arms should wish to be?' William
Wordsworth, 'Character of the Happy Warrior', 1807.

128

Clarinet sang into 'Hundred Pipers and a''
Aveluy's pipers answered with pipers' true call
'Happy we've been a'-tegether' when nothing, nothing
Stayed of war-weariness or winter-loathing.
Cracker with stockings hung in the quaint Heavens
Orion and the seven stars comical at odds and evens —
Gaiety split discipline in sixes or sevens —
Hunger mixed strangely with magical leavens.
It was as if Cinderella had opened the Ball
And music put aside the time's saddened clothing.
It was as if Sir Walter were company again
In the late night — 'Antiquary' or 'Midlothian' —
Or 'Redgauntlet' bringing Solway clear to the mind.
After music, and a day of walking or making
To return to music, or to read the starred dark dawn-blind.

IVOR GURNEY

A variety of attitudes to officers and 'top brass' are shown in the poems
which follow. The infantryman in 1916 did not expect to like his
officers, knew almost instantly those he was prepared to respect, and by
and large obeyed orders from those and any others with a maximum of
grumbling and considerable efficiency. Commentators have latched on
to the distance between top generals and their men with great vigour and
determination, as if it was something new in warfare. Very few men of
Wellington's army would have spoken to their general, or wanted to,
and Wellington fought battles of attrition as much as did French and
Haig. The point about the complaints against officers is that they were
not new in the Great War. Sassoon's 'The General' does show a form of
relationship between men and their leaders, but it is a relationship that
had been around for many hundreds of years.

It is not the province of a poetry anthology to discuss the military
wisdom of the tactics used by the leadership in the Great War, but it is
relevant to an understanding of that poetry. Generals were sometimes
hated by their men, but more hatred seems to have been directed at staff
officers, for the age-old reason that they were not fighting, and yet were
giving orders to men who were (Hotspur's reaction to a courtly
messenger in *Henry IV Part 1* is a much earlier but standard response
to staff officers). As regards the tactics used on the Western Front, there
was certainly bitterness at the carnage of the Somme, but it has to be

129

remembered that a majority of the officers in the front line believed, as did Haig, that the barrage would cut the wire, and that the Germans would be pounded to dust in their trenches. The stories whereby officers in the trenches pleaded with higher authority to be allowed to change the main battle plan to adapt to local conditions have become a part of folk-myth, as has the image of officers leading their men over the top kicking footballs.* Such stories are used to illustrate the idiocy of higher command, and the wholly unthinking manner in which offensives were planned and executed. The problem with this view is that it is too simple. It is very easy, and very tempting, to overlook the huge size of the army in Flanders, and the extent to which that size meant that either the army acted as one unit, or stood in danger of not acting at all. It is easy for us to argue that a certain regiment or battalion should have been allowed to start its attack earlier or later, or change to another easily reached objective. Looked at from base, it raises the appalling spectre of troops running into their own artillery bombardments, or opening up their flanks to counter-attack by launching offensives without proper support. It is often stated that the conventional assault, as seen at Loos, on the Somme, and in a host of other offensives, failed because artillery bombardment could not cut the enemy's wire, and because massed, straight-line attacks were not able to pick areas of weakness on the opposing front and funnel men into them. The German offensive of 1918 is often cited as an example of how it should be done — no preliminary bombardment, men brought up to assault positions under cover of darkness, and the flexibility whereby attacking troops could by-pass strongpoints and concentrate on weak areas. What is less often cited is that heavy fog greatly assisted this offensive, and that without it the German success might very well have been much less. As far as massed action goes, there had been no time to train Kitchener's volunteer army to anywhere near the same extent as the BEF, and the former's combat experience was often heavily weighted towards the static, defensive war. The troops at the Somme had to be kept together and treated in some respects like a massed band, because they were not battle-hardened veterans who could be expected to fight their way through a battlefield on the basis of individual initiative. Even had they been so, primitive communications made this a dangerous activity. None of this excuses the carnage of the Somme, but it helps to explain why it happened, and why at grass-roots level there is rather less bitterness against high-ranking officers than one might expect.

---

*One officer did indeed provide his men with footballs on 1 July 1916. He was killed. See Martin Middlebrook, *The First Day on the Somme* (1971).

Gold Braid

Same old crossing, same old boat,
    Same old dust round Rouen way,
Same old narsty one-franc note,
    Same old 'Mercy, sivvoo play;'
Same old scramble up the line,
    Same old 'orse-box, same old stror,
Same old weather, wet or fine,
    Same old blooming War.

Ho Lor, it isn't a dream,
    It's just as it used to be, every bit;
Same old whistle and same old bang,
    And me to stay 'ere till I'm 'it.

*

'Twas up by Loos I got me first;
    I just dropped gently, crawled a yard
And rested sickish, with a thirst —
    The 'eat, I thought, and smoking 'ard …
Then someone offers me a drink,
    What poets call 'the cooling draft,'
And seeing 'im I done a think:
    '*Blighty*,'* I thinks — and laughed.

I'm not a soldier natural,
    No more than most of us to-day;
I runs a business with a pal
    (Meaning the Missis) Fulham way;
Greengrocery — the cabbages
    And fruit and things I take meself,
And she has daffs and crocuses
    A-smiling on a shelf.

---

*'Blighty' meaning 'England' or 'home' became common in the Great War, but originated much earlier with soldiers in India. It derives from the Urdu *vilayati* or *bilati*, meaning 'provincial, removed at some distance', and hence 'home' to the soldiers. Thus a 'Blighty one' was a wound sufficiently severe to ensure a return to England, but not so bad as to maim or disable.

'Blighty,' I thinks. The doctor knows;
  'E talks of punctuated damn-the-things.
It's me for Blighty. Down I goes;
  I ain't a singer, but I sings;
'Oh, 'oo goes 'ome?' I sort of 'ums;
  'Oh, 'oo's for dear old England's shores?'
And by-and-by Southampton comes —
  'Blighty!' I says and roars.

I s'pose I thort I done my bit;
  I s'pose I thort the War would stop;
I saw myself a-getting fit
  With Missis at the little shop;
The same like as it used to be,
  The same old markets, same old crowd,
The same old marrers, same old me,
  But 'er as proud as proud ...

*

The regiment is where it was,
  I'm in the same old ninth platoon;
New faces most, and keen becos
  They 'ope the thing is ending soon;
I ain't complaining, mind, but still,
  When later on some newish bloke
Stops one and laughs, 'A Blighty, Bill,'
  I'll wonder, 'Where's the joke?'

Same old trenches, same old view,
  Same old rats and just as tame,
Same old dug-outs, nothing new,
  Same old smell, the very same,
Same old bodies out in front,
  Same old *strafe** from 2 till 4,
Same old scratching, same old 'unt,
  Same old bloody War.

---

*From German *strafen*, to punish. Hence to bombard with shells or bombs, harry with sniping etc.

Ho Lor, it isn't a dream
  It's just as it used to be, every bit;
Same old whistle and same old bang
  And me out again to be 'it.

A.A. MILNE

The Infantryman

The gunner rides on horseback, he lives in luxury,
The sapper has his dug-out as cushy as can be,
The flying man's a sportsman, but his home's a long way back,
In painted tent or straw-spread barn or cosy little shack;
Gunner and Sapper and flying man (and each to his job, say I)
Have tickled the Hun with mine or gun or bombed him from on
    high,
But the quiet work, and the dirty work, since ever the War began
Is the work that never shows at all, the work of the infantryman.

The guns can pound the villages and smash the trenches in,
And the Hun is fain for home again when the T.M.B.'s begin,
And the Vickers gun* is a useful one to sweep a parapet,
But the real work is the work that's done with bomb and bayonet.
Loam him down from heel to crown with tools and grub and kit,
He's always there where the fighting is — he's there unless he's hit;
Over the mud and the blasted earth he goes where the living can;
He's in at the death while he yet has breath, the British infantryman!

Trudge and slip on the shell-hole's lip, and fall in the clinging mire —
Steady in front, go steady! Close up there! Mind the wire!
Double behind where the pathways wind! Jump clear of the ditch,
    jump clear!
Lost touch at the back? Oh, halt in front! and duck when the shells
    come near!

---

* TMB trench-mortar barrage; Vickers gun — British belt-fed heavy machine-gun, similar
to the German Maxim.

Carrying parties all night long, all day in a muddy trench,
With your feet in the wet and your head in the rain and the sodden
    khaki's stench!
Then over the top in the morning, and onward all you can —
This is the work that wins the War, the work of the infantryman.

E.F. CLARKE

I Saw French* Once

I saw French once — he was South Africa cavalry —
And a good leader and a successful, clever one to me.
A knight of Romance — for the knight of Veldt was about him
Who outwitted Bors — few could — who laid traps and got him.
Egypt and Aldershot — Commander of the Forces
And Mons Leader — and Ypres of the Worcestershires.
Now Captain of Deal Castle — so my book advises.
We were paraded for six mortal long hours of shoulders strain
And after hours of cleaning up of leather and brasses —
(O! never, never may such trial be on soldiers again!)
And it was winter of weather and bitter chill,
Outside of Tidworth on a barren chalk slope — Wiltshire Hill.
Six long hours we were frozen with heavy packs —
Brasses cleaned bright, biscuits in haversacks.
At last horses appeared hours late, and a Marshal
Dismounted, our shoulders so laden we were impartial
Whether he shot or praised us — Whether France of the Line
Or soft fatigues at Rouen or Abbeville or Boulogne.
Slow along the ranks of stiff boys pained past right use
Egypt and Veldt — Ulster — Mons, Ypres came

* Field-Marshal Sir John French(1852-1925), later 1st Earl of Ypres, commanded the cavalry in the Boer War (1899-1901) with Douglas Haig as his Chief of Staff, and was chief of the Imperial General Staff, 1912-14. Commanded the British Expeditionary Force from the outbreak of the Great War until replaced by Haig (some say because of the latter's machinations) after the Battle of Loos in the autumn of 1915, and then commanded the troops in the UK until the war's end. Other references are to French's service in the Sudan campaign, 1884-5, and in Ireland, to the battle of and retreat from Mons, and to the first two Battles of Ypres (autumn 1914 and spring 1915). During First Ypres the 2nd Worcestershire Regiment made a famous charge at Gheluvelt which saved the British line. Général J.J.C. Joffre was Commander-in-Chief of the French armies from the outbreak of war until December 1916. See also footnote on p.129.

And none to shout out of Ypres or cry his name —
Hell's pain and silence gripping our shoulders hard
And none speaking — all stiff — in the knifed edged keen blast.
He neared me (Police used electricity) Ypres neared me
The praises of Worcestershires, Joffre's companion Captain he
Who the Médaille-Militaire — the soldier known of France wore,
Scanned me, racked of my shoulders, with kind fixed face
Passed, to such other tormented ones, pain-kept-in-place
To stare so — and be satisfied with these young Gloucesters
Who joined to serve, should have long ago seen Armentières,
As Ypres, but at least Richebourg or near Arras.
But they would not send — youth kept us rotting in a town
Easy and discipline worried — better by far over by Ovillers —
Or Béthune — or St Omer — or Lys, Scarpe, those rivers
To keep a line better than march by meadow and down.
Chelmsford army training to bitterness heart turning
Without an honour — or a use — and such drear bad days
Without body's use, or spirit's use — kept still to rot and laze,
Save when some long route march set our shoulders burning
Blistered our heels — and for one day made body tired.
Anyway, on the chill slope we saw Lord French, Commander on the
    hill
Of short turf, and knew History and were nearer History
Soon for scarred France — to find what Chance was to be feared,
To leave those damned Huts and fall men in shell blast and shots.
To live belt-hungry — to freeze close in narrow cuts
Of trenches — to go desperate by barbed wire and stakes
And (fall not) keep an honour by the steel and the feel
Of the rifle wood kept hard in the clutch of the fingers, blood pale
The coming of French after freezing so long on the slope.
Tidworth was Hell — men got Blighties — at least equal hope.
This was March — in May we were overseas at La Gorgue —
And the Welshmen took us, and were kind, past our hoping mind —
Signallers found romance past believing of War's chance.
But the leader of Mons we had seen, and of History a mien,
South Africa and the first days, Mons, Ypres and between.

IVOR GURNEY

Grand-père

And so when he reached my bed
The General made a stand:
'My brave young fellow,' he said,
    'I would shake your hand.'

So I lifted my arm, the right,
With never a hand at all;
Only a stump, a sight
    Fit to appal.

'Well, well, Now that's too bad!
That's sorrowful luck,' he said;
'But there! You give me, my lad,
    The left instead.'

So from under the blanket's rim
I raised and showed him the other,
A snag as ugly and grim
    As its ugly brother.

He looked at each jagged wrist;
He looked but he did not speak;
And then he bent down and kissed
    Me on either cheek.

You wonder now I don't mind
I hadn't a hand to offer ...
They tell me (you know I'm blind)
    'Twas Grand-père Joffre.

ROBERT SERVICE

Untitled

The General inspecting the trenches
Exclaimed with a horrified shout,
'I refuse to command a Division
Which leaves its excreta about.'

But nobody took any notice
No one was prepared to refute,
That the presence of shit was congenial
Compared with the presence of Shute.

And certain responsible critics
Made haste to reply to his words
Observing that his Staff advisers
Consisted entirely of turds.

For shit may be shot at odd corners
And paper supplied there to suit,
But a shit would be shot without mourners
If somebody shot that shit Shute.*

A.P. HERBERT

After the Battle

So they are satisfied with our Brigade
   And it remains to parcel out the bays!
And we shall have the usual Thanks Parade,
   The beaming General, and the soapy praise.

You will come up in your capacious car
   To find your heroes sulking in the rain,
To tell us how magnificent we are,
   And how you hope we'll do the same again.

And we, who knew your old abusive tongue,
   Who heard you hector us a week before,
We who have bled to boost you up a rung —
   A K.C.B. perhaps, perhaps a Corps† —

---

* This poem is attributed to A.P. Herbert in Lyn Macdonald's *Somme*. Herbert served with the Royal Naval Division 1914-17 in Gallipoli and in France, where he was wounded. Major-General C.D. (later Lieutenant-General Sir Cameron, KCB, KCMG) Shute complained about the state of trenches which the Naval Division had just taken over from Portuguese units — this poem was the troops' reply. Shute was honoured after the war, and in 1927 was GOC-in-C, Northern Command, having been Lieutenant of the Tower of London 1926-7. Died 1936.

† KCB — Knight Commander of the Order of the Bath, and thus to be addressed as 'Sir Somebody'. Corps - i.e., to be promoted from command of a division (major-general) to command of a corps (lieutenant-general). If this verse refers to Shute, then he achieved both.

We who must mourn those spaces in the Mess,
  And somehow fill those hollows in the heart,
We do not want your Sermon on Success,
  Your greasy benisons on Being Smart.

We only want to take our wounds away
  To some warm village where the tumult ends,
And drowsing in the sunshine many a day,
  Forget our aches, forget that we had friends.

Weary we are of blood and noise and pain;
  This was a week we shall not soon forget;
And if, indeed, we have to fight again,
  We little wish to think about it yet.

We have done well; we like to hear it said.
  Say it, and then, for God's sake, say no more.
Fight, if you must, fresh battles far ahead,
  But keep them dark behind your château door!

A.P. HERBERT

The following section contains a batch of poems about injury and disablement. The British medical service in France was excellent; the French troops suffered appalling agonies through the weakness of their army in this area. One result of this medical excellence was that men who in other wars would have died on the field were allowed to live, sometimes without arms and legs, or with other horrific injuries. The better-known poetry of the war cites madness or mental illness as a major fear, as in Owen's 'The Chances'. This does not seem to be reflected to nearly the same extent in the work of other poets, and the ordinary soldier either prayed for a 'Blighty' (a wound that would get him sent home), or not to be wounded at all.

Going Home

I'm goin' 'ome to Blighty — ain't I glad to 'ave the chance!
I'm loaded up wiv fightin', and I've 'ad my fill o' France;
I'm feelin' so excited-like, I want to sing and dance,
  For I'm goin' 'ome to Blighty in the mawnin'.

I'm goin' 'ome to Blighty: can you wonder as I'm gay?
I've got a wound I wouldn't sell for 'alf a year o' pay;
A harm that's mashed to jelly in the nicest sort o' way,
    For it takes me 'ome to Blighty in the mawnin'.

'Ow everlastin' keen I was on gettin' to the front!
I'd ginger for a dozen, and I 'elped to bear the brunt;
But Cheese and Crust!* I'm crazy, now I've done me little stunt,
    To sniff the air of Blighty in the mawnin'.

I've looked upon the wine that's white, and on the wine that's red;
I've looked on cider flowin', till it fairly turned me 'ead;
But oh, the finest scoff will be, when all is done and said,
    A pint o' Bass in Blighty in the mawnin'!

I'm goin' back to Blighty, which I left to strafe the 'Un;
I've fought in bloody battles, and I've 'ad a 'eap of fun;
But now me flipper's busted, and I fink me dooty's done,
    And I'll kiss me gel in Blighty in the mawnin'.

Oh, there be furrin' lands to see, and some of 'em be fine;
And there be furrin' gels to kiss, and scented furrin' wine;
But there's no land like England, and no other gel like mine:
    Thank Gawd for dear old Blighty in the mawnin'.

ROBERT SERVICE

The Veteran
May, 1916

We came upon him sitting in the sun,
    Blinded by war, and left. And past the fence
There came young soldiers from the *Hand and Flower*,
    Asking advice of his experience.

And he said this, and that, and told them tales,
    And all the nightmares of each empty head

---

* i.e. Jesus Christ.

Blew into air; then, hearing us beside,
   'Poor chaps, how'd they know what it's like?' he said.

And we stood there, and watched him as he sat,
   Turning his sockets where they went away,
Until it came to one of us to ask
   'And you're — how old?'
   'Nineteen, the third of May.'

MARGARET POSTGATE

The Death-Bed

He drowsed and was aware of silence heaped
Round him, unshaken as the steadfast walls;
Aqueous like floating rays of amber light,
Soaring and quivering in the wings of sleep.
Silence and safety; and his mortal shore
Lipped by the inward, moonless waves of death.

Someone was holding water to his mouth.
He swallowed, unresisting; moaned and dropped
Through crimson gloom to darkness; and forgot
The opiate throb and ache that was his wound.
Water — calm, sliding green above the weir.
Water — a sky-lit alley for his boat,
Bird-voiced, and bordered with reflected flowers
And shaken hues of summer; drifting down,
He dipped contented oars, and sighed, and slept.

Night, with a gust of wind, was in the ward,
Blowing the curtain to a glimmering curve.
Night. He was blind; he could not see the stars
Glinting among the wraiths of wandering cloud;
Queer blots of colour, purple, scarlet, green,
Flickered and faded in his drowning eyes.

Rain — he could hear it rustling through the dark;
Fragrance and passionless music woven as one;

140

Warm rain on drooping roses; pattering showers
That soak the woods; not the harsh rain that sweeps
Behind the thunder, but a trickling peace,
Gently and slowly washing life away.

He stirred, shifting his body; then the pain
Leapt like a prowling beast, and gripped and tore
His groping dreams with grinding claws and fangs.
But someone was beside him; soon he lay
Shuddering because that evil thing had passed.
And death, who'd stepped toward him, paused and stared.

Light many lamps and gather round his bed.
Lend him your eyes, warm blood, and will to live.
Speak to him; rouse him; you may save him yet.
He's young; he hated War; how should he die
When cruel old campaigners win safe through?

But death replied: 'I choose him.' So he went,
And there was silence in the summer night;
Silence and safety; and the veils of sleep.
Then, far away, the thudding of the guns.

SIEGFRIED SASSOON

Stretcher Case

He woke; the clank and racket of the train
Kept time with angry throbbings in his brain.
Then for a while he lapsed and drowsed again.
At last he lifted his bewildered eyes
And blinked, and rolled them sidelong; hills and skies,
Heavily wooded, hot with August haze,
And, slipping backward, golden for his gaze,
Acres of harvest.

Feebly now he drags
Exhausted ego back from glooms and quags

And blasting tumult, terror, hurtling glare,
To calm and brightness, havens of sweet air.
He sighed, confused; then drew a cautious breath;
This level journeying was no ride through death.
'If I were dead,' he mused, 'there'd be no thinking —
Only some plunging underworld of sinking,
And hueless, shifting welter where I'd drown.'

Then he remembered that his name was Brown.

But was he back in Blighty? Slow he turned,
Till in his heart thanksgiving leapt and burned.
There shone the blue serene, the prosperous land,
Trees, cows and hedges; skipping these, he scanned
Large, friendly names, that change not with the year,
Lung Tonic, Mustard, Liver Pills and Beer.

SIEGFRIED SASSOON

Disabled

He sat in a wheeled chair, waiting for dark,
And shivered in his ghastly suit of grey,
Legless, sewn short at elbow. Through the park
Voices of boys rang saddening like a hymn,
Voices of play and pleasure after day,
Till gathering sleep had mothered them from him.

*

About this time Town used to swing so gay
When glow-lamps budded in the light blue trees,
And girls glanced lovelier as the air grew dim, —
In the old times, before he threw away his knees.
Now he will never feel again how slim
Girls' waists are, or how warm their subtle hands.
All of them touch him like some queer disease.

*

There was an artist silly for his face,
For it was younger than his youth, last year.
Now, he is old; his back will never brace;
He's lost his colour very far from here,
Poured it down shell-holes till the veins ran dry,
And half his lifetime lapsed in the hot race
And leap of purple spurted from his thigh.

*

One time he liked a blood-smear down his leg,
After the matches, carried shoulder-high.
It was after football, when he'd drunk a peg,
He thought he'd better join. — He wonders why.
Someone had said he'd look a god in kilts,
That's why; and maybe, too, to please his Meg,
Aye, that was it, to please the giddy jilts
He asked to join. He didn't have to beg;
Smiling they wrote his lie: aged nineteen years.
Germans he scarcely thought of; all their guilt,
And Austria's, did not move him. And no fears
Of Fear came yet. He thought of jewelled hilts
For daggers in plaid socks; of smart salutes;
And care of arms; and leave; and pay arrears;
Esprit de corps; and hints for young recruits.
And soon, he was drafted out with drums and cheers.

*

Some cheered him home, but not as crowds cheer Goal.
Only a solemn man who brought him fruits
Thanked him; and then enquired about his soul.

*

Now, he will spend a few sick years in institutes,
And do what things the rules consider wise,
And take whatever pity they may dole.
Tonight he noticed how the women's eyes
Passed from him to the strong men that were whole.
How cold and late it is! Why don't they come
And put him into bed? Why don't they come?

WILFRED OWEN+

143

Conscious

His fingers wake, and flutter; up the bed.
His eyes come open with a pull of will,
Helped by the yellow mayflowers by his head.
The blind-cord drawls across the window-sill ...
What a smooth floor the ward has! What a rug!
Who is that talking somewhere out of sight?
Three flies are creeping round the shiny jug ...
'Nurse! Doctor!' — 'Yes, all right, all right.'

But sudden evening blurs and fogs the air.
There seems no time to want a drink of water.
Nurse looks so far away. And here and there
Music and roses burst through crimson slaughter.
He can't remember where he saw blue sky ...
The trench is narrower. Cold, he's cold; yet hot —
And there's no light to see the voices by ...
There is no time to ask ... he knows not what.

WILFRED OWEN+

Futility

Move him into the sun —
Gently its touch awoke him once,
At home, whispering of fields unsown.*
Always it woke him, even in France,
Until this morning and this snow.
If anything might rouse him now
The kind old sun will know.

Think how it wakes the seeds —
Woke, once, the clays of a cold star.
Are limbs so dear-achieved, are sides

---

* Stallworthy (see Bibliography) has 'half-sown' in line 3.

Full-nerved, — still warm, — too hard to stir?
Was it for this the clay grew tall?
O what made fatuous sunbeams toil
To break earth's sleep at all?

WILFRED OWEN+

The Dug-Out

Why do you lie with your legs ungainly huddled,
And one arm bent across your sullen, cold,
Exhausted face? It hurts my heart to watch you,
Deep-shadow'd from the candle's guttering gold;
And you wonder why I shake you by the shoulder;
Drowsy, you mumble and sigh and turn your head . . .
You are too young to fall asleep for ever;
And when you sleep you remind me of the dead.

SIEGFRIED SASSOON
St Venant, July 1918

The Kirk Bell

When oor lads gaed ower the tap
  It was nine o' a Sabbath morn.
I felt as my hert wad stap,
  And I wished I had ne'er been born;
  I wished I had ne'er been born
For I feared baith the foe and mysel',
  Till there fell on my ear forlorn
The jow o' an auld kirk bell.
For a moment the guns were deid,
  Sae I heard it faint and far;
And that bell was ringin' inside my heid
  As I stauchered into the war.

I heard nae ither soun',
  Though the air was a wild stramash,

And oor barrage beat the grun'
   Like the crack o' a cairter's lash,
   Like the sting o' a lang whup lash;
And ilk breath war a prayer or an aith,
   And whistle and drone and crash
Made the pitiless sang o' death.

But in a' that deavin' din
   Like the cry o' the lost in Hell,
I was hearkenin' to a peacefu' tüne
   In the jow o' a far-off bell.

I had on my Sabbath claes,
   And was steppin' doucely the gait
To the kirk on the broomy braes;
   I was standin' aside the yett,
   Crackin' aside the yett;
And syne I was singin' lood
   'Mang the lasses snod and blate
Wi' their roses and southernwood.
I hae nae mind o' the tex'
   For the psalm was the thing for me,
And I gied a gey wheen Huns their paiks
To the tüne o' auld 'Dundee'.

They tell me I feucht like wud,
   And I've got a medal to shaw,
But in a' that habble o' smoke and bluid
   My mind was far awa';
   My mind was far awa'
In the peace o' a simmer glen,
   Daunderin' hame ower the heathery law,
Wi' twae-three ither men....
But sudden the lift grew red
   Ere we wan to the pairtin' place;
And the next I kenned I was lyin' in bed
And a Sister washin' my face.

My father was stench U.P.;
   Nae guid in Rome could he fin';

But, this war weel ower, I'm gaun back to see
 That kirk ahint the line —
 That kirk ahint oor line,
And siller the priest I'll gie
 To pray for the sauls o' the deid langsyne
Whae bigged the steeple for me.
It's no that I'm chief wi' the Pape,
 But I owe the warld to yon bell;
And the beadle that swung the rape
 Will get half a croon for himsel'.*

JOHN BUCHAN

Killed in Action[†]

Your 'Youth' has fallen from its shelf,
And you have fallen, you yourself.
They knocked a soldier on the head,
I mourn the poet who fell dead.
And yet I think it was by chance,
By oversight you died in France.
You were so poor an outward man,
So small against your spirit's span,
That Nature, being tired awhile,
Saw but your outward human pile;
And Nature, who would never let
A sun with light still in it set,
Before you even reached your sky,
In inadvertence let you die.

ANONYMOUS

*jow — ringing; stauchered — stagger; stramash — disturbance; grun — ground; ilk — each, every; aith — oath; deavin' — deafening; claes — clothes; doucely — sedately; yett — gate; crackin' — conversing; syne — then, afterwards; snod — neat, trim; blate — bashful; gey wheen — considerable number; paik — drubbing; like wud — eagerly, vehemently; habble — mob-fight, confusion; daundering — wandering; law — hill; lift — sky; stench — staunch; U.P. — United Presbyterian, a church which had seceded from the main body of the Church of Scotland; siller — silver, money; bigged — built; rape — rope.

[†]This poem was attributed to Isaac Rosenberg in *An Anthology of War Poems*, edited by Frederick Brereton (see Bibliography). It is not listed in the *Collected Works*, and is entirely different from Rosenberg's normal style. *Youth* was a privately printed pamphlet of poems by Rosenberg. I have so far been unable to trace the author of this poem, but wonder if it might be Harold Monro.

On Leave

I had auchteen months o' the war,
  Steel and pouther and reek,
Fitsore, weary and wauf, —
  Syne I got hame for a week.

Daft-like I entered the toun,
  I scarcely kenned for my ain.
I sleepit twae days in my bed,
  The third I buried my wean.

The wife sat greetin' at hame,
  While I wandered oot to the hill,
My hert as cauld as a stane,
  But my heid gaun roond like a mill.

I wasna the man I had been, —
  Juist a gangrel dozin' in fits; —
The pin had faun oot o' the warld,
  And I doddered amang the bits.

I clamb to the Lammerlaw
  And sat me doun on the cairn; —
The best o' my freends were deid,
  And noo I had buried my bairn; —

The stink o' the gas in my nose,
  The colour o' bluid in my ee,
And the biddin' o' Hell in my lug
  To curse my Maker and dee.

But up in that gloamin' hour,
  On the heather and thymy sod,
Wi' the sun gaun down in the Wast
  I made my peace wi' God. . . .

*

I saw a thoosand hills,
   Green and gowd i' the licht,
Roond and backit like sheep,
   Huddle into the nicht.

But I kenned they werena hills,
   But the same as the mounds ye see
Doun by the back o' the line
   Whaur they bury oor lads that dee.

They were juist the same as at Loos
   Whaur we happit Andra and Dave. —
There was naething in life but death,
   And a' the warld was a grave.

A' the hills were graves,
   The graves o' the deid langsyne,
And somewhere oot in the Wast
   Was the grummlin' battle-line.

*

But up frae the howe o' the glen
   Came the waft o' the simmer een.
The stink gaed oot o' my nose,
   And I sniffed it, caller and clean.

The smell o' the simmer hills,
   Thyme and hinny and heather,
Jeniper, birk and fern,
   Rose in the lown June weather.

It minded me o' auld days,
   When I wandered barefit there,
Guddlin' troot in the burns,
   Howkin' the tod frae his lair.

If a' the hills were graves
    There was peace for the folk aneath
And peace for the folk abune,
    And life in the hert o' death. ....

Up frae the howe o' the glen
    Cam the murmur o' wells that creep
To swell the heids o' the burns,
    And the kindly voices o' sheep.

And the cry o' a whaup on the wing,
    And a plover seekin' its bield. —
And oot o' my crazy lugs
    Went the din o' the battlefield.

*

I flang me doun on my knees
    And I prayed as my hert wad break,
And I got my answer sune,
    For oot o' the nicht God spake.

As a man that wauks frae a stound*
    And kens but a single thocht,
Oot o' the wind and the nicht
    I got the peace that I socht.

Loos and the Lammerlaw,
    The battle was feucht in baith,
Death was roond and abune,
    But life in the hert o' death.

A' the warld was a grave,
    But the grass on the graves was green,
And the stanes were bields for hames,
    And the laddies played atween.

*auchteen — eighteen; pouther — gunpowder; reek — smoke; fitsore — footsore; wauf — worn out; wean — child; greetin' — weeping; gangrel — vagrant; happit — covered, buried; howe — hollow; caller — fresh; lown — calm; guddlin' — 'tickling': howkin' — digging; tod — fox; abune — above; whaup — curlew; bield — shelter; wauks frae a stound — wakes from painful thoughts.

Kneelin' aside the cairn
On the heather and thymy sod,
The place I had kenned as a bairn,
I made my peace wi' God.

JOHN BUCHAN
1916

Apologia Pro Poemate Meo

I too, saw God through mud,
The mud that cracked on cheeks when wretches smiled.
War brought more glory to their eyes than blood,
And gave their laughs more glee than shakes a child.

Merry it was to laugh there —
Where death becomes absurd and life absurder.
For power was on us as we slashed bones bare
Not to feel sickness or remorse of murder.

I, too, have dropped off Fear —
Behind the barrage, dead as my platoon,
And sailed my spirit surging light and clear
Past the entanglement where hopes lay strewn;

And witnessed exultation —
Faces that used to curse me, scowl for scowl,
Shine and lift up with passion of oblation,
Seraphic for an hour; though they were foul.

I have made fellowships —
Untold of happy lovers in old song.
For love is not the binding of fair lips
With the soft silk of eyes that look and long,

By Joy, whose ribbon slips, —
But wound with war's hard wire whose stakes are strong;
Bound with the bandage of the arm that drips;
Knit in the webbing of the rifle-thong.

151

I have perceived much beauty
    In the hoarse oaths that kept our courage straight;
    Heard music in the silentness of duty;
    Found peace where shell-storms spouted reddest spate.

Nevertheless, except you share
    With them in hell the sorrowful dark of hell,
    Whose world is but the trembling of a flare
    And heaven but as the highway for a shell,

You shall not hear their mirth:
    You shall not come to think them well content
    By any jest of mine. These men are worth
    Your tears. You are not worth their merriment.

WILFRED OWEN+

The Shell

Shrieking its message the flying death
Cursed the resisting air,
Then buried its nose by a battered church,
A skeleton gaunt and bare.

The brains of science, the money of fools
Had fashioned an iron slave
Destined to kill, yet the futile end
Was a child's uprooted grave.

PRIVATE H. SMALLEY SARSON

Carrion

It is plain now what you are. Your head has dropped
Into a furrow. And the lovely curve
Of your strong leg has wasted and is propped
Against a ridge of the ploughed land's watery swerve.

You are swayed on waves of the silent ground;
You clutch and claim with passionate grasp of your fingers
The dip of earth in which your body lingers;
If you are not found,
In a little while your limbs will fall apart;
The birds will take some, but the earth will take most of your heart.

You are fuel for a coming spring if they leave you here;
The crop that will rise from your bones is healthy bread.
You died — we know you — without a word of fear,
And as they loved you living I love you dead.

No girl would kiss you. But then
No girls would ever kiss the earth
In the manner they hug the lips of men:
You are not known to them in this, your second birth.

No coffin-cover now will cram
Your body in a shell of lead;
Earth will not fall on you from the spade with a slam,
But will fold and enclose you slowly, you living dead.

Hush, I hear the guns. Are you still asleep?
Surely I saw you a little heave to reply.
I can hardly think you will not turn over and creep
Along the furrows trenchward as if to die.

HAROLD MONRO

No One Cares Less than I

'No one cares less than I,
Nobody knows but God,
Whether I am destined to lie
Under a foreign clod,'
Were the words I made to the bugle call in the morning.

But laughing, storming, scorning,
Only the bugles know

What the bugles say in the morning,
And they do not care, when they blow
The call that I heard and made words to early this morning.

EDWARD THOMAS+

A Soldier

He is that fallen lance that lies as hurled,
That lies unlifted now, come dew, come rust,
But still lies pointed as it ploughed the dust.
If we who sight along it round the world,
See nothing worthy to have been its mark,
It is because like men we look too near,
Forgetting that as fitted to the sphere,
Our missiles always make too short an arc.
They fall, they rip the grass, they intersect
The curve of earth, and striking, break their own;
They make us cringe for metal-point on stone.
But this we know, the obstacle that checked
And tripped the body, shot the spirit on
Further than target ever showed or shone.

ROBERT FROST

My reasons for giving here the older version of Rosenberg's 'Dead Man's Dump', rather than the revised version edited by Ian Parsons, are given as a preface to Owen's 'Spring Offensive' later in this section. However, in this instance the differences between the version usually printed and the most modern one are very slight, limited to a handful of minor punctuation marks and some small re-arrangement of stanzas. Rosenberg's 1936 *Collected Works* contained a rather confused eighth stanza, omitted here and in the reading by Ian Parsons. Gordon Bottomley also excluded this stanza in his *Collected Poems* of Rosenberg, and this is essentially the version given here.

Dead Man's Dump

The plunging limbers over the shattered track
Racketed with their rusty freight,
Stuck out like many crowns of thorns,
And the rusty stakes like sceptres old
To stay the flood of brutish men
Upon our brothers dear.

The wheels lurched over sprawled dead
But pained them not, though their bones crunched;
Their shut mouths made no moan,
They lie there huddled, friend and foeman,
Man born of man, and born of woman;
And shells go crying over them
From night till night and now.

Earth has waited for them,
All the time of their growth
Fretting for their decay:
Now she has them at last!
In the strength of her strength
Suspended — stopped and held.

What fierce imaginings their dark souls lit?
Earth! Have they gone into you?
Somewhere they must have gone,
And flung on your hard back
Is their souls' sack,
Emptied of God-ancestralled essences.
Who hurled them out? Who hurled?

None saw their spirits' shadow shake the grass,
Or stood aside for the half-used life to pass
Out of those doomed nostrils and the doomed mouth,
When the swift iron burning bee
Drained the wild honey of their youth.

What of us who, flung on the shrieking pyre,
Walk, our usual thoughts untouched,
Our lucky limbs as on ichor fed,
Immortal seeming ever?
Perhaps when the flames beat loud on us,
A fear may choke in our veins
And the startled blood may stop.

The air is loud with death,
The dark air spurts with fire,
The explosions ceaseless are.
Timelessly now, some minutes past,
These dead strode time with vigorous life,
Till the shrapnel called 'An end!'
But not to all. In bleeding pangs
Some borne on stretchers dreamed of home,
Dear things, war-blotted from their hearts.

A man's brains splattered on
A stretcher-bearer's face;
His shook shoulders slipped their load,
But when they bent to look again
The drowning soul was sunk too deep
For human tenderness.

They left this dead with the older dead,
Stretched at the cross roads.

Burnt black by strange decay
Their sinister faces lie,
The lid over each eye;
The grass and coloured clay
More motion have than they,
Joined to the great sunk silences.

Here is one not long dead.
His dark hearing caught our far wheels,
And the choked soul stretched weak hands
To reach the living word the far wheels said;

The blood–dazed intelligence beating for light,
Crying through the suspense of the far torturing wheels
Swift for the end to break
Or the wheels to break,
Cried as the tide of the world broke over his sight,
'Will they come? Will they ever come?'
Even as the mixed hoofs of the mules,
The quivering-bellied mules,
And the rushing wheels all mixed
With his tortured upturned sight.

So we crashed round the bend,
We heard his weak scream,
We heard his very last sound,
And our wheels grazed his dead face.

ISAAC ROSENBERG+

The version of 'Spring Offensive' given below is the traditional one, current until the new edition of Owen's work by Jon Stallworthy (see Bibliography). Stallworthy gives a new reading for lines 2-3, inserts 'ridge' in place of 'line' in line 11, and inserts 'buttercups' for 'the buttercups' in line 14. Stallworthy also reads 'When' for 'Where' in line 16, 'arms' for 'hands' in line 17, and has 'Breasted the surf of bullets' in line 34 in place of 'Leapt to swift unseen bullets'.

I have operated in defiance of all standard academic procedure by printing the 'old' version here, as I have for Isaac Rosenberg's 'Dead Man's Dump'. Modern scholarship has produced a revised version of what the authors apparently intended to write, and I do not doubt or question the accuracy of the editing work done by Jon Stallworthy and Ian Parsons. It is true to say that, in a number of cases where editors have worked from manuscripts that were not final versions prepared by the poet, an element of guesswork creeps in as to the poet's actual intentions — if indeed the poet knew himself what he intended at that time. My reasons for giving the older versions are not, however, based on profound critical insight. 'Spring Offensive' and 'Dead Man's Dump', in their earlier forms, provided my first intro-duction to Great War poetry. Rather in the manner of someone who prefers the language of the old Lord's Prayer whilst recognising the greater accuracy of the new, modern-English version, I respect the revised versions of both these poems, but in my mind will always continue to think of them and remember them in the form in which I came to love them. The revised versions are not difficult to find for any reader who prefers them, and the older settings will no doubt be swept out to sea in future anthologies. I am reduced to begging for understanding of what is effectively a grossly sentimental decision.

Spring Offensive

Halted against the shade of a last hill,
They fed, and, lying easy, were at ease
And, finding comfortable chests and knees
Carelessly slept. But many there stood still
To face the stark, blank sky beyond the ridge,
Knowing their feet had come to the end of the world.

Marvelling they stood, and watched the long grass swirled
By the May breeze, murmurous with wasp and midge,
For though the summer oozed into their veins
Like the injected drug for their bones' pains,
Sharp on their souls hung the imminent line of grass,
Fearfully flashed the sky's mysterious glass.

Hour after hour they ponder in the warm field —
And the valley far behind, where the buttercups
Had blessed with gold their slow boots coming up.
Where even the little brambles would not yield,
But clutched and clung to them like sorrowing hands;
They breathe like trees unstirred.

Till like a cold gust thrilled the little word
At which each body and its soul begird
And tighten them for battle. No alarms
Of bugles, no high flags, no clamorous haste —
Only a lift and flare of eyes that faced
The sun, like a friend with whom their love is done.
O larger shone that smile against the sun, —
Mightier than his whose bounty these have spurned.

So, soon they topped the hill, and raced together
Over an open stretch of herb and heather
Exposed. And instantly the whole sky burned
With fury against them; and soft sudden cups
Opened in thousands for their blood; and the green slopes
Chasmed and steepened sheer to infinite space.

Of them who running on that last high place
Leapt to swift unseen bullets, or went up
On the hot blast and fury of hell's upsurge,
Or plunged and fell away past this world's verge,
Some say God caught them even before they fell.

But what say such as from existence' brink
Ventured but drave too swift to sink.
The few who rushed in the body to enter hell,
And there out-fiending all its fiends and flames
With superhuman inhumanities,
Long-famous glories, immemorial shames —
And crawling slowly back, have by degrees
Regained cool peaceful air in wonder —
Why speak they not of comrades that went under?

WILFRED OWEN+

159

IV

'We Sha'n't See Willy Any More'

THE ROMANTIC TRADITION: ANIMALS AND NATURE

If the Romantic movement in Britain was dead by 1914, no one appears to have told the poets who were writing then. Of course, Romantic poetry dealt with a great deal more than just nature, but the titles of some of its most famous poems — 'Daffodils', 'Ode to a Skylark', 'Ode to a Nightingale' — illustrate the extent to which that movement has come to be associated with nature. There had been other poetic movements since the Romantics (the Pre-Raphaelites and the Imperialist school among them), and other great poets, most notably Thomas Hardy, but Wilfred Owen was not alone in looking to Shelley for much of his inspiration. The fact was that, whatever they thought they were doing, a large number of young poets were, prior to the war, following firmly in a tradition that harked back to Wordsworth. They wrote with relative simplicity about birds, animals, and the rural landscape, used common speech, and put 'ordinary' people at the centre of their poems. Their verse was also very subjective, and often gave the impression of seeking to express a transcendental moment of insight, an explosion of the inner soul visited upon the outer world.

At the same time as this post-Romantic tradition was flourishing, there was growing that style of poetry which led directly to T.S. Eliot's 'smells of steaks in passageways'. Every force provokes a counter-force. So the preponderance of nature poetry in pre-war England encouraged a body of writing that was altogether harder, more objective, and much more firmly based in and on urban Britain. This counter-force is sometimes associated with the great rival to Georgian poetry, the Imagist* school, though in reality the movement against Romanticism went much beyond Imagism and its followers. The Georgians won the war, in poetic terms; the Imagists won the peace. T.S. Eliot wrote

* See biographical note on Ezra Pound.

poetry deliberately designed to exclude the last vestiges of Romanti-
cism, and it is his style of writing that has dominated critical thinking
about modern poetry for the past fifty years.

A background as a Nature poet cut both ways for those who fought
in and wrote about the war. A number of poets, notably Siegfried
Sassoon and Robert Graves, reacted to the shock of fighting in the
early stages by retreating into a vision, after a few cursory references to
the war, of an idyllic pastoral world. Other poets continued to write
poetry, fanciful nature poetry, and found themselves becoming
rapidly divorced from the mood of the times. Nature poetry also pro-
duced poets who were prepared to look at what they saw, record it,
but rarely comment on it.

On the credit side, the Nature poet went to war with a number of
advantages. His subject went back to the dawn of time, and so, if
properly handled and integrated, could give his war poetry a sense of
breadth and depth lacking in other verse. Thomas Hardy always had a
magnificent sense of history. Isaac Rosenberg, not normally thought
of as a Nature poet, managed to give the war both an awful majesty
and a pathetic, ironical twist by writing of it in the context of nature.
Owen's 'Spring Offensive' (included in the previous section of this book)
is one of the most complex poems of the war, with much of that fruitful
complexity achieved by use of natural imagery. An efficient poet
could make the war seem less terrifying by suggesting that it was all
part of a natural cycle, a cycle which included birth, death, and also
re-birth. Edward Thomas, Charles Sorley, and Edmund Blunden were
particularly skilful at this. Alternatively, he or she could make it
appear more terrifying by suggesting that the war had overwhelmed
the natural cycle, as Rosenberg does in 'Spring 1916', or simply by
contrasting the images of healthy nature with the carnage of the
trenches. The various poems contrasting bird-song with trench life
show what powerful effects can be wrought by relatively simple
juxtaposition.

Some poems which feature animals are more or less shamelessly
sentimental, but one such as J.C. Squire's 'To a Bulldog' seems, to me
at least, to be plainly effective. Squire came, after the war, to be asso-
ciated with the conservative, right-wing element in poetry. The tail-
end of the Georgian movement was derisively named 'the Squirearchy'
after him. Yet his poetry shows him at times to have been surprisingly
unlike his image, something perhaps shown more strongly in the
poems in the 'Home Front' section of this work. Given the fuss made
about the perception of the British as a race which thinks more about
the RSPCA than the NSPCC, one might have expected the First

World War to produce a great many more poems about suffering cavalry chargers and the like. In practice, it was the loss of human life that dominated poetry.

If the preceding section is the most conventional in this book, then what follows here is the most difficult to marshal into one separate entity. An awareness of nature permeates, quite literally, thousands of the poems written during the Great War. One reason, of course, is that the landscape of trench warfare was so obviously and immediately gripping. Another is that the front-line soldier in that war lived very close to the elements. Living in mud, often protected only by the clothing on his back from the cold and the wet, and at the mercy of the weather in a military as well as a personal sense (a major reason for the success of the German offensive in 1918 was that it was launched on a morning of thick fog), the soldier had a sharpened awareness of nature. This applied particularly to dawn. Dawn 'stand-to', where the soldiers manned the firing-step on the trenches, was a regular feature of each day of war, because offensives were often launched either at dawn or in the early morning. Night-time often saw more action in no man's land, under cover of darkness, than daytime in the trenches. Patrols, wire-cutting parties, attempts to rescue the wounded or to take a prisoner, and false alarms frequently meant that dawn, when spirits were often at a low ebb anyway, became a moment of extreme exhaustion. Dawn had also been traditionally a symbol of new hope and a new day. That in itself was an ironic comment for the soldier who woke every morning to look out over a front line that had remained static for years and years.

Rats and lice were permanent reminders of the natural world, as was shown in the preceding section. One survivor of the First World War proudly produced for me his huge .455 service revolver, some fifty years after the war had ended. It had six live rounds in the chambers, and with it, once a week, he used to shoot at rats on a nearby compost heap from out of his bedroom window, carrying on a sport he had learnt in his dug-out on the Somme. War Office records do not detail how many officers and men lost their lives through getting in the way of bullets meant for rats; memoirs suggest it may have been a considerable number. The rats could grow to the size of small dogs. Few soldiers doubted what food it was that gave them their size. Hair- and body-lice were an inseparable part of trench life, too. Clothes could be scoured or scorched free of lice, and bodies washed, but a return to the trenches was also a return to the lice. Only one author, Isaac Rosenberg, managed to combine humour and seriousness in poems dealing with rats and lice, emphasising his ability, above all others, to make serious poetry out of very basic elements. There is humour in this section, too, as in all the others; again, it does not diminish the seriousness of what is said, and sometimes, by so obviously demonstrating defence mechanisms, it can enhance it. The poets who relied heavily on nature for their war poetry were inheritors of the pastoral tradition in English verse. It is a noble tradition, and very rarely did they let it down.

On Receiving News Of The War

Snow is a strange white word;
No ice or frost
Have asked of bud or bird
For Winter's cost.

Yet ice and frost and snow
From earth to sky
This Summer land doth know,
No man knows why.

In all men's hearts it is.
Some spirit old
Hath turned with malign kiss
Our lives to mould.

Red fangs have torn His face.
God's blood is shed.
He mourns from His lone place
His children dead.

O! ancient crimson curse!
Corrode, consume.
Give back this universe
Its pristine bloom.

ISAAC ROSENBERG+
Cape Town, 1914

To A Bulldog

(W.H.S., Capt. [Acting Major] R.F.A;* killed April 12, 1917.)

We sha'n't see Willy any more, Mamie,
　　He won't be coming any more:
He came back once and again and again,
　　But he won't get leave any more.

We looked from the window and there was his cab,
　　And we ran downstairs like a streak,
And he said 'Hullo, you bad dog', and you crouched to the floor,
　　Paralysed to hear him speak,

And then let fly at his face and his chest
　　Till I had to hold you down,
While he took off his cap and his gloves and his coat
　　And his bag and his thonged Sam Browne.

We went upstairs to the studio
　　The three of us, just as of old,
And you lay down and I sat and talked to him
　　As round the room he strolled.

Here in the room where, years ago
　　Before his old life stopped,
He worked all day with his slippers and his pipe,
　　He would pick up the threads he'd dropped.

Fondling all the drawings he had left behind,
　　Glad to find them all still the same,
And opening the cupboards to look at his belongings
　　… Every time he came.

But now I know what a dog doesn't know,
　　Though you'll thrust your head on my knee,
And try to draw me from the absent-mindedness
　　That you find so dull in me.

* Royal Field Artillery.

165

And all your life you will never know
 What I wouldn't tell you even if I could,
That the last time we waved him away
 Willy went for good.

But sometimes as you lie on the hearthrug
 Sleeping in the warmth of the stove,
Even through your muddled old canine brain
 Shapes from the past may rove.

You'll scarcely remember, even in a dream,
 How we brought home a silly little pup,
With a big square head and little crooked legs
 That could scarcely bear him up.

But your tail will tap at the memory
 Of a man whose friend you were,
Who was always kind though he called you a naughty dog
 When he found you in his chair;

Who'd make you face a reproving finger
 And solemnly lecture you
Till your head hung downwards and you looked very sheepish!
 And you'll dream of your triumphs too.

Of summer evening chases in the garden
 When you dodged us all about with a bone:
We were three boys, and you were the cleverest,
 But now we're two alone.

When summer comes again,
 And the long sunsets fade,
We shall have to go on playing the feeble game for two
 That since the war we've played.

And though you run expectant as you always do
 To the uniforms we meet,
You'll never find Willy among all the soldiers
 In even the longest street,

Nor in any crowd; yet, strange and bitter thought,
   Even now were the old words said,
If I tried the old trick and said 'Where's Willy?'
   You would quiver and lift your head,

And your brown eyes would look to ask if I were serious,
   And wait for the word to spring.
Sleep undisturbed: I sha'n't say *that* again,
   You innocent old thing.

I must sit, not speaking, on the sofa,
   While you lie asleep on the floor;
For he's suffered a thing that dogs couldn't dream of,
   And he won't be coming here any more.

                                                    J.C. SQUIRE

The Burdened Ass
(An Allegory)

One day, as I travelled the highway alone,
I heard, on in front, a most dolorous groan;
And there, round the corner, a weary old ass
Was nuzzling the hedge for a mouthful of grass.
The load that he carried was piled up so high
That it blocked half the road and threatened the sky.
Indeed, of himself I could see but a scrap,
And expected each minute to see that go snap;
For beneath all his load I could see but his legs,
And they were as thin as the thinnest clothes-pegs.

I said, 'O most gentle and innocent beast,
Say, — why is your burden so greatly increased?
Who loads you like this, beyond reason and right?
Is it done for a purpose, or just out of spite?
Is it all your own treasures you have in your pack,
That crumples your backbone and makes your ribs crack?
It is really too much for an old ass's back.'

'Treasures!' — he groaned, through a lump of chewed grass,
'*Are* they treasures? I don't know. I'm only the ass
That carries whatever they all like to pack
On my load, without thought of my ribs or my back.
I know there are heaps of things there that I hate,
But it's always been so. I guess it's my fate.'
And he flicked his long ears, and switched his thin tail,
And rasped his rough neck with a hinder-foot nail.

'There are fighting-men somewhere up there, and some fools,
And talking-men — heaps — who have quitted their stools
To manage the state and direct its affairs,
And see, I suppose, that we all get our shares, —
And ladies and lords, and their offspring and heirs,
And their flunkeys and toadies, and merchants and wares. —
And parsons and lawyers, — O heaps, — in that box,
And big folk and small folk, and all kinds of crocks.

'*That mighty big bale?* — Poison, that, — for the people;
Whatever else lacks they must still have their tipple.
That's The Trade, don't you know, that no one can shackle, —
"Vested Int'rests," they call it, and that kind of cackle.
Why the Bishops themselves dare not tackle the tipple,
For it props up the church and at times builds a steeple.'

(A strangely ingenuous old ass, you perceive,
Whom any shrewd rascal could easily deceive.)

'*That other big bale?* — What I said, — fighting things, —
Ammunition and guns and these new things with wings,
O yes, they bulk big, but we need them, — for why? —
If we hadn't as much as the others have — why,
They say we might just as well lie down and die.

'*Yon big bale on top?* — Ah! that *is* a big weight.
And that's just the one of the lot I most hate.
That's Capital, that is, — and landlords and such;
And there seems to me sometimes a bit overmuch
In *that* bale. But there, — I'm perhaps wrong again,
Such matters are outside an old ass's ken.

'*My fodder?* Oh well, you see, — no room for that.
I pick as I go, and no chance to get fat.
That poison bulks large, — and the landlords, you see; —
And that Capital's heavy as heavy can be.
Someone's bound to go short, and of course that one's ME.'

He kicked up one heel with a snort of disgust,
And — sudden as though by a giant hand thrust,
The top-heavy pack on his lean back revolved,
Came crashing to earth, and in fragments dissolved.

Much surprised, — the old ass, thus set free from his load,
Picked out a soft spot in the nice dusty road,
And laid him down on it and rolled in high glee,
And, as he kicked this way and that, said to me, —

'Say, Man, I have never enjoyed such a roll
Since the day I was born, a silly young foal.
Seems to me, if I'd had half the sense of an ass,
I'd have long since got rid of that troublesome mass.
But now that it's down, why — down it shall stop.
All my life's been down under, but now I'm on top.'
Then he came right-side up, pranced about on his load,
And kicked it to pieces all over the road.

And what all this means, I really can't say.
It may not mean much. But — again, — why, it may.

JOHN OXENHAM

Elegy On The Death Of Bingo Our Trench Dog

WEEP, weep, ye dwellers in the delvèd earth,
    Ah, weep, ye watchers by the dismal shore
Of No Man's Land, for Bingo is no more;
He is no more, and well ye knew his worth,
    For whom on bully-beefless days were kept
Rare bones by each according to his means,

169

And, while the Quartermaster-Sergeant slept,
The elusive pork was rescued from the beans.
   He is no more and, impudently brave,
   The loathly rats sit grinning on his grave.

Him mourn the grimy cooks and bombers ten,
   The sentinels in lonely posts forlorn,
   The fierce patrols with hands and tunics torn,
The furtive band of sanitary men.
   The murmuring sound of grief along the length
Of traversed trench the startled Hun could hear;
   The Captain, as he struck him off the strength,
Let fall a sad and solitary tear;
   'Tis even said a batman passing by
   Had seen the Sergeant-Major wipe his eye.

The fearful fervour of the feline chase
   He never knew, poor dog, he never knew;
   Content with optimistic zeal to woo
Reluctant rodents in this murky place,
   He never played with children on clean grass,
Nor dozed at ease beside the flowing embers,
   Nor watched with hopeful eye the tea-cakes pass,
Nor smelt the heather-smell of Scotch Septembers,
   For he was born amid a world at war
   Although unrecking what we struggled for.

Yet who shall say that Bingo was unblest
   Though all his Sprattless life was passed beneath
   The roar of mortars and the whistling breath
Of grim nocturnal heavies going West?
   Unmoved he heard the evening hymn of hate,
Unmoved would gaze into his master's eyes,
   For all the sorrows men for men create
In search of happiness wise dogs despise,
   Finding ecstatic joy in every rag
   And every smile of friendship worth a wag.

                  MAJOR E. DE STEIN

An Appeal

I'm only a cavalry charger,
  And I'm dying as fast as I can
(For my body is riddled with bullets —
  They've potted both me and my man);
And though I've no words to express it,
  I'm trying this message to tell
To kind folks who work for the Red Cross —
  Oh, please help the Blue one as well!

My master was one in a thousand,
  And I loved him with all this poor heart
(For horses are built just like humans,
  Be kind to them — they'll do their part);
So please send out help for our wounded,
  And give us a word in your prayers;
This isn't so strange as you'd fancy —
  The Russians do it in theirs.

I'm only a cavalry charger,
  And my eyes are becoming quite dim
(I really don't mind, though I'm 'done for',
  So long as I'm going to *him*);
But first I would plead for my comrades,
  Who're dying and suffering too —
Oh, please help the poor wounded horses!
  I'm sure that you would — if you knew.

'SCOTS GREYS'

Commandeered

Last year he drew the harvest home
  Along the winding upland lane,
The children twisted marigolds
  And clover flowers to deck his mane.
    Last year he drew the harvest home.

To-day, with puzzled, patient face,
 With ears a-droop and weary feet
He marches to the sound of drums
 And draws the gun along the street.
 To-day he draws the guns of war!

L.G. MOBERLEY

Nature came into its own in the Great War. Its eternal, cyclic pattern
could be used as a source of great reassurance, the stopping of that
pattern by the war as a sign of the war's immensity and power. Dawn
birdsong (pp. 177-9), in the middle of so much carnage, destruction, and
machine-made noise, was an irony, a stimulant, and sometimes even a
shock, and was written about certainly as widely as any other
single natural feature of trench life.

A Private

This ploughman dead in battle slept out of doors
Many's a frozen night, and merrily
Answered staid drinkers, good bedmen, and all bores:
'At Mrs. Greenland's Hawthorn Bush,' said he,
'I slept.' None knew which bush. Above the town,
Beyond 'The Drover', a hundred spot the down
In Wiltshire. And where now at last he sleeps
More sound in France — that, too, he secret keeps.

EDWARD THOMAS+

The Guard's Mistake

The chapel at the crossways bore no scar,
There never a whining covey of shells yet pounced;
The calm saints in the chapel knew no war,
No meaning there the horizon's roars announced;
 We halted, and were glad; the country lay,
 After our marching, like a sabbath day.

Round the still quandrangle of the great farm
The company soon had settled their new home;

172

The cherry-clusters beckoned every arm,
The brook ran wrinkling by with playful foam,
    And when the guard was at the main gate set,
    Surrounding pastoral urged them to forget.

So out upon the road, gamekeeper-like,
The cowman now turned warrior measured out
His up-and-down *sans* fierce 'bundook and spike',*
Under his arm a cudgel brown and stout;
    With pace of comfort and kind ownership,
    And philosophic smile upon his lip.

It seemed a sin to soil the harmonious air
With the parade of weapons built to kill.
But now a flagged car came ill-omened there;
The crimson-mottled monarch, shocked and shrill,
    Sent our poor sentry scampering for his gun,
    Made him once more 'the terror of the Hun'.

EDMUND BLUNDEN

As the Team's Head-Brass

As the team's head-brass flashed out on the turn
The lovers disappeared into the wood.
I sat among the boughs of the fallen elm
That strewed the angle of the fallow, and
Watched the plough narrowing a yellow square
Of charlock. Every time the horses turned
Instead of treading me down, the ploughman leaned
Upon the handles to say or ask a word,
About the weather, next about the war.
Scraping the share he faced towards the wood,
And screwed along the furrow till the brass flashed
Once more.

---

* Rifle and bayonet, a Regular Army term from about 1850. *Bundook* is Hindi for a rifle; earlier a musket, and earlier still a cross-bow. It derives originally from the Arabic *banadik*, Venice, where cross-bows were made.

The blizzard felled the elm whose crest
I sat in, by a woodpecker's round hole,
The ploughman said. 'When will they take it away?'
'When the war's over.' So the talk began —
One minute and an interval of ten,
A minute more and the same interval.
'Have you been out?' 'No.' 'And don't want to, perhaps?'
'If I could only come back again, I should.
I could spare an arm, I shouldn't want to lose
A leg. If I should lose my head, why, so,
I should want nothing more. . . . Have many gone
From here?' 'Yes.' 'Many lost?' 'Yes, a good few.
Only two teams work on the farm this year.
One of my mates is dead. The second day
In France they killed him. It was back in March,
The very night of the blizzard, too. Now if
He had stayed here we should have moved the tree.'
'And I should not have sat here. Everything
Would have been different. For it would have been
Another world.' 'Ay, and a better, though
If we could see all all might seem good.' Then
The lovers came out of the wood again:
The horses started and for the last time
I watched the clods crumble and topple over
After the ploughshare and the stumbling team.

EDWARD THOMAS+

'If The War Keeps On'

It can't keep a-goin' —
I told Farmer Scott;
We're too near to ruin,
'Twill crack the ole pot.
Our men an' our boys is all marchin',
An' wimin can't manage the lot.

But Scott says it will —
(He's said so a year —)

174

Noa food'll be grawn,
Noa barley, noa beer,
Noa wheat, nor noa beef, nor yet mutton —
A terrible business, I fear.

Our farms'll run wild,
But weeds'll go free
Wi' nettles an' thistles
As far as the sea,
The land'll be choaked up wi' rubbish,
An' only the crows'll agree.

The Fens'll be flooded,
The Wolds'll stan' dry,
The blackbird'll sing,
An' the cuckoo'll cry,
Our dogs an' our cats'll turn savage
An' live on the chance passers-by.

It must a bin once,
So why not agen?
'Twas so afore farmers
Come into the Fen,
The oak an' th' ash'll stan' steady,
They've bin 'ere sin' goodness knows when.

The villages all
Their doors'll be shut,
Their folk to the towns
'll gallop full butt,
But how they will live when they get there —
I could tell you no more'n my foot.

'Twill be a strange sight —
Ole England gone back
For thousands of years
To ruin an' wrack,
But I doan't care a farden what 'appens,
'Coz now't will bring back my poor Jack.

BERNARD GILBERT

Spring 1916

Slow, rigid, is this masquerade
That passes as through a difficult air;
Heavily — heavily passes.
What has she fed on? Who her table laid
Through the three seasons? What forbidden fare
Ruined her as a moral lass is?

I played with her two years ago,
Who might be now her own sister in stone,
So altered from her May mien,
When round vague pink a necklace of warm snow
Laughed to her throat where my mouth's touch had gone.
How is this, ruined Queen?

Who lured her vivid beauty so
To be that strained chilled thing that moves
So ghastly midst her young brood
Of pregnant shoots that she for men did grow?
Where are the strong men who made these their loves?
Spring! God pity your mood.

ISAAC ROSENBERG+

Break Of Day In The Trenches

The darkness crumbles away.
It is the same old druid Time as ever,
Only a live thing leaps my hand,
A queer sardonic rat,
As I pull the parapet's poppy
To stick behind my ear.
Droll rat, they would shoot you if they knew
Your cosmopolitan sympathies
(And God knows what antipathies).
Now you have touched this English hand

You will do the same to a German
Soon, no doubt, if it be your pleasure
To cross the sleeping green between.
It seems you inwardly grin as you pass
Strong eyes, fine limbs, haughty athletes,
Less chanced than you for life,
Bonds to the whims of murder,
Sprawled in the bowels of the earth,
The torn fields of France.
What do you see in our eyes
At the shrieking iron and flame
Hurled through still heavens?
What quaver — what heart aghast?
Poppies whose roots are in man's veins
Drop, and are ever dropping;
But mine in my ear is safe —
Just a little white with the dust.

ISAAC ROSENBERG+

Returning, We Hear The Larks

Sombre the night is.
And though we have our lives, we know
What sinister threat lurks there.

Dragging these anguished limbs, we only know
This poison-blasted track opens on our camp —
On a little safe sleep.

But hark! joy — joy — strange joy.
Lo! heights of night ringing with unseen larks.
Music showering our upturned list'ning faces.

Death could drop from the dark
As easily as song —
But song only dropped,
Like a blind man's dreams on the sand

By dangerous tides,
Like a girl's dark hair for she dreams no ruin lies there,
Or her kisses where a serpent hides.

ISAAC ROSENBERG+

A Thrush In The Trenches

Suddenly he sang across the trenches,
   vivid in the fleeting hush
as a star-shell through the smashed black branches,
   a more than English thrush.

Suddenly he sang, and those who listened
   nor moved nor wondered, but
heard, all bewitched, the sweet unhastened
   crystal Magnificat.

One crouched, a muddied rifle clasping,
   and one a filled grenade,
but little cared they, while he went lisping
   the one clear tune he had.

Paused horror, hate and Hell a moment,
   (you could almost hear the sigh)
and still he sang to them, and so went
   (suddenly) singing by.

Suddenly singing — and thus, out of hate and horror,
   the greater impulse than those that it can move by
shakes itself free, and death becomes a mirror,
   held up by angels, for man to see God's love by,
     and this we were,
   and, thus we challenge you, Michael, says the soldier.

HUMBERT WOLFE

The Question

I wonder if the old cow died or not.
　　Gey bad she was the night I left, and sick.
Dick reckoned she would mend. He knows a lot —
　　At least he fancies so himself, does Dick.

Dick knows a lot. But maybe I did wrong
　　To leave the cow to him, and come away.
Over and over like a silly song
　　These words keep humming in my head all day.

And all I think of, as I face the foe
　　And take my lucky chance of being shot,
Is this — that if I'm hit, I'll never know
　　Till Doomsday if the old cow died or not.

WILFRID WILSON GIBSON

The Kingfisher

A flash of blue
And a flicker of fire —
A thought of you,
And the heart's desire.

A pencil-stroke
By the unseen drawn, —
A sigh that spoke
Of a hope's young dawn.

Jewel of blue
And of fire-raped red,
Past me, past you
The Kingfisher sped.

DYNELEY HUSSEY

Chemin Des Dames

In silks and satins the ladies went
Where the breezes sighed and the poplars bent,
Taking the air of a Sunday morn
Midst the red of poppies and gold of corn —
Flowery ladies in stiff brocades,
With negro pages and serving maids,
In scarlet coach, or in gilt sedan,
With brooch and buckle and flounce and fan,
Patch and powder and trailing scent,
Under the trees the ladies went —
Lovely ladies that gleamed and glowed,
As they took the air on the Ladies' Road.

Boom of thunder and lightning flash —
The torn earth rocks to the barrage crash;
The bullets whine and the bullets sing
From the mad machine-guns chattering;
Black smoke rolling across the mud,
Trenches plastered with flesh and blood —
The blue ranks* lock with the ranks of grey,
Stab and stagger and sob and sway;
The living cringe from the shrapnel bursts,
The dying moan of their burning thirsts,
Moan and die in the gulping slough —
Where are the butterfly ladies now?

CROSBIE GARSTIN

From Albert To Bapaume

Lonely and bare and desolate,
Stretches of muddy filtered green,
A silence half articulate
Of all that those dumb eyes have seen.

* Most of France's infantrymen wore a blue uniform (*bleu horizon*), in contrast to the British khaki and German field grey (*feldgrau*). The Chemin des Dames is a road that runs along ridges near the River Aisne, and was the scene of heavy fighting in 1917 and again in 1918.

A battered trench, a tree with boughs
Smutted and black with smoke and fire,
A solitary ruined house,
A crumpled mass of rusty wire.

And scarlet by each ragged fen
Long scattered ranks of poppies lay,
As though the blood of the dead men
Had not been wholly washed away.

ALEC WAUGH

Three Hills

There is a hill in England,
    Green fields and a school I know,
Where the balls fly fast in summer,
    And the whispering elm-trees grow,
        A little hill, a dear hill,
    And the playing fields below.

There is a hill in Flanders,
    Heaped with a thousand slain,
Where the shells fly night and noontide
    And the ghosts that died in vain,
        A little hill, a hard hill
    To the souls that died in pain.

There is a hill in Jewry,
    Three crosses pierce the sky,
On the midmost He is dying
    To save all those who die,
        A little hill, a kind hill
    To souls in jeopardy.

EVERARD OWEN

Fingal's Weeping*

Because they were so brave and young
    Who now are sleeping,
His old heart wrung, his heart unstrung,
    Fingal's a-weeping.

There's warble of waters at morning in Etive glen,
    And the mists are flying;
Chuckles of Spring in the wood, on the moor, on the ben,
    No heed for their dying!
So Fingal's weeping, the young brave sleeping,
    Fingal's weeping.

      They'll be forgot in time — forgot!
        Time that goes sweeping;
      The wars they fought remembered not,
        And Fingal's weeping.

Hearken for voices of sorrow for them in the forest den
    Where once they were rovers —
Only the birds of the wild at their building again,
    Whispering of lovers!
So Fingal's weeping, his old grief keeping,
    Fingal's weeping.

      They should be mourned by the ocean wave
        Round lone isles creeping,
      But the laughing wave laments no grave,
        And Fingal's weeping.

Morven and Moidart, glad, gallant and gay in the sun,
    Rue naught departed;
The moon and the stars shine out when the day is done,
    Cold, stony-hearted,
And Fingal's weeping war's red reaping,
    Fingal's weeping.

NEIL MUNRO

*Fingal is the great Gaelic semi-mythological hero, father of Ossian. His kingdom was the north-west of Scotland — Loch Etive, Morven (now Morvern) and Moidart are all in that area.

Retreat

Broken, bewildered by the long retreat
   Across the stifling leagues of southern plain,
     Across the scorching leagues of trampled grain,
Half-stunned, half-blinded by the trudge of feet
And dusty smother of the August heat,
He dreamt of flowers in an English lane,
Of hedgerow flowers glistening after rain —
All-heal and willow-herb and meadow-sweet.

All-heal and willow-herb and meadow-sweet —
The innocent names kept up a cool refrain —
All-heal and willow-herb and meadow-sweet,
Chiming and tinkling in his aching brain,
Until he babbled like a child again —
All-heal and willow-herb and meadow-sweet.

WILFRID WILSON GIBSON

Au Champ d'Honneur

Mud-stained and rain-sodden, a sport for flies and lice,
Out of this vilest life into vile death he goes;
  His grave will soon be ready, where the grey rat knows
There is fresh meat slain for her. Our mortal bodies rise,
In those foul scampering bellies, quick ... And yet those eyes
  That stare on life still out of death and will not close,
  Seeing in a flash the Crown of Honour, and the Rose
Of Glory wreathed about the Cross of Sacrifice,
Died radiant. May some English traveller to-day,
  Leaving his London cares behind him, journeying West
To the brief solace of a carnal holiday,
   Quicken again with boyish ardour, as he sees,
For a moment, Windsor Castle towering on the crest
And Eton still enshrined amid remembered trees.

CHARLES SCOTT MONCRIEFF

The Unreturning Spring

A leaf on the grey sand-path
Fallen, and fair with rime!
A yellow leaf, a scarlet leaf,
And a green leaf ere its time.

Days rolled in blood, days torn,
Days innocent, days burnt black,
What is it the wind is sighing
As the leaves float, swift or slack?

The year's pale spectre is crying
For beauty invisibly shed,
For the things that never were told
And were killed in the minds of the dead.

LAURENCE BINYON

Magpies in Picardy

The magpies in Picardy
Are more than I can tell.
They flicker down the dusty roads
And cast a magic spell
On the men who march through Picardy,
Through Picardy to Hell.

(The blackbird flies with panic,
The swallow goes like light,
The finches move like ladies,
The owl floats by at night;
But the great and flashing magpie
He flies as artists might.)

A magpie in Picardy
Told me secret things —

Of the music in white feathers,
And the sunlight that sings
And dances in deep shadows —
He told me with his wings.

(The hawk is cruel and rigid,
He watches from a height;
The rook is slow and sombre,
The robin loves to fight;
But the great and flashing magpie
He flies as lovers might.)

He told me that in Picardy,
An age ago or more,
While all his fathers were still eggs,
These dusty highways bore
Brown singing soldiers marching out
Through Picardy to war.

He said that still through chaos
Works on the ancient plan,
And two things have altered not
Since first the world began —
The beauty of the wild green earth
And the bravery of man.

(For the sparrow flies unthinking
And quarrels in his flight;
The heron trails his legs behind,
The lark goes out of sight;
But the great and flashing magpie
He flies as poets might.)

           T.P. CAMERON WILSON+

The Birds Of Steel

This apple tree, that once was green,
    Is now a thousand flowers in one!
And, with their bags strapped to their thighs,
    There's many a bee that comes for sweets,
To stretch each bag to its full size.

And when the night has grown a moon,
    And I lie half-asleep in bed,
I hear those bees again — ah no,
    It is the birds of steel instead,
Seeking their innocent prey below.

Man-ridden birds of steel, unseen,
    That come to drop their murdering lime
On any child or harmless thing
    Before the early morning time:
Up, nearer to God, they fly and sing.

W.H. Davies

Soldiers In A Small Camp

There is a camp upon a rounded hill
Where men do sleep more closely to the stars,
And tree-like shapes stand at its entrances,
Beside the small, dark, shadow-soldiery.

Deep in the gloom of days of isolation,
Withdrawn, high up from the low, murmuring town,
Those shadows sit, drooping around their fires,
Or move as winds dark-waving in a wood.

Staring at cattle on a neighbouring hill
They are oblivious as is stone or grass —
The clouds passed voiceless over, and the sun
Rose, and lit trees, and vanished utterly.

Then in the awful beauty of the world,
When stars are singing in dark ecstasy,
Those ox-like soldiers sit collected round
A thin, metallic echo of human song:

And click their feet and clap their hands in time,
And wag their heads, and make the white ghost owl
Flit from its branch — but still those tree-like shapes
Stand like archangels dark-winged in the sky.

And presently the soldiers cease to stir;
The thin voice sinks and all at once is dead;
They lie down on their planks and hear the wind,
And feel the darkness fumbling at their souls.

They lie in rows as stiff as tombs or trees,
Their eyeballs imageless, like marble still;
And secretly they feel that roof and walls
Are gone and that they stare into the sky.

It is so black, so black, so black, so black,
Those black-winged shapes have stretched across the world,
Have swallowed up the stars, and if the sun
Rises again, it will be black, black, black.

W.J. TURNER

Moonrise Over Battlefield

After the fallen sun the wind was sad
like violins behind immense old walls.
Trees were musicians swaying round the bed
Of a woman in gloomy halls.

In privacy of music she made ready
with comb and silver dust and fard;
under his silken vest her little belly
shone like a bladder of sweet lard.

She drifted with the grand air of a punk
on Heaven's streets soliciting white saints;
then lay in bright communion on a cloud-bank
as one who near extreme of pleasure faints.

Then I thought, standing in the ruined trench,
(all round, dead Boche white-shirted lay like sheep),
'Why does this damned entrancing bitch
seek lovers only among them that sleep?'

EDGELL RICKWORD

V

'The Hot Red Rocks of Aden'

FOREIGN FIELDS

September 1914: British and Indian Army forces attack Tanga, German East Africa, but are driven off in confusion, with heavy losses in men, weapons and equipment, by a far smaller German and African force.

October 1914: Turkey enters the war on Germany's side.

19 February 1915: Royal Navy and French ships begin bombardment of outer forts of the Dardanelles.

25 April 1915: British and Empire — notably Anzac — and French forces land at Gallipoli against fierce opposition from Turkish troops.

24 May 1915: Italy joins the war on the Allied side.

6 August 1915: Further troops land at Gallipoli; no significant gains.

28 September 1915: Anglo-Indian force under Townshend captures Kut-al-Amara, Mesopotamia.

5 October 1915: British and French forces land at Salonika, in neutral Greece, to aid the Serbians against the Bulgarians. Half a million Allied troops are in Salonika by the end of the campaign.

22 November 1915: Townshend successfully attacks Ctesiphon, but is forced by the arrival of Turkish reinforcements to retire into Kut-al-Amara on 3 December, where he is beseiged.

20 December 1915– 9 January 1916: Gallipoli beaches evacuated. Losses are: British and Commonwealth, 41,000 killed and missing, 78,500 wounded; French, 9,000 killed, 13,000 wounded; Turks, 66,000 killed and missing,

152,000 wounded. In addition, the Allies suffer another 100,000 casualties through sickness.

December 1915–29 April 1916: Repeated attempts to relieve Townshend fail, and the garrison, weakened by sickness and starvation, finally surrenders. 8,000 prisoners are taken by the Turks.
Almost from the outset of the war British Empire forces — principally Indian Army — have been engaged against the Turks in Mesopotamia and Palestine, to safeguard the Persian oil wells. By the end of the war Mesopotamia involves 600,000 Allied troops, Palestine 500,000.

17 February–11 March 1917: British and Indian forces assault and capture Baghdad.

26 March–19 April 1917: British attacks on Gaza, Palestine, driven off with heavy casualties.

6 April 1917: America enters the war against Germany, although it will be nearly a year before their troops can make a significant contribution.

28-29 September 1917: Anglo-Indian forces attack Ramadi, overwhelming and capturing most of the Turkish garrison. This is the last major action in Mesopotamia, although pressure is still kept up on the remaining Turkish forces there.

November 1917: British troops (five divisions) sent to Italy, to help the Italian Army repulse German and Austro-Hungarian offensives after the disaster at Caporetto.

31 October–9 December 1917: Renewed British attacks under Allenby capture Beersheba, Gaza, Junction Station and, finally, the heights overlooking Jerusalem.

9 December 1917: British forces capture Jerusalem.

15 December 1917: The Treaty of Brest-Litovsk puts Russia out of the war.

15-22 June 1918: Five Anglo-French divisions take part in the defence of the Piave River line. Strong counter-attacks, principally by the Italians, force the Austrians back and inflict heavy casualties on them.

19 September 1918: Allenby attacks Megiddo, forcing the Turks back across the River Jordan.

30 September 1918: Bulgaria signs an armistice. Allied casualties in the Salonika campaign amount to 18,000 from battle, and 481,000 from malaria.

1 October 1918: Anzac and Arab forces, the latter under T.E. Lawrence, occupy Damascus; Allenby enters the city on the following day.

30 October 1918: Turkey negotiates an armistice. British, Anzac and Indian casualties in the Palestine campaign are 550,000, 90 per cent from disease.

24 October–3 November 1918: Italian and Allied forces, after hard fighting, win crossings over the Piave and capture Vittorio Veneto. Austro-Hungarian resistance begins to crumble, and finally their forces are routed.

3 November 1918: Austria-Hungary signs an armistice.

25 November 1918: Undefeated, Colonel Paul von Lettow-Vorbeck agrees to an honourable surrender of his remaining forces in German East Africa — 155 Europeans, 1,168 *askari* (African soldiers) and 3,000 carriers. The maximum Allied strength ranged against him has been 139 generals, 150,000 fighting troops from seven nations, and 200,000 porters. The ratio of casualties from disease to those from battle during the campaign is 31:1.

It is difficult to think of the First World War as taking place anywhere other than in the trenches of France and Flanders. The few details above show how significant the involvement in other theatres of war was. It does not include much about the conflict in German East Africa, which went on until after Armistice in 1918, and in which a tiny army, mainly of African troops under German officers, remained undefeated by a huge force commanded by Smuts, or the other wars fought by Empire troops for German colonies in Africa and elsewhere. Technically, of course, France and Belgium are 'foreign fields', but the title of this section has been taken to mean battles and warfare outside Western Europe. There is one exception to this. For Canadian troops coming over to France the experience was equally as different as that facing the English soldier going to fight in Mesopotamia, and for purposes of comparison two poems by a Canadian have been included here. It should also be remembered that, as well as the Canadians, Indian, Gurkha, Australian, South African and New Zealand troops were all engaged on the Western Front.

The Dardanelles and Gallipoli have acquired considerable notoriety, and with good reason. The idea of a second front has often been put down to Churchill, although in reality he was not alone in his support for action outside Europe. Kitchener, for one, realised from an early stage in the war that it was going to be very difficult to make anything significant happen on the Western Front (and, almost alone among senior commanders, he foresaw in 1914 that the war would be long). It was not the idea that killed the attempt to force the Dardanelles and move out from the Gallipoli beaches, but ineptitude on the part of the commanders in question. The expedition was doomed to disaster almost from the start. The ships bombarding the outer forts of the Dardanelles took considerable damage from mines, but had run down the ammunition of the Turks and were within hours of being able to steam past unharmed. The Allied commanders lost their nerve before the Turks fired their last shell. The naval bombardment ended without result. Then came the landings at Gallipoli. The attacking force had no experience of seaborne landings, and it showed. Transports were wrongly packed, with non-essential equipment at the top and vital supplies buried in the holds, and had to be returned to port to be re-stowed. At every stage the Allies gave the Turkish defenders time and warning enough for them to build up sufficient forces, and keep the attackers pinned down on the beaches. Some of the initial landings were made with minimal losses, and with virtually empty ground before the attacking troops. Commanders slept and had lunch, troops began to unload on to the beach-heads, and by the time an advance was ordered Turkish forces were in command of the heights overlooking the beaches. It took a long while for the troops to be extricated from their exposed positions, long enough for savage casualties to be taken. Above all, perhaps, the higher command seriously underestimated the superb fighting qualities of the Turkish soldier, although how an army that itself relied heavily upon 'native' troops could have done so remains a mystery.

Poetry about Gallipoli and other faraway campaigns is less distinctive than that written about the Western Front, reinforcing the impression that it was the static nature of the war in Flanders and Northern France that gave it much of its uniqueness. In that sense, the poetry from the Dardanelles and other campaigns is similar to some of the poetry produced in the Second World War. A more jokey, off-hand manner creeps into much of it, as if heat, sand, and flies were in some vague way not quite so offensive as mud, rain, and lice (and in some campaigns, such as Mesopotamia, there were plenty of the latter as well). Perhaps the British and their soldiers had been used to sweating it out in sandy deserts for so long that the experience was not quite so much of a shock. There was 'Vitaï Lampada' to look back on, after all. (As for the individual quality of unpleasantness, very little happened on the Western Front that was more bestial than some of things inflicted on (and by) British troops during the Indian Mutiny, or in Afghanistan; it was merely that the scale was much greater. It is true, too, that the treatment of the wounded and prisoners by the Turks was infinitely worse than anything meted out by the Germans and Austrians. Sheer boredom comes through as a strong element in much of this poetry. Another feature, common to many British overseas campaigns, is also expressed, that of the 'forgotten army'.* By and large the 'side shows' in Mesopotamia and Palestine, or the general policing of the Empire which still had to go on despite the war, were viewed as being less glamorous, for obvious reasons, both by the military themselves and by the people at home. Had they been seen as more glamorous and important, then the War Office might have sent better generals to Gallipoli. As it was, they chose simply by seniority and availability.

Not all the other engagements were different from those in France; both Gallipoli and Kut-al-Amara, among other actions, developed into a species of trench warfare. Arguably one of the most crass-brained exercises of the war was the sending of a significant body of Allied troops to land in Salonika, against the wishes of the Greeks, to aid Serbia against the ravening Bulgarian hordes. In fact these ravening hordes came to be rather popular with the British soldiers, or at least as popular as any enemy is likely to be. One instance is recorded of British and Bulgarian troops stopping fighting so that both sides could cheer on a British officer involved in racing after a runaway horse. This occasional *camaraderie* did not disguise the fact that the whole expedition was a futile waste of resources, keeping many thousands of valuable troops as bogged down in trenches as their counterparts were in France. The difference was that the Bulgarians were much less of a real threat than

---

* A notion by no means confined to the Great War. The soldiers of General Sir William Slim's magnificent Fourteenth Army, which defeated the Japanese in Burma from 1942-1945, almost invariably referred (and refer) to themselves as the 'Forgotten Army'.

any enemy likely to be met with in France. The extract from 'The Song of Tiadatha' could easily be taken for a reference to the Western Front, if a few names were changed. The difference was that the campaign against Bulgaria had even less point than the one in France.

Home Thoughts

The hot red rocks of Aden
Stand from their burnished sea;
The bitter sands of Aden
Lie shimmering in their lee.

We have no joy of battle,
No honour here is won;
Our little fights are nameless,
With Turk and sand and gun.

East and West the greater wars
Swirl widely up and down;
Forgotten here and sadly
We hold the port and town.

The great round trees of England
Hurt us with vain desire;
The little wayside cottage,
The clanging blacksmith's fire.

The salt dry sands of Aden,
The bitter sun-cursed shore;
Forget us not in England,
We cannot serve you more.

ANONYMOUS*

---

* This poem appeared in *The Times* in 1916.

Concert Party
(*Egyptian Base Camp*)

They are gathering round ...
Out of the twilight; over the grey-blue sand,
Shoals of low-jargoning men drift inward to the sound —
The jangle and throb of a piano ... tum–ti–tum ...
Drawn by a lamp, they come
Out of the glimmering lines of their tents, over the shuffling sand.

O sing us the songs, the songs of our own land,
You warbling ladies in white.
Dimness conceals the hunger in our faces,
This wall of faces risen out of the night,
These eyes that keep their memories of the places
So long beyond their sight.

Jaded and gay, the ladies sing; and the chap in brown
Tilts his grey hat; jaunty and lean and pale,
He rattles the keys ... some actor-bloke from town ...
God send you home; and then *A long, long trail;*
I hear you calling me; and *Dixieland ...*
Sing slowly ... now the chorus ... one by one
We hear them, drink them; till the concert's done.
Silent, I watch the shadowy mass of soldiers stand.
Silent, they drift away, over the glimmering sand.

SIEGFRIED SASSOON
Kantara, April 1918

The Forest of the Dead
(*Baghdad Military Cemetery*)

There are strange trees in that pale field
Of barren soil and bitter yield:
They stand without the city walls;
Their nakedness is unconcealed.

Cross after cross, mound after mound,
And no flowers blossom but are bound,
The dying and the dead, in wreaths,
Sad crowns for kings of Underground.

The Forest of the Dead is still,
No songs of birds can ever thrill
Among the sapless boughs that bear
No fruit, no flower, for good or ill.

The sun by day, the moon by night
Give terrible or tender light,
But night or day the forest stands
Unchanging, desolately bright.

With loving or unloving eye
Kinsman and alien pass them by;
Do the dead know, do the dead care,
Under the forest as they lie?

To each the tree above his head,
To each the sign in which is said ...
'By this thou art to overcome':
Under this forest sleep no dead.

These, having life, gave life away:
Is God less generous than they?
The spirit passes and is free:
Dust to the dust; Death takes the clay.

J. GRIFFYTH FAIRFAX

Salonika Campaign
From *The Song of Tiadatha*

Four days long the guns had thundered,
When one starlit April evening
Came the Dudshires' mighty battle.
Not a man in all the Dudshires,

None who lived to see the daylight,
Ever could forget that evening,
Least of all my Tiadatha.

Very clear it was and starlight,
And a nightingale was singing
Somewhere in among the bushes;
Many of the soldiers heard it
In the little lulls of firing,
Heard its silver notes go throbbing
Out into the April evening.

Watch on wrist stood Tiadatha,
Gazing anxious at the minutes
As the starting time came nearer.
He was clad in Tommy's tunic,
Tommy's breeches and equipment,
In his hands he bore a rifle,*
On his head a shrapnel helmet.
Then at last he gave the signal,
And his men filed out behind him.
Through the gaps they wound like serpents,
Into No Man's Land they sallied,
Through the din of bursting shrapnel,
Through the bursting high explosives.
Down the steep Patte d'Oie he led them,
Down that steep and rocky gully,
Rocky as a Cornish headland,
Steeper than a traveller's story:
There the dread trench mortar barrage
Swept upon them like a hailstorm,
Storm with stones as big as footballs,
Stones alive with death and torture.
Through that blinding storm he led them,
Up the farther side he led them —
All that were not killed or wounded.

*Infantry officers in the Great War quite quickly adopted the other ranks' equipment and
weaponry, since the loss of officers to sniper fire was great.

There upon the flashing hillside
Tiadatha crouched and waited,
Waited for the Zero hour,
When the barrage would be lengthened,
Lifted from the front line trenches.

As the moment came he leapt up,
Gave a shout to all the Dudshires,
And the Dudshires rose and followed,
Charged beside my Tiadatha —
All who were not killed or wounded.
Through the broken wire they scrambled,
Some men cursing, some men shouting,
Some men muttering little prayers,
Some in grim and deadly silence.

They were met by bombs and bullets,
Heard the Bulgars in their trenches,
Heard them crying: 'Come on, Johnny,
Come on, come on, English Johnny.'
And three times the Royal Dudshires
Swept upon the Bulgar trenches,
Every time the line was thinner,
Every time its heart was steadfast.
And the third time Tiadatha,
With a little band behind him,
Leapt into the battered trenches,
Got to work with bomb and bayonet,
In his heart the lust of battle;
Then felt something hit his shoulder,
Felt his shoulder wet and burning,
Found he'd stopped a shrapnel bullet,
Set his teeth and staggered onwards,
Led his party round a traverse,
Bombed a dug-out full of Bulgars,
Bombed until his bombs were finished,
Carried on with German stink-bombs
That the Bulgar'd left behind him.

On and on the little party
Pushed along the Bulgar trenches,
Till there came a deadly sickness
Stealing over Tiadatha,
And he knew his strength was failing,
Knew that he could get no farther,
So he shouted to his corporal,
'Take them on and do your damnedest.'
Flopped down in the trench and fainted.

Then came Woggs, the soldier servant,
Trusty Woggs, the ever-ready,
And produced a flask of brandy,
Poured it down my Tiadatha.
'Curse you, Woggs,' said Tiadatha,
'Go on with your section leader.
Every man of you'll be wanted,
I'll crawl back and get my wound dressed,
Then I'll come again and find you.'

*

Had you been there when the dawn broke
Had you looked from out the trenches,
You'd have seen that Serbian hillside,
Seen the aftermath of battle.
Seen the scattered picks and shovels,
Seen the scraps of stray equipment,
Here and there a lonely rifle,
Or a Lewis gun all twisted.
Seen the little heaps of khaki
Lying huddled on the hillside,
Huddled by the Bulgar trenches
Very still and very silent,
Nothing stirring, nothing moving,
Save a very gallant doctor
And his band of stretcher bearers
Working fearless in the open,
Giving water to the dying,
Bringing in those broken soldiers.

You'd have seen the sunlight streaming,
And perhaps you would have wondered
How the sun could still be shining,
How the birds could still be singing,
While so many British soldiers
Lay so still upon the hillside.

MAJOR OWEN RUTTER

The Gift

Marching on Tanga,* marching the parch'd plain
Of wavering spear-grass past Pangani River,
England came to me — me who had always ta'en
But never given before — England, the giver,
In a vision of three poplar-trees that shiver
On still evenings of summer, after rain,
By Slapton Ley, where reed-beds start and quiver
When scarce a ripple moves the upland grain.
Then I thanked God that now I had suffered pain,
And, as the parch'd plain, thirst, and lain awake
Shivering all night through till cold daybreak:
In that I count these sufferings my gain
And her acknowledgement. Nay, more, would fain
Suffer as many more for her sweet sake.

FRANCIS BRETT YOUNG

The Sand of Palestine

The sand one meets in Palestine's an all-pervading sediment,
To really cleanly feeding it is always an impediment,
For stew and tea and bacon have habitually a grittiness
That tends to turn one's language from its customary prettiness.

* In the East African campaign, which was fought between a very small German/African force under Colonel Paul von Lettow-Vorbeck, and a very large Allied force of British, Indian, African, South African, Rhodesian, Belgian and Portuguese troops under a succession of commanders, including Smith-Dorrien and Smuts. Von Lettow-Vorbeck remained undefeated, and agreed to an honourable surrender on 25 November 1918, two weeks after the Armistice.

The sand one meets in Palestine at first will make you wonder where
The cause is of the raspiness apparent in your underwear;
We've seen a suffering novice after hasting to inspect his hide
Erroneously indent for half a hogshead of insecticide.

The sand one meets in Palestine — 'twere folly to be lenient —
Deserves no weaker censure than extremely inconvenient,
But though about its qualities each single soldier carries on
It has its little merits — one unearths them by comparison.

The sand one meets in Palestine's an unadhesive article,
It's not so hard to brush away each desiccated particle,
But the sticky mud of Flanders can have nothing to rebel at if
I say it clings as closely as an impecunious relative.

The sand one meets in Palestine (where JAEL did for SISERA)
Does not create a mudbank in the region of your viscera,
But Flanders has the sort of soil that leaves on each comestible
Alluvial deposits that are vilely indigestible.

Having tried them both I've formed — and I submit it with all
   deference —
The view that I am right in giving Palestine the preference,
For I hold its arid vistas as comparatively gladdening
Alternative to landscapes that are soddening and saddening.

T. HODGKINSON

Somewhere East of Suez

Nothing delights me as I sit
   In this pestiferous clime;
Mosquitoes plague me and the horrid
Sand-flies make raids upon my forehead;
I hit and curse and wildly hit,
   And miss them every time.

When all things trooped to ADAM'S door
   Their several names to ask,

He must have suffered from a very
Inadequate vocabulary;
Scarcely our Sergeant-Major's lore
    Suffices for the task.

And NOAH, oh, what a chance he had
    When two and two they met!
To think that with a single digit
He might have squashed the mother-midget
And saved his sons from going mad
    By stinging swarms beset!

I am regarded as a mere
    Canteen by every pest;
They're all hard drinkers — none are wowsers;
That splotch of blood upon my trousers
Shows where one bloated profiteer
    Has suddenly gone West.

Nothing delights me, *nothing* does;
    There cannot be much bliss
Where all the animals created
Seem only differentiated
Between the brutes that fly and buzz
    And those that crawl and hiss.

                    H.W. BERRY

Gallipoli
(*Anniversary*)

Ghosts man the phantom ships that ply between.
White ships with sails of mist and bleaching prows,
Ply through the night, with freight of unkept vows
And haggard men. The waters stretching green
Into the distant bay, roll to the shore
With ominous music, and the dawn creeps slow
On frightened feet across the hills, till lo,

The ghastly prows are turned, and there once more
The boats are lowered and filled, and through the dark
Bewildered waters crouching men cling close
On anxious oars. 'A landing! Now!' Dim rows
Bleeding, insensate, mark the waiting sand,
Heedless they rush, blanched, frenzied, staring, stark,
Dead men, — eternally, they land, they land!

MARY MORISON WEBSTER

Abdul

We've drunk the boys who rushed the hills
    The men who stormed the beach,
The sappers and the A.S.C.,*
    We've had a toast for each;
And the guns and stretcher-bearers —
    But before the bowl is cool,
There's one chap I'd like to mention,
    He's a fellow called ABDUL.

We've heard the twigs a-crackling,
    As we crouched upon our knees,
And his big, black shape went smashing,
    Like a rhino, through the trees.
We've seen him flung in, rank on rank,
    Across the morning sky;
And we've had some pretty shooting,
    And — he knows the way to die.

So though your name be black as ink
    For murder and rapine
Carried out in happy concert
    With your Christians from the Rhine,
We will judge you, Mr Abdul,

---

* ASC — Army Service Corps, a body whose task was to bring food, ammunition and other supplies forward to the fighting troops. Known as 'Aly Sloper's Cavalry' after a popular cartoon character, and as the 'Jam-Stealers' (for obvious reasons).

By the test by which *we* can —
That , with all your breath, in life, in death,
You've played the Gentleman.

Anonymous

The Turkish Trench Dog

Night held me as I crawled and scrambled near
The Turkish lines. Above, the mocking stars
Silvered the curving parapet, and clear
Cloud-latticed beams o'erflecked the land with bars;
I, crouching, lay between
Tense-listening armies, peering through the night,
Twin giants bound by tentacles unseen.
Here in dim-shadowed light
I saw him, as a sudden movement turned
His eyes towards me, glowing eyes that burned
A moment ere his snuffling muzzle found
My trail; and then as serpents mesmerise
He chained me with those unrelenting eyes,
That muscle-sliding rhythm, knit and bound
In spare-limbed symmetry, those perfect jaws
And soft-approaching pitter-patter paws.
Nearer and nearer like a wolf he crept —
That moment had my swift revolver leapt —
But terror seized me, terror born of shame
Brought flooding revelation. For he came
As one who offers comradeship deserved,
An open ally of the human race,
And sniffing at my prostrate form unnerved
He licked my face!

Geoffrey Dearmer

Five Souls

FIRST SOUL

I was a peasant of the Polish plain;
I left my plough because the message ran: —
Russia, in danger, needed every man
To save her from the Teuton; and was slain.
I gave my life for freedom — This I know:
For those who bade me fight had told me so.

SECOND SOUL

I was a Tyrolese, a mountaineer;
I gladly left my mountain home to fight
Against the brutal, treacherous Muscovite;
I died in Poland on a Cossack spear.
I gave my life for freedom — This I know:
For those who bade me fight had told me so.

THIRD SOUL

I worked at Lyons at my weaver's loom,
When suddenly the Prussian despot hurled
His felon blow at France and at the world;
Then I went forth to Belgium and my doom.
I gave my life for freedom — This I know:
For those who bade me fight had told me so.

FOURTH SOUL

I owned a vineyard by the wooded Main,
Until the Fatherland, begirt by foes
Lusting her downfall, called me, and I rose
Swift to the call — and died in fair Lorraine.
I gave my life for freedom — This I know:
For those who bade me fight had told me so.

FIFTH SOUL

I worked in a great shipyard by the Clyde,
There came a sudden word of wars declared,

Of Belgium, peaceful, helpless, unprepared,
Asking our aid: I joined the ranks, and died.
I gave my life for freedom — This I know:
For those who bade me fight had told me so.

W.N. EWER

Untitled

If you think it crude to be rough and rude.
This tale is not for you.
There's nothing nice about rats and mice
From any point of view.

Yes, the rats do roam and make their home
In the fields where the dead men lie.
Yes, the lice do bite all day and night
And never quit till you die.

Here the human moles from their stinking holes
Crawl up through the muck and slime
To hide all day, then work all night
Till there is no sense to time.

The great shells roar through the leaden skies
As their targets crouch in the drains,
Then burst with a roar and the shrapnel flies,
And it rains and rains and rains.

On a dirty night when your nerves draw tight
And you rouse to the gas alarms,
In a dank shell hole you'd sell your soul
For a night in a woman's arms.

When the grey green mass of chlorine gas
Drifts down from the eastern sky,
You choke and spit till your lungs are split
And you hear your best friends die.

In the stinking stench of a rotten trench
Mid the swarms of filthy flies,
Some men got caught so their bodies rot,
And the maggots eat their eyes.

Here tattered bums from city slums
With pampered sons of the rich,
All lie with God on that sodden sod,
And you can't tell which is which.

In that sea of mud you can feel your blood
Go cold as you shake with fright,
And among the dead you raise your head
To stand to your post to fight.

So a few survive and are still alive
When at last relief breaks through,
And the press reports all quiet,
As they bury the lads they knew.

Theirs was the fate from German hate,
Its greed and mistaken pride.
In far-off days, a soldier prays,
'Forget not why they died.'

ROBERT SWAN

Trench Fever

Discussions in the trenches often coupled pleasant wenches
With attempts to learn the language of the land.
Life could be very merry with a sleeping dictionary
To pass the time and get to understand.

They could talk among their pals of dodging loving gals
Who had gently tried to trap them into marriage.
They were good at fast romance, but shuddered at the chance
Of being nailed to push a baby carriage.

To improve the army diet, they would snatch a hen and fry it
With potatoes which they also got for free.
There was bully beef and cheese which could be flogged with ease
For more tasteful liquid products than their tea.

When they tangled with a limey, he was quick to holler 'Blimey!'
As they bashed his blinkin' head against a wall.
Why would any bloomin' gent foster further discontent
By more gentle ways to quell a free-for-all?

When a message from on high urged them forth to do or die,
There was little they could do except to cuss,
And among themselves to wonder how to dodge this latest blunder,
While the senders held a five-mile start on us.

For the language of the forces never came from college courses,
Nor resulted from intensive foreign studies.
It was fractured, it was bent, it was borrowed, it was lent,
But they never brought themselves to swallow butties.

In times of sudden stress, it was anybody's guess
How the wicked always managed to survive,
While their more deserving brothers, along with all the others,
Scratched and scrambled just to stay alive.

When fighting chores were done, they manufactured fun,
Avoiding ways to harm their precious skin.
Without damage to the nation they would take a short vacation,
And risk a call to answer for their sins.

So before you turn aside, remember this with pride:
In the game of war they played the hands they drew.
You will never understand how they loved their native land,
But they proved it as they lived and died for you.

ROBERT SWAN*

---

* Swan served in the Canadian Army.

Sidney Walter Powell's epic but little known poem 'Gallipoli' (of which only five pages are printed here) had to wait until 1933 to gain publication, and then only succeeded because in 1932 its author submitted it to a competition for poets under forty years of age. Powell, then aged fifty-four, won, and then owned up — to the annoyance of the competition's judge, John Masefield — and returned the prize, but his ruse was enough to get his poem printed in the *Poetry Review* the following year. It also appeared in a collection of his verse, *One-Way Street*, published in 1934. Since then Powell and his work have faded from public view, although a paperback edition of his remarkable memoir *Adventures of a Wanderer*, with the complete seventeen-page text of 'Gallipoli' included in it, was published in 1986. The poem seems to deserve a better fate than to be forgotten.

Gallipoli
(*Extracts*)
PRELUDE

What is this thing you would do?
Would you sing a song?
But why?
Will any man hear you?
Nay, but the gods will hear me,
The old gods of the Beginning,
Of Light and Darkness;
Not man in his grey twilight. . . .

*

So I will sing to them
Of the earth in these days,
Sundering light from darkness.
I will sing to them a song of blood.
Of things I have seen and things I have done I will sing to them,
Cleaving their weariness:
And nothing lost if no man hear me.

A SONG OF BLOOD

*

… Light grows, and grows less tender,
Following the law.
The new day is with us,
Come at a glide so subtle that we saw it not.
Day was not and now is,
Full-dressed in his blue and gold.
With a wipe he has burnished the sea's dull armour,
To use it for his looking-glass.
In his young pride he peacocks before us,
And the sight gladdens us.
A day of goodly appearance this our gift.
Bravely it shines, and the shine of it honours us.
Bravely the water glitters,
Bravely the guns roar
And the fountains rise.
Bravely the loaded boats drive at the shore.
The clopple, clopple, clopple, clopple, clopple
Is off to the hills,
But we shall follow it —
If we are permitted.
That fountain spouted nigh. It sprayed us!
Our serpent is disturbed and draws away.
And there goes a boat caught up in a fountain.
How funnily its ends tossed,
Closing like a pair of scissors
And spilling its passengers.
But gaily! Is not this a play?
A water-carnival, a regatta?
With the launches darting, the boats racing,
Spangles on the water, sparkle in the air,
Blue above, blue below, gold and blue everywhere,
Except on the hills which curiously gloom, rejecting the day.
Festive it is, but the hills refuse to be festive.
Brooding they are, and sour, and barren and graceless.

Yes, but this is make-believe.

The hills gloom as hills gloom from a back-scene.
Artistic contrast!
This is a theatre, and we are the spectators.
In the water-filled arena is mimic war.
See these ones with infant voices* commanding the launches,
From whose mouths issue orders to men.
Look at their gigantic tobacco-pipes!
Were ever infants seen with pipes
But as figures of comedy?
Midshipmen! Tut, tut! Little drolls they are.
Comic relief to the seemingly dangerous spouting fountains.
They are quite unconcerned, these babies.
So may we be.
Let us enjoy the show.
There goes another boat.
This shuts up like a jack-knife, the blade upon the handle,
And disrupts, leaving a dark molecular bobbing residue.
The actors are getting a bath.
But most of them have dived, for verisimilitude —
Eh? They could not get rid of their packs?
So they drown. They would, of course, in ugly reality.
But there is no ugliness about this
We are spectators of an exhilarating show
Perfectly staged under brilliant conditions.
Surely that was a dream of a day for others.
What gift do we make of this day?

What? Is there a rôle for us?
Do we enter the boats and go where the fountains spout?
Unbuckle your belts and loosen your packs, my fellows.
Accidents happen, even at play.

Shall we, or shall we not?
We are halfway.
More. A little more.
Nay, nay.

*The ships' boats from which many troops were landed were commanded by midshipmen.
Some of them were very young indeed.

We are men of dry land. To drown is no sort of death.
We did not come here to drown. It was not in our bargain.
Damned stupid anticlimax!
Ah, shallow water, Lord be praised!
We are spared that bathos.
The mountain conceived of God, but had a miscarriage!
Queer it should stick in the gizzard —
But it was as if the gift should be snatched from the hand.

Who are these upon the beach
Laid in an orderly row in the sunshine,
Head to the hills, feet to the sea?
Their eyes are wide, but they blink not.
The sun roasts them, but they sweat not.
He scorches them, but they do not redden.
Their colour is clay.

Now we know that this is no play. ...

*

It is the moment. It is reality.
Nothing is real till the moment gives birth to it.
And yet this is familiar. We have enacted it before.
There is nothing untaught in our instant procedure.
We do not pause. We stoop low and rush.
They are the goal. We are the ball.
Propelled, we go. There is no more to it,
Except sensation,
Now too dazzling-swift to impress.
That wild altissimo again.
It is ourselves. It is our spirit in the air.
We soar. Death is out of sight.
We are the destroyers, not the destructible;
Born to destroy, born for this moment of death-giving,
Reborn for this reborn moment,
As well known to us as our faces.
Thus in the past a thousand times we fell upon our enemies
With claw, with club, with spear.
Their eyes flinch, they would flee.

It is too late for them.
They would drop their guns and fling up their arms.
It is too late for them.
The madness of undrawn blood is upon us.

We kill.

What have we done? We have killed those who would surrender.
Then why were they too late? Can the cat stay her spring in mid-air?
The fault was not ours.

They would have cheated us. And our dead are many.

It was an orgy. I will not remember it.
(But I am gladder than I was.)
Wipe off the mess upon your steel.

We move on, following the direction of the beacon,
Which flares distantly again.
My gladness is fizzling out of me
As from an uncorked bottle.

I grow flat. I am tired and thirsty ...
I wish this field-day would end.
Surely it is time to march back to camp.
We have had enough of these exercises.
We are ready for the canteen.
I could drink a gallon of beer without stopping.
When will the 'Cease Fire' sound? ...
Oh hell, but this is war.
Am I going to have delusions now?
Shall I be seeing a mirage of pale ale next?
My God, but I would lie down in it!
Come, pull yourself together.
This — is — War.
Unlimited. Calling for unlimited endurance.
Take a prudent pull at your precious warm water,
And don't glue your mouth to the spout.
This day will never end.

It is at least forty-eight hours long already,
And the sun is still high;
And the land is waterless.

No more the beacon flares,
But we have guidance.
We hear as it were the crackle of it;
Its flames roar.
There is a mighty fire ahead of us.
It spreads, by the sound of it, to right and left of us.
In this deep fold of the land it is a sound only.
The hornets are high in the air.
Now another sound regularly punctures it.
One, two, three, four bangs.
Pause, and da capo.
Indeed a lively combustion ahead;
Even unseen, sufficient to wither illusions.
We shall be there.
This day grows more rational.
I have a nascent suspicion there is purpose in it,
At present hidden in the womb.

Over this mangy hog's back — curse its bristles —
We should have view.
It breaks.
An amphitheatre.
But the ring is empty;
The actors are all in the gallery beyond.
We do not stand to gaze:
There is no standing-room up here
For the pests of the air that swarm fanwise upon it.
We hurtle into the empty arena
(Not quite empty: it is opening as a scrap-heap)
And are borne by momentum across it and switchbacked up a bit.

The lost whelp has found its dam.

The lost whelp has found its dam beleaguered,
Bloodily snapping at a pack.

The horns of our enemies encompass us.
As the claws of a crab they close to crack us, cooping us within.
(Now does the day grow big!)
But why did you stay, brothers?
It was the word.
We have fought with an army this day.
For that went we out, that our brothers who fought through the
     morning
Might hold to their gain of the morning.
We fell on this army and stood in its way.
Safe is the gain of the morning now, dear bought,
And our turn to pay.

Now is the day delivered of its purpose.
Now is all made clear.
And now the hour of the gift's deliverance

Too is near.
(Do you fear?
Nay. There is nothing that cannot be spent, and fear is spent.
I have no more fear.)

Take. It was pledged freely and is given freely —
But they who buy me shall pay dear!
I will have my brokerage of them.
They shall wish they had brought in another market ere the deal be

They shall make no profit of this purchase....

Now is the end here.
Sing, for the day is over!
(Does a red veil blind you?
What but the curtain falling on the play?)
Sing, for the day is over!
Red the sunset?
Happy omen, so men say.
Red the steel? The pain red-hot?
You dream, my children. All is over.
Death is slain.

All is over, dream or not,
Of gaining, giving, dying, living.
Sing once again.
Birds at evening, sing your lay:
'Good has been our short spring day!'

High in air it drifts away.
High it drifts and dies, dies away.

SIDNEY WALTER POWELL

VI

'England's Pride'

WAR AT SEA AND WAR IN THE AIR

22 September 1914: British cruisers HMSS *Aboukir*, *Cressy* and *Hogue* sunk in one day by a German U-boat.

28 August 1914: Battle of Heligoland Bight. Germans lose three light cruisers, *Mainz*, *Köln* and *Ariadne*, and a destroyer, with over 1,000 men, and three more cruisers are badly damaged; British lose thirty-five men killed and no ships. The effect on the sea war is crucial — the Kaiser orders that there will be no further risking of ships, and that his navy will stay within the Bight, except with his special permission.

1 November 1914: Battle of Coronel. German raiding force under von Spee overwhelms two British cruisers, *Good Hope* and *Monmouth*, under Cradock, who goes down with his flagship, *Good Hope*. All *Monmouth's* company are lost; German casualties are three sailors wounded.

9 November 1914: German raider *Emden*, a light cruiser, sunk by Australian cruiser HMAS *Sydney*.

8 December 1914: Battle of the Falkland Isles. Von Spee's force of two armoured and three light cruisers in turn overwhelmed by British battle-cruisers and cruisers under Sturdee. Von Spee and the entire crew of his flagship, *Scharnhorst*, are lost. Only one German light cruiser escapes.

24 January 1915: Battle of Dogger Bank. British battle-cruisers under Beatty sink the German armoured cruiser *Blücher*. British losses fifteen men killed, no ships; German losses almost 1,000 men killed, one armoured cruiser sunk, and other ships, including battle-cruisers, damaged.

7 May 1915:   Cunard luxury liner SS *Lusitania*, out of New York, torpedoed without warning by *U20* off the south coast of Ireland. 1,201 passengers and crew die, 128 of them American. Dispute about whether *Lusitania* was armed or carrying munitions continues to this day, abetted by official secrecy.

1 March 1916:   Admiral von Capelle, commanding the German U-boats, widens his campaign to include all shipping in the Atlantic.

31 May 1916:   Battle of Jutland. British and German fleets meet at full strength for the only time in the war. British losses: three battle-cruisers, three armoured cruisers, one light cruiser, seven destroyers; 6,097 men killed. German losses: one battleship, one battle-cruiser, four light cruisers, five destroyers; 2,551 men killed. German fleet breaks off action and retires to port, never again to be an effective force in the war.

1 February 1917:   Germany declares unrestricted submarine warfare.

26 April 1917:   Lloyd George initiates convoys for merchant ships, against the wishes of the Admiralty, after disastrous losses. Almost immediately, losses to U-boats and raiders decline from 600,000 tons a month to 200,000 tons.

23 April 1918:   Admiral Scheer sets sail with the German fleet for the last time, but misses the target convoy. Rear-Admiral Keyes sinks block-ships at Zeebrugge.

17 October 1918:   Unrestricted submarine warfare called off.

29 October 1918:   German High Seas Fleet mutinies and refuses to sail. Mutiny spreads to the town of Kiel, which is taken over by the mutineers by 3 November.

11 November 1918:   Armistice — all offensive action ceases.

21 November 1918:   Imperial German High Seas fleet sails out to internment and demilitarisation in Scapa Flow.

21 June 1919:   Crews remaining on the German ships in Scapa Flow open the sea-cocks to scuttle their vessels.

Many are sunk, including some of the great capital ships.

*

1912:	Royal Flying Corps formed.
1 July 1914:	Royal Naval Air Service formed from Naval Wing, RFC.
13 August 1914:	First bombing attack — German Taube monoplane two-seater drops grenades on Paris.
14 August 1914:	French bomb the Zeppelin sheds at Metz.
22 August 1914:	British aircraft spot and report German outflanking movement and sudden French withdrawal during Battle of Mons, thus allowing BEF to escape.
3 September 1914:	French aircraft spot gap between German armies, information which leads to Allied victory on the Marne.
5 October 1914:	First true air-to-air victory: French Voisin two-seater armed with a Hotchkiss machine-gun destroys German Aviatik two-seater.
October 1914:	Flight Sub-Lieutenant Marix bombs and destroys Zeppelin ZIX in her shed at Düsseldorf.
19 January 1915:	First Zeppelin raid against Britain, hitting Yarmouth and King's Lynn.
24 May 1915:	Italy joins the war on the Allied side. Italian bombing policy, tactical and strategic, is aggressive, forward-looking and imaginative. The Italians gain and retain air supremacy in that theatre throughout the war. Inspired to a considerable extent by the poet Gabriele d'Annunzio (whose son was killed with the French Foreign Legion during the war), Italian bombers provide much-needed ground support, as well as initiating true long-range bombing. On 9 August 1918, an Ansaldo SVA5 with d'Annunzio in the observer's cockpit flies to Vienna and, to the consternation of the Austrians, drops propaganda leaflets on the city.

	This entails a round flight of more than 600 miles.
June 1916:	French bomber squadrons begin attacks on Germany.
7 June 1916:	First Zeppelin to be destroyed in aerial combat. Flight Sub-Lieutenant Warneford attacks L237 over Ghent, dropping six 20-pound bombs along the airship's length. Warneford receives the VC.
July 1916:	Appearance of German Fokker EI monoplane, first aircraft to be equipped with interrupter gear allowing a machine-gun to be fired forward through the airscrew. The 'Fokker Scourge' continues to the end of the year, taking a heavy toll of Allied pilots and machines. Rise to fame of German aces Oswald Boelcke and Max Immelman. Boelcke recruits from the cavalry Rittmeister Freiherr Manfred von Richthofen, the highest-scoring pilot of the war, with 80 confirmed victories.
July 1916:	Naval aircraft 'spot' the cruiser *Königsberg* (blocked up by the British in the Rufiji River delta, German East Africa) for two Royal Navy monitors, which succeed in sinking the German warship.
Spring 1916:	'Fokker Scourge' ended by appearance of Allied aircraft such as the Nieuport 11 and the British DH2, the latter a 'pusher' biplane which allowed a gun to be mounted in the nose.
May 1916:	British and French air forces regain air supremacy in response to Pétain's call for support during his counter-attack at Verdun. New British aircraft arrive equipped with Constaninesco gun-synchronising gear.
July-November 1916:	Allied air supremacy continues throughout battle of the Somme, in marked contrast to the stalemate on the ground.
2 September 1916:	First Zeppelin — SL11 — destroyed over Britain by Lieutenant Leefe-Robinson, who is awarded the VC. Some days later two more Zeppelins are brought down — the airship menace declines from this point.

28 November 1916: As the Zeppelins decline, Germans send heavy bombers to Britain, the first daylight raid being made on this date.

1917: New German aircraft in service, notably the Albatros DI and DII fighters. The balance of air power swings back towards the Germans.

April 1917: Called 'Bloody April' by the RFC. In attempting to support the Allied offensives at and around Arras, the British pilots suffer heavy casualties, amounting to one-third of the RFC's total strength. Life expectancy of an RFC subaltern at this time is from eleven to twenty-one days. First appearance of German *Jagdgeschwader (Jg)*, a fixed unit of four *Jagdstaffeln* (*Jastas* — fighter squadrons) mustering up to fifty aircraft at any given time. The spectacle of so many variously coloured aircraft of different types milling about the sky earns the *Jgs* the nickname 'Flying Circuses'. Desperately pressed, the RFC calls for help from the RNAS. The latter responds with eight squadrons of Sopwith Triplanes, which achieve considerable success.

20 May 1917: Felixstowe flying-boat sinks the German *UC-36*, the first U-boat to be sunk by aircraft.

April to July 1917: Appearance of new Allied aircraft which begin to restore the balance; the French Spad XIII, the SE5 and its successor, the SE5A, the Bristol F2B two-seater and the Sopwith Camel — the last the most successful aircraft of the war, accounting for 1,294 enemy machines.

Spring and summer 1917: Rise to fame of such German aces as Manfred von Richthofen, Kurt Wolff, Werner Voss, Hermann Göring, Ernst Udet, and Lothar von Richthofen. British and Dominion aces include: Lanoe Hawker, Albert Ball, Mick Mannock, Billy Bishop, Raymond Collishaw, James McCudden, William Barker; French: Charles Nungesser, René Fonck, Georges Guynemer; American: Edward Rickenbacker, Frank Luke, Raoul Lufbery. Mannock is the highest-scoring British ace (73 victories); Fonck the highest-scoring French and Allied ace (75 victories); Rickenbacker the highest-scoring

American (26); Collishaw the highest-scoring naval pilot (60); and Willy Coppens the highest-scoring Belgian (37, including 26 balloons).

2 August 1917: Squadron Commander Dunning achieves first successful landing of an aircraft on a ship under way, but is tragically killed five days later while attempting the feat again.
German daylight raids on Britain by bombers increase throughout the year, but so do their losses.

September 1917: German bombers switch to night bombing.

31 October 1917: Twenty-two Gothas drop eighty-five bombs on London, Essex and Kent. Damage is light, and five aircraft are damaged or destroyed in landing back at their bases.

November-December 1917: German two-seater aircraft used in a ground-attack role contribute greatly to halting the successful British advance at Cambrai.

6 December 1917: Nineteen German aircraft bomb London, Dover, Ramsgate, Sheerness and Margate, starting some fires. Two aircraft damaged by AA fire crash-land in England; two more crash outside their base; a fifth goes missing at sea; and a sixth is destroyed on landing.

18 December 1917: Fifteen German bombers do more serious damage to London. But Captain Murlis-Green in a Sopwith Camel destroys one, and others are damaged or destroyed on landing. Despite some hysteria in Britain, the 'Gotha Menace' declines from this point, stopping altogether in May 1918. The German bombing of Britain has achieved little material damage, but it does succeed in tying up aircraft, pilots and AA weapons from France and other theatres, and in disrupting war production.

1918: British bombing raids against Germany, first by the RFC and RNAS, later by the RAF, began in direct reprisal for the Gotha raids. By October 1917 day and night raids are being undertaken by the RFC, and by early 1918 RFC and RNAS squadrons are bombing German cities, airfields, manufacturing plants and military targets.

March 1918: Germans regain air supremacy during the Ludendorff Offensive, which nearly breaks the Allied line.

1 April 1918: RAF formed from the amalgamation of the RFC and RNAS

21 April 1918: Manfred von Richthofen, the 'Red Baron', shot down and killed. Dispute as to whether he was brought down by air or ground fire contines to this day.

6 June 1918: Independent Bombing Force, RAF formed by Trenchard. An increase in strategic bombing is called for by the formation of the RAF and the arrival of the American bombing squadrons, but French opposition, and Haig's insistence on tactical support for his armies, limits the IBF's effectiveness. It numbers only nine squadrons by the Armistice.

19 July 1918: First full-scale aircraft-carrier attack, when HMS *Furious* launches her aircraft against the airship sheds at Tondern, destroying two Zeppelins.

August 1918: During Allied offensives at Amiens, French, American and RAF squadrons achieve complete air supremacy, which they maintain until the Armistice.

September 1918: Macedonia — three RAF squadrons catch a Bulgarian force in a narrow pass, and succeed in completely demoralising the enemy, inflicting heavy damage and casualties.

There is much less poetry about the air and sea wars than there is about the corresponding war on land. There is a variety of reasons for this. The numbers of men involved in both the war at sea and the war in the air were minuscule compared with those involved in the land campaigns. Unlikely soldiers such as Wilfred Owen and Isaac Rosenberg might well join the Army, but pre-war poets were much less likely to find themselves in the Royal Flying Corps, the Royal Naval Air Service, or the Royal Navy, with the Navy, in particular, tending to retain its traditional intake; there was no 'New Navy' to go with Kitchener's 'New Army', nor a need for one. Since 1906 the Royal Navy had been involved in a massive race to give itself enough ships and men to fight a major war, and of all the armed services it was the one best prepared for it, and best able to cope when war came.

Nor was there the same need among the airmen and sailors to write poetry as there was for the soldiers. Air warfare was completely new in 1914.* There was a pioneering spirit to it, and a sense both of chivalry and excitement. There are various recorded instances of British pilots deliberately aiming at German aircraft so as to disable the machine but leave the pilot unharmed, and of pilots refusing to shoot at the observers of barrage balloons as they tried to escape from the 'blimps' after they had been hit. Other instances, such as the treatment of downed pilots, were very much in this tradition. The war in the air became dirtier as time went on, however, and more savage, exacerbated by General Trenchard's aggressive policies. German aircraft were often better than their British counterparts (although technological supremacy swung back and forth throughout the war), few of the 'aces' on either side survived the war, and the life expectancy of a new pilot, barely able to fly his aircraft in a straight line, could sometimes be measured in minutes.

For all this, however, the war in the air remained a highly individual exercise, and a highly exciting affair. Whilst logically that excitement should have produced poetry, in practice it seems to have been the grinding and razor-edged boredom of trench life that provoked some of the best verse, coupled with the proximity of the writers to the blood-letting. Air warfare remained, for all its horror, a much cleaner affair, where death was usually more-or-less instant, and the chances of that death much more dependent on the individual skills of the pilot. It was harder to blame someone else for tragedy, and the decrease in bitterness led to a corresponding decrease in the need for self-expression. Despite this, the war in the air did produce one poet who is worth serious critical attention. Jeffery Day was similar in some respects to Charles Sorley, in that he was a man who inspired instant affection and respect among those who knew him, and was at the same time, potentially at least, a major poet. His

---

*Before 1914, the Americans had used aircraft against Pancho Villa, the Mexican bandit or freedom-fighter (depending on one's point of view), as had the Italians against the Bulgarians, gaining for themselves the dubious distinction of being the first nation to undertake aerial bombardment. There was, however, no proper aerial warfare or bombing until the war got under way.

poem 'On the Wings of the Morning'* is a standard anthology piece. This is slightly surprising, since it is effectively a eulogy of flying, and has very little to do with the First World War. Day was for the first part of the war a naval flier, transferring at his own request to France later on. Some of his other work, most notably the poem 'Dawn', is virtually unique in applying to the air war the style and sentiments of poetry written about the war on land. There are echoes of Rupert Brooke in his verse, including an annoying tendency to diminish the impact of a poem by using slang or colloquial language, but it has an energy and acuteness of observation that mark out Day as a man with exceptional promise. There is a pathetic aptness in a poem such as Hutcheon's 'The Flight to Flanders'. New pilots were often packed off to fly their machines to France, with minimal training not only in the basics of machine-handling, but also in navigation and in piloting a front-line aircraft rather than a trainer. With hindsight, these flights appear to have been something of an initiation test — get there, and you had the makings of a pilot. Pilots frequently did not make it, at least to where they were meant to go, and when they did arrive often showed their inexperience by crashing the aircraft on landing. Aircraft design was a matter of trial and error (or, as one survivor put it, error and trial), and some of the aircraft used in the First World War — notably the Sopwith Camel — were beasts to handle, particularly for inexperienced pilots. They were also often very rugged, and an aura of individual initiative permeates the air war in a way it never did with the war on land or at sea. Stories about the air war are legion. It was not unusual for an aircraft to take damage, land in a field, have the pilot mend it, and take off again as if nothing had happened. One story is told of an observer who, when he noticed that his pilot had been wounded, climbed out of the aircraft, sat on the wing, and roused his pilot back to semi-consciousness, thereafter yelling instructions that allowed the pair of them to land back at base. On a more sombre side, the British were reluctant to issue pilots with parachutes (and indeed never did so), for fear that having a 'safety net' would take away their concentration and sharpness. Balloon observers, however, had parachutes for most of the war, as did the Germans towards the end. It took a while for the Industrial Revolution to come to terms with the human side of machines. In the same way, the early railway-engine drivers were refused enclosed cabs because it was felt that if they

---

* A singularly apt title, from the 139th Psalm: 'If I take the wings of the morning: and remain in the uttermost parts of the sea; even there also shall thy hand lead me ...' Day was a Royal Naval Air Service pilot.

225

became too comfortable, they would not concentrate sufficiently on the job.

The air war was new; there was no tradition for poets to fall back on either when involved in it, or when writing about it from back at home. The opposite was true of the war at sea. The country took tremendous and overwhelming pride in its Navy, and pre-war writers had not been backward in producing a significant quantity of stirring stuff about Britain's Pride. Without a visible ripple, a number of these writers transferred to the war in hand, as if nothing had changed since Nelson's day. It is interesting that the disillusion which became notable on the Western Front never really found its way into poetry about the sea war. One reason was that in the early days there were a number of British victories to confirm writers in the opinion that Britain ruled the waves. Another was that, after Jutland, the war increasingly became one of small-scale Channel skirmishes and submarine warfare in the oceans, shrouded in secrecy and lacking glamour and drama with which to fuel poetry.

Jutland was another story. In terms of ships and men the British lost the battle,* but scored a strategic victory because, after the engagement, the Germans were the ones to run away and remained in their bases thereafter, making only one more major, abortive, foray. The tactical battle was lost because British shells failed to pierce German armour; had they done so, the Germans would have lost another six capital ships. It was also lost because British cordite exploded rather than flamed off when ignited by enemy fire, crippling or destroying ships, and because in the race to keep up the rate of fire the British left too many shells in turrets and hoists, and too many open channels down to magazines, with the same result to ships when enemy shells struck. The truth about this was not to emerge for many years. The failure was technical and therefore unexciting, and public knowledge of it was delayed as well. One literary result of Jutland was a sharp decline in the 'Rule Britannia' style of poetry, but the disappointment was not sufficient of a push to produce its opposite, gritty verse about the real war. Poetry about the war at sea therefore tends either to be heroic and romantic, or rather low-key, although this did not stop some fine pieces being written. The fact that this poetry was included as a matter of course in anthologies published up to 1935, and then increasingly dropped in favour of the land campaign, is partly a reflection of its relative quality. But it is also a reflection of the fact that, increasingly since the mid-1930s, we have

---

* It was said of Jellicoe at Jutland that he had the capacity to win or lose the war in an afternoon — and did neither.

tended to have a specific and immutable image of the First World War, and have then sought to confirm that image by being selective about what is printed. Poetry about the war at sea lacked the war-revulsion that we have seen as typifying trench poetry, and so has often been ignored. Notwithstanding its difference from trench poetry, the feelings of poetry from the sea war are an accurate guide to what was being felt and written at the time, and an accurate view of Great War verse demands that it be included.

Disillusion does in fact come through into the poetry of the war at sea, but in a rather sideways manner. For years the battleship had been the symbol of sea power and the measure of a navy's strength, as well as the focus of much public attention. After Jutland, the battleships of both fleets for the most part swung at their moorings in harbour, the Germans for fear of being beaten, the British because there was no German fleet to fight, and because increasingly the German sub-marines penned the big ships in harbour. As a result there was a concentration of poetry on to the smaller ships, the destroyers, the submarines, and the minesweepers, which bore most of the action after Jutland. Poets wrote war poetry when action or combat high-lighted certain areas. With an absence of battleship-against-battleship combats to stimulate the imagination, the ships of the merchant fleet like the smaller Royal Naval vessels, came to be popular subjects. There was considerable justice in this. In both world wars the sacri-fices made by merchant seamen have tended to be overlooked in favour of the more glamorous naval engagements, but apart from the Grand Fleet being wiped out, the only thing that could have lost Britain the sea war — perhaps the whole war — was the loss of its merchant fleet. People came to realise more and more, as rationing and shortages focused their minds, that the lowly tramp steamer was as important in its way (if not more so) than the battleship. Modern criticism can be sharp about poems glorifying the 'dirty British coaster', perhaps sharper than such poems deserve. Poets who wrote in this vein were the inheritors of a long tradition, and the feelings they expressed were not dressed-up morale-boosters, but often both genuinely felt and accurate as regards the importance of the merchant vessels and the courage and sacrifice of those who sailed them.

One poem needs to be selected for special mention. 'Battle of the Falkland Isles' is a classic example of the heroic mode of naval writing, and shows how insufferably pompous poets could be when fed from youth on a staple diet of Trafalgar. The poet suggests that Admiral Cradock's fatal decision to attack the German raiders *Scharnhorst* and *Gneisenau* — which culminated in the disaster at Coronel — was highly courageous, which it was. He then conjures up a marvellously efficient Board of Admiralty, which sends Sir Doveton Sturdee off to wreak revenge. The truth was that Sturdee was only sent off in command of two battle-cruisers because he was held responsible for the preceding débâcle at Coronel; getting rid of him in this manner was a political compromise that allowed Churchill and Fisher (respectively First Lord of the Admiralty and First Sea Lord) to remain on speaking terms. The two British battle-cruisers left port amid scenes of chronic chaos and confusion, and then dawdled on their way south with inexplicable slowness, in the meantime announcing to the world by their wireless traffic that they were coming. When Admiral von Spee came upon the British force it was in Port Stanley, coaling. In those days this was a filthy, laborious, and lengthy business, and one which also meant that the ships did not have steam up. If von Spee had chanced his luck and gone straight in against the British he might have had them for supper, and thereby scored one of the greatest naval victories of all time. As it was, the ancient battleship *Canopus*, beached at Port Stanley, lobbed off a few shells, one of which bounced off the ocean and went through a German cruiser's funnel. This was enough to turn von Spee away. Frantic efforts by the British got them out of harbour a considerable while later, and what followed was an unglamorous and protracted stern chase, in which the British battle-cruisers showed a remarkable capacity for missing the German ships, while several German shells went straight through the British ships' plate. Sturdee demonstrated a fixation with food throughout the battle, and orders for breakfast and lunch occupy as much space in the history of the chase as does action; it was therefore ironic that an unexploded German shell should have come to rest nestling against a jar of Sturdee's marmalade. The German forces showed remarkable courage and fortitude throughout and it is a pity that no German poet seems to have written a 'Battle of the Falkland Isles' from his country-men's point of view.

Battle of the Falkland Isles

The Isle Juan Fernandez off Valparaiso Bay,
    Twas there that Cradock sought
    The action that he fought —
For he said: 'To run from numbers is not our English way,
    Nor do we question why
    We are fore-ordained to die.'

Though his guns were scooping water and his tops were blind with
    spray.

In the red light of the sunset his ships went down in flame,
    He and his brave men
    Were never seen again,
And von Spee he stroked his beard, and said: 'Those Englishmen are
    game,
    But their dispositions are
    More glorious than war;
Those that greyhounds set on mastiffs are surely much to blame.'

Then the Board of Admiralty to Sir Doveton Sturdee said:
    'Take a proper naval force
    And steer a sou'west course,
And show the world that England is still a power to dread.'
    Like scorpions and whips
    Was vengeance to his ships,
And Cradock's guiding spirit flew before their line ahead.

Through tropic seas they shore like a meteor through the sky,
    And the dolphins in their chase
    Grew weary of the race;
The swift grey-pinioned albatross behind them could not fly,
    And they never paused to rest
    Upon the ocean's breast
Till their southern shadows lengthened and the Southern Cross rode
    high.

Then Sir Doveton Sturdee said in his flagship captain's ear:
    'By yon kelp and brembasteen
    'Tis the Falkland Isles, I ween,
Those mollymauks and velvet-sleeves they signal land is near,
    Give your consorts all the sign
    To swing out into line,
And keep good watch 'twixt ship and ship till Graf von Spee appear.'

The Germans like grey shadows came stealing round the Horn,
    Or as a wolf-pack prowls

With blood upon its jowls,
Their sides were pocked with gun-shots and their guns were battle-
    worn,
    And their colliers down the wind
    Like jackals trailed behind,
'Twas thus they met our cruisers on a bright December morn.

Like South Atlantic rollers half a mile from crest to crest,
    Breaking on basalt rocks
    In thunderous battle shocks,
So our heavy British metal put their armour to the test.
    And the Germans hurried north,
    As our lightnings issued forth,
But our battle-line closed round them like a sickle east and west.

Each ship was as a pillar of grey smoke upon the sea,
    Or mists upon a fen,
    Till they burst forth again
From their wraiths of battle-vapour by wind and speed made free;
    Three hours the action sped,
    Till, plunging by the head,
The *Scharnhorst* drowned the pennant of Admiral von Spee.

At the end of two hours more her sister ship went down
    Beneath the bubbling wave,
    The *Gneisenau* found her grave,
And *Nurnberg* and *Leipzig*, those cities of renown,
    Their cruiser god-sons too,
    Were both pierced through and through,
There was but one of all five ships our gunners did not drown.

'Twas thus that Cradock died, 'twas thus von Spee was slain,
    'Twas thus that Sturdee paid
    The score those Germans made,
'Twas thus St George's Ensign was laundered white again,
    Save the Red Cross over all
    The graves of those who fall,
That England as of yore may be Mistress of the Main.

'I.C.'

Off Coronel

Since Sturdee cleared the Southern Seas
Cradock's 'Good Hope' sleeps deep and well,
And he, avenged, can take his ease
Among his men off Coronel.

A.T. NANKIVELL

The Sailing of the Fleet

A signal flutters at the Flagship's fore,
And a deep pulse
Stirs in the mighty hulls
Slow wheeling seaward, where, beyond the Bar,
Half veiled in gloom,
Those messengers of doom
The lean destroyers are.

From the thronged piers
Faintly, the sound of cheers
Tossed by the winds afar ...

With gathering speed
The grey, grim shapes proceed —
The Might of England — to uphold the Law
'Gainst blackest treachery.
And the same courage high
That fired those valiant hearts at Trafalgar,
Burning from age to age,
Our proudest heritage,
Pierces disquieting war-clouds like a star,
As, burdened with a Nation's hopes and fears,
The Battle Fleet of England sweeps to war.

LIEUTENANT N.M.F. CORBETT, RN

Kilmeny
(A Song of the Trawlers)*

Dark, dark lay the drifters, against the red west,
  As they shot their long meshes of steel overside;
And the oily green waters were rocking to rest
  When *Kilmeny* went out, at the turn of the tide.
And nobody knew where that lassie would roam,
  For the magic that called her was tapping unseen.
It was well nigh a week ere *Kilmeny* came home,
  And nobody knew where *Kilmeny* had been.

She'd a gun at her bow that was Newcastle's best,
  And a gun at her stern that was fresh from the Clyde,
And a secret her skipper had never confessed,
  Not even at dawn, to his newly-wed bride;
And a wireless that whispered above like a gnome,
  The laughter of London, the boasts of Berlin.
O, it may have been mermaids that lured her from home,
  But nobody knew where *Kilmeny* had been.

It was dark when *Kilmeny* came home from her quest
  With her bridge dabbed red where her skipper had died;
But she moved like a bride with a rose at her breast;
  And 'Well done, *Kilmeny*!' the admiral cried.
Now at sixty-four fathom a conger may come,
  And nose at the bones of a drowned submarine;
But late in the evening *Kilmeny* came home,
  And nobody knew where *Kilmeny* had been.

There's a wandering shadow that stares at the foam,
  Though they sing all the night to old England, their queen,
Late, late in the evening *Kilmeny* came home,
  And nobody knew where *Kilmeny* had been.

ALFRED NOYES

* In the Great War (and again in the Second, and even nowadays) many fishing vessels were used for patrol duties, principally minesweeping.

Destroyers Off Jutland

They had hot scent across the spumy sea,
    Gehenna and her sister, swift *Shaitan*,
      That in the pack, with *Goblin*, *Elbis* ran
And many a couple more, full cry, foot-free;
The dog-fox and his brood were fain to flee,
    But bare of fang and dangerous to the van
      That pressed them close. So when the kill began
Some hounds were lamed and some died splendidly.

But from the dusk along the Skaggerack,
    Until dawn loomed upon the Reef of Horn
      And the last fox had slunk back to his earth,
They kept the great traditions of the pack,
    Staunch-hearted through the hunt, as they were born,
      These hounds that England suckled at the birth.

REGINALD McINTOSH CLEVELAND

Destroyers

On this primeval strip of western land,
With purple bays and tongues of shining sand,
Time, like an echoing tide,
Moves drowsily in idle ebb and flow;
The sunshine slumbers in the tangled grass
And homely folk with simple greeting pass
As to their worship or their work they go.
Man, earth, and sea
Seem linked in elemental harmony
And my insurgent sorrow finds release
In dreams of peace.

But silent, grey,
Out of the curtained haze,
Across the bay

233

Two fierce destroyers glide with bows afoam
And predatory gaze,
Like cormorants that seek a submerged prey.
An angel of destruction guards the door
And keeps the peace of our ancestral home;
Freedom to dream, to work, and to adore,
These vagrant days, nights of untroubled breath,
Are bought with death.

HENRY HEAD

The Search-Lights
From '*A Salute from the Fleet*'

Shadow for shadow, stripped for fight,
   The lean black cruisers search the sea.
Night-long their level shafts of light
   Revolve, and find no enemy.
Only they know each leaping wave
May hide the lightning, and their grave.

And in the land they guard so well
   Is there no silent watch to keep?
An age is dying, and the bell
   Rings midnight on a vaster deep.
But over all its waves, once more,
The search-lights move, from shore to shore.

And captains that we thought were dead,
   And dreamers that we thought were dumb,
And voices that we thought were fled,
   Arise, and call us, and we come;
And 'Search in thine own soul', they cry;
'For there, too, lurks thine enemy'.

ALFRED NOYES

234

Mine-Sweeping Trawlers

Not ours the fighter's glow,
    the glory, and the praise.
Unnoticed to and fro
    we pass our dangerous ways.

We sift the drifting sea,
    and blindly grope beneath;
obscure and toilsome we,
    the fishermen of death.

But when the great ships go
    to battle through the gloom,
our hearts beat high to know
    we cleared their path of doom.

E. HILTON YOUNG

Destroyers

Through the dark night
And the fury of battle
Pass the destroyers in showers of spray.
As the wolf-pack to the flank of the cattle,
We shall close in on them — shadows of grey.
In from ahead,
Through shell-flashes red,
We shall come down to them, after the Day.
Whistle and crash
Of salvo and volley
Round us and into us while we attack.
Light on our target they'll flash in their folly,
Splitting our ears with the shrapnel-crack.
Fire as they will,
We'll come to them still,
Roar as they may at us — Back — Go Back!
White though the sea
To the shell-splashes foaming,

235

We shall be there at the death of the Hun.
Only we pray for a star in the gloaming
(Light for torpedoes and none for a gun).
Lord — of Thy Grace
Make it a race,
Over the sea with the night to run.

'KLAXON'

Submarines

When the breaking wavelets pass all sparkling to the sky,
When beyond their crests we see the slender masts go by,
When the glimpses alternate in bubbles white and green,
And funnels grey against the sky show clear and fair between,
When the word is passed along — 'Stern and beam and bow' —
'Action stations fore and aft — all torpedoes now!'
When the hissing tubes are still, as if with bated breath
They waited for the word to loose the silver bolts of death,
When the Watch beneath the Sea shall crown the great Desire,
And hear the coughing rush of air that greets the word to fire,
We'll ask for no advantage, Lord — but only would we pray
That they may meet this boat of ours upon their outward way.

'KLAXON'

Eyes in the Air

Our guns are a league behind us, our target a mile below,
And there's never a cloud to blind us from the haunts of our lurking
    foe —
Sunk pit whence his shrapnel tore us, support-trench crest-concealed,
As clear as the charts before us, his ramparts lie revealed.
His panicked watchers spy us, a droning threat in the void;
Their whistling shells outfly us — puff upon puff, deployed
Across the green beneath us, across the flanking grey,
In fume and fire to sheath us and baulk us of our prey.
Below, beyond, above her,
Their iron web is spun:

236

Flicked but unsnared we hover,
    Edged planes against the sun:
Eyes in the air above his lair,
    The hawks that guide the gun!

No words from earth may reach us, save, white against the ground,
The strips outspread to teach us whose ears are deaf to sound:
But down the winds that sear us, athwart our engine's shriek,
We send — and know they hear us, the ranging guns we speak.
Our visored eyeballs show us their answering pennant, broke
Eight thousand feet below us, a whorl of flame-stabbed smoke —
The burst that hangs to guide us, while numbed gloved fingers tap
From wireless key beside us the circles of the map.
    Line — target — short or over —
        Come, plain as clock hands run,
    Words from the birds that hover,
        Unblinded, tail to sun:
    Words out of air to range them fair,
        From hawks that guide the gun!

Your flying shells have failed you, your landward guns are dumb:
Since earth hath naught availed you, these skies be open! Come,
Where, wild to meet and mate you, flame in their beaks for breath,
Black doves! the white hawks wait you on the wind-tossed boughs of
    death.
These boughs be cold without you, our hearts are hot for this,
Our wings shall beat about you, our scorching breath shall kiss;
Till, fraught with that we gave you, fulfilled of our desire,
You bank — too late to save you from biting beaks of fire —
    Turn sideways from your lover,
        Shudder and swerve and run,
    Tilt; stagger; and plunge over
        Ablaze against the sun:
    Doves dead in air, who clomb to dare
        The hawks that guide the gun!*

GILBERT FRANKAU

* The main work of aircraft in the Great War was reconnaissance, artillery spotting, as in this poem, and observation, which was mainly carried out by slow and poorly armed two-seaters. The single-seat 'scouts' were developed in order to protect their own two-seaters and shoot down the enemy's. Two-seater flying was dangerous and unglamorous, but vital.

North Sea

Dawn on the drab North Sea! —
colourless, cold, and depressing,
with the sun that we long to see
refraining from his blessing.
To the westward — sombre as doom:
to the eastward — grey and foreboding:
Comes a low, vibrating boom —
the sound of a mine exploding.

Day on the drear North Sea! —
wearisome, drab, and relentless.
The low clouds swiftly flee;
bitter the sky, and relentless.
Nothing at all in sight
save the mast of a sunken trawler,
fighting her long, last fight
with the waves that mouth and maul her.

Gale on the bleak North Sea! —
howling a dirge in the rigging.
Slowly and toilfully
through the great, grey breakers digging,
thus we make our way,
hungry, wet, and weary,
soaked with the sleet and spray,
desolate, damp, and dreary.

Fog in the dank North Sea! —
silent and clammily dripping.
Slowly and mournfully,
ghostlike, goes the shipping.
Sudden across the swell
come the fog-horns hoarsely blaring
or the clang of a warning bell,
to leave us vainly staring.

Night on the black North Sea! —
black as hell's darkest hollow.

Peering anxiously,
we search for the ships that follow.
One are the sea and sky,
dim are the figures near us,
with only the sea-bird's cry
and the swish of the waves to cheer us.

Death on the wild North Sea! —
death from the shell that shatters
(death we will face with glee,
'tis the weary wait that matters): —
death from the guns that roar,
and the splinters weirdly shrieking.
'Tis a fight to the death; 'tis war;
and the North Sea is redly reeking!

JEFFERY DAY+

The war at sea was, in journalistic terms, pretty boring. There were skirmishes early on in the war, and the greatest naval anti-climax of all time at Jutland, but the great Nelsonian blood-baths that would have made marvellous copy were noticeably absent from the Great War. Gradually the public came to realise that it was the war against the submarine that mattered more than the war against the battleship. One device used to trap submarines was the Q-boat. This was a merchant ship armed with hidden guns, packed to the hilt with wood or other buoyant cargo, and sent off masquerading as an innocent merchantman. On sighting a lone merchant ship a U-boat had two options. It could fire a torpedo, in which case the Q-ship might not sink, given its buoyant cargo. However, the hope was that the U-boat would decide to save a precious torpedo, surface, and sink the merchant ship by gunfire. If this happened, the shutters would come down and the Q-ship would open fire on the U-boat. Victory for the Q-boat was by no means assured. If it did not hit the U-boat suffi-ciently seriously to stop it submerging, the submarine could then pick the ship off at its leisure with a torpedo. There were a number of bloody battles between these ships and submarines. The drama of the battles has tended to obscure the fact that it was a very hit-and-miss method of anti-submarine warfare, and a measure born out of desperation.

The Q-Boat

She's the plaything of the Navy, she's the nightmare of the Hun,
    She's the wonder and the terror of the seas,
She's a super-censored secret that eludes the prying sun
    And the unofficial wireless of the breeze;
        She can come and go unseen
        By the foredoomed submarine;
    She's the Mystery-Ship, the Q-boat, if you please.

She can weave a web of magic for the unsuspecting foe,
    She can scent the breath of Kultur leagues away,
She can hear a U-Boat thinking in Atlantic depths below
    And disintegrate it with a Martian ray;
        She can feel her way by night
        Through the minefield of the Bight;
    She has all the tricks of science, grave and gay.

In the twinkle of a searchlight she can suffer a sea-change
    From a collier to a *Shamrock* under sail,
From a hyper-super-Dreadnought, old Leviathan at range,
    To a lightship or a whaler or a whale;
        With some canvas and a spar
        She can mock the morning star
    As a haystack or the flotsam of a gale.

She's the derelict you chartered North of Flores outward-bound,
    She's the iceberg that you sighted coming back,
She's the salt-rimed Biscay trawler heeling home to Plymouth Sound,
    She's the phantom-ship that crossed the moon-beams' track;
        She's the rock where none should be
        In the Adriatic Sea,
    She's the wisp of fog that haunts the Skagerrack.

She can dive in twenty seconds, she can lie submerged for weeks,
    She can burrow in the shingle or the sand,
She can scale the rocky foreshore, she can thread the mazy creeks,

She can waddle like a Tank along the strand;
    She can spread a pair of planes,
    If necessity obtains,
And cruise aloft at watch o'er sea and land.

H.E. WILKES

The Surrender of the Hun Fleet
(After 'The Ancient Mariner')

As idle as a German ship
Upon the 'German' Ocean.*

ANONYMOUS

The Mystery Ships†
To 'The Coasters and Merchantmen who accompany the Lord High Admiral'

There's order and law in a battleship's might;
    The cruisers proceed on a logical plan;
While even destroyers go gay to the fight
    By tactical units as well as they can;
But far away out in a world of their own,
    Where logic and limit are shivered to bits,
You'll light on the ladies who labour alone,
    The jocular gipsies who live by their wits.

Disciples of DRAKE and DUNDONALD,
    The sea in their blood and their bones,
They sail in the wake of BOSCAWEN and BLAKE
    And hail as an ally PAUL JONES;
For better than honour and glory
    They reckon the frolics and quips
Which daily illumine the story
    That comes from the Mystery Ships.

* The North Sea was also sometimes known as the German Ocean.

† i.e. Q-ships.

They're nautical zealots who never suppose
    That right is defended by leisure and ease;
The submarine, quaking wherever she goes,
    Can tell they're abroad by the feel of the seas;
There's ominous oil in the wake of their work;
    The soles on the Dogger take cover amain,
And cry, as the stranger alights with a jerk,
    'The Mystery Ships have been at it again!'

Untutored, but versed in the oldest of creeds,
    The King's Regulations decay on their shelves;
Between the Addenda, which nobody reads,
    The Mystery Ships are a law to themselves;
Their pictures and pranks are denied to the Press,
    Till out of the offing as blithe as can be
A weather-worn sea-dog of twenty or less
    Blows in to the Palace to get a V.C.

The family fought in ELIZABETH'S time
    From Bristol and Dover and Harwich and Leigh;
From Barnstaple, Yarmouth and London and Lyme
    They hurried away at the call of the sea;
Their titles are writ in the Rolls of their Race,
    With laughter and love we can picture them still;
Is mystery work to be done for HER GRACE?
    My lord in the Flagship can summon at will

The *Lark* and the *Lamb* and the *Moonshine*,
    The *Hazard* and *Happy Pretence*,
The *Wraith* and the *Smoke* and the *Merlin* and *Joke*,
    The *Riddle* and *Royal Defence*;
As quick as a cradle could spare them
    They scuttled away from the slips,
For England, the mother who bare them,
    The first of the Mystery Ships.

CAPTAIN R.A. HOPWOOD, RN

242

Admiral Dugout*

He had done with fleets and squadrons, with the restless roaming
  seas,
  He had found the quiet haven he desired,
And he lay there to his moorings with the dignity and ease
  Most becoming to Rear-Admirals (retired);
He was bred on 'Spit and Polish' — he was reared to 'Stick and
  String' —
  All the things the ultra-moderns never name;
But a storm blew up to seaward, and it meant the Real Thing,
  And he had to slip his cable when it came.

So he hied him up to London for to hang about Whitehall,
  And he sat upon the steps there soon and late,
He importuned night and morning, he bombarded great and small,
  From messengers to Ministers of State;
He was like a guilty conscience, he was like a ghost unlaid,
  He was like a debt of which you can't get rid,
Till the Powers that Be, despairing, in a fit of temper said,
  'For the Lord's sake give him something' — and they did.

They commissioned him a trawler with a high and raking bow,
  Black and workmanlike as any pirate craft,
With a crew of steady seamen very handy in a row,
  And a brace of little barkers fore and aft;
And he blessed the Lord his Maker when he faced the North Sea
  sprays
  And exceedingly extolled his lucky star
That had given his youth renewal in the evening of his days
  (With the rank of Captain Dugout, R.N.R.).

He is jolly as a sandboy, he is happier than a king,
  And his trawler is the darling of his heart
(With her cuddy like a cupboard where a kitten couldn't swing,

* Retired officer recalled to service (i.e. dug out of retirement).

And a smell of fish that simply won't depart);
He has found upon occasion sundry targets for his guns;
    He could tell you tales of mine and submarine;
Oh, the holes he's in and out of and the glorious risks he runs
    Turn his son — who's in a Super-Dreadnought — green.

He is fit as any fiddle; he is hearty, hale and tanned;
    He is proof against the coldest gales that blow;
He has never felt so lively since he got his first command
    (Which is rather more than forty years ago);
And of all the joyful picnics of his wild and wandering youth —
    Little dust-ups from Taku to Zanzibar —
There was none to match the picnic, he declares in sober sooth,
    That he has as Captain Dugout, R.N.R.

MISS C. FOX-SMITH

Years Ahead

Years ahead, years ahead,
    Who shall honour our sailor-dead?
For the wild North Sea, the bleak North Sea,
Threshes and seethes so endlessly.
Gathering foam and changing crest
Heave and hurry, and know no rest:
    How can they mark our sailor-dead
        In the years ahead?

Time goes by, time goes by,
    And who shall tell where our soldiers lie?
The guiding trench-cut winds afar,
Miles upon miles where the dead men are;
A cross of wood, or a carven block,
A name-disc hung on a rifle-stock —
    These shall tell where our soldiers lie
        As the time goes by.

Days to come, days to come —
But who shall ask of the wandering foam,

The weaving weed, or the rocking swell,
The place of our sailor-dead to tell?
From Jutland reefs to Scapa Flow
Tracks of the wary warships go,
    But the deep sea-wastes lie green and dumb
      All the days to come.

    Years ahead, years ahead,
      The sea shall honour our sailor-dead!
No mound of mouldering earth shall show
The fighting place of the men below,
But a swirl of seas that gather and spill;
And the wind's wild chanty whistling shrill
    Shall cry 'Consider my sailor-dead!'
      In the years ahead.

GUY N. POCOCK

A Drifter Off Tarentum

He from the wind-bitten North with ship and companions
    descended,
Searching for eggs of death spawned by invisible hulls.
Many he found and drew forth. Of a sudden the Fishery ended
In flame and a clamorous breath not new to the eye-pecking gulls.

RUDYARD KIPLING

A Minesweeper Sunk
(The Duty Chief Petty Officer to the Duty Writer)

Only one drifter down in the patrol!
Well that's damned fine! — Don't stand and stare
Writer, for God's sake pile the coal;
You'll find their service sheets filed over there.
Is that the list of 'em? Make a rough note
In pencil on page three before you go;
Use some of them buff forms and when you've wrote

To stop allotments mind you let me know
Down in the C.P.O.'s canteen below.

Give us a hand on with me bloody coat.

EDWARD L. DAVISON

A Poor Aviator Lay Dying

Oh, a poor aviator lay dying
At the end of a bright summer's day,
His comrades were gathered around him
To carry the fragments away.

The engine was piled on his wishbone,
The Hotchkiss* was wrapped round his head,
A spark-plug stuck out of each elbow
It was plain that he'd shortly be dead.

He spat out a valve and a gasket
And stirred in the sump where he lay,
And then to his wond'ring comrades,
These brave parting words he did say;

'Take the manifold out of my larynx
And the butterfly valve off my neck
Remove from my kidneys the camrods,
There's a lot of good parts in his wreck.

'Take the piston rings out of my stomach,
And the cylinders out of my brain,
Extract from my liver the crankshaft,
And assemble the engine again.

'I'll be riding a cloud in the morning
With no rotary* before me to cuss,

* Hotchkiss — machine-gun; rotary — type of aircraft engine. The last two stanzas come from a much earlier Army ballad, supposedly written during a cholera epidemic in India or about the time of the Mutiny (1857).

So shake the lead from your feet and get busy,
There's another lad wanting this 'bus'

Who minds to the dust returning?
Who shrinks from the sable shore?
Where the high and the lofty yearning
Of the soul shall be no more?

So stand to your glasses steady,
This world is a world full of lies,
Here's a health to the dead already,
And hurrah for the next man who dies!

ANONYMOUS

The Royal Aircraft Factory BE2C aircraft was viewed by many pilots as an engineering and fighting death trap. A two-seater used primarily for reconnaissance and artillery spotting, it was extremely stable but slow, poorly armed, cumbersome in turns, and had an unreliable engine and poor forward and downward vision for the pilot. It was one of a number of aircraft produced by all the combatants in the war which were kept in service long after their uselessness was revealed, a tendency which in the case of the BE2C cost many lives.

They Called Them RAF* 2C's

Oh! they found a bit of iron what
Some bloke had thrown away,
And the RAF said, 'This is just the thing
We've sought for many a day,'

They built a weird machine,
The strangest engine ever seen,
And they'd quite forgotten that the thing was rotten,
And they shoved it in a flying machine.

* The Royal Air Force did not come into being until 1 April 1918, by the amalgamation of the Royal Flying Corps and the Royal Naval Air Service. Until then, 'RAF' stood for Royal Aircraft Factory; 'BE' stands for 'Bombing Experimental'.

Then they ordered simply thousands more,
And sent them out to fight.
When the blokes who had to fly them swore,
The RAF said, 'They're all right
The 'bus is stable as can be;
We invented every bit ourselves, you see!'

They were so darn' slow, they wouldn't go,
And they called them RAF 2C's!

ANONYMOUS

The Pilot's Psalm

The BE2C is my 'bus; therefore I shall want.
He maketh me to come down in green pastures.
He leadeth me where I will not go.
He maketh me to be sick; he leadeth me astray on all cross-country
    flights.
Yea, though I fly over No-man's land where mine
    enemies would compass me about, I fear much evil
    for thou art with me; thy joystick and thy prop discomfort me.
Thou preparest a crash before me in the presence
    of thy enemies; thy RAF anointeth my hair with oil, thy tank leaketh
    badly.
Surely to goodness thou shalt not follow me all
    the days of my life; else I shall dwell in the House of Colney Hatch
    forever.

ANONYMOUS

Every Little While

Every little while I crash a Camel,
Every little while I hit a tree,
I'm always stalling — I'm always falling,
Because I want to fly a posh SE.*

* The SE (Scout Experimental) 5A, perhaps the Royal Aircraft Factory's most successful design
of the war, and one of the best aircraft of any side.

Every little while my engine's conking,
Every little while I catch on fire.
All the time I've got my switch up*
I've always got the wind up,
Every, every, little while.

ANONYMOUS RFC SONG

The 'PBO' in the poem below stands for 'Poor Bloody Observer'. The observer in a First World War two-seater reconnaissance (or, later, bombing) aircraft was carried, as his name suggests, to undertake the reconnaissance duties and spotting which at the start of the war were seen as the main function of aircraft. In addition, the observer was a machine-gunner, particularly in the days when the absence of a gun that could fire through the propeller meant that there could only be a fixed forward-firing gun mounted on the top plane to fire outside the propeller arc, and another on a movable mounting in the observer's cockpit, which obviously could not be fired forward, or through the wings, tail assembly, or fuselage. Although originally observers had been officers who commanded the aircraft and its pilot, they later tended to be of lower rank than the pilots, and were certainly lower in status. The other miseries of an observer's life are clearly catalogued in the poem.

You're Only a PBO

When you're doing an escort stunt and the Huns get on your tail
You fire and aim till you see 'em flame and down they go like hail.
Alas, the pilot's jealous scorn is a thing we learn to know,
You may get twenty Huns in flames
Don't think that they'll believe your claims,
For you're only a PBO, yes, only a PBO.

Chorus: At seventeen, etc.,

We all of us know the case when the pilot came home alone,
No doubt it was only a slight mistake, but his attitude's clearly shown.
He suddenly shoved his joystick down as far as it would go.

---

* i.e., the ignition circuit on.

'Hello, you seem to have gone,' he said.
'I fear you must be somewhat dead,
But you're only a PBO, yes, only a PBO.'

Chorus. At seventeen, etc.,

I managed to get my leave, and was trying to drown the past,
When I chanced on a maiden passing fair, and thought I had clicked
    at last.
To my joy she said 'The RFC are the nicest boys I know'
When I said 'Well, I'm an Observer, dear,'
She said 'There's nothing doing here,
You're merely a PBO, a miserable PBO.'

Chorus. At seventeen, etc.,

When you climb in the old machine to start on a damned OP,*
You cover yourself with tons of clothes and they're all of them NBG,
The pilot sits near the engine's warmth, his body with heat aglow,
Whilst you must stand in the back and cuss
Till the ice on your whiskers stalls the bus,
You're only a PBO, yes, only a PBO.

Chorus

At seventeen thou. he's shooting rather badly at a Pfalz of tender blue,
At fifteen thou. you see him point out sadly some Huns of a different
    hue,
At ten or twelve he's shooting rather madly at six or eight or more.
When he fancies he is past hope
Fires a long burst as a last hope
And a Hun spins down on fire to the floor!

ANONYMOUS RFC/RAF MESS SONG

On the Wings of the Morning

A sudden roar, a mighty rushing sound,
    a jolt or two, a smoothly sliding rise,
    a tumbled blur of disappearing ground,

---

* Observation patrol.

and then all sense of motion slowly dies.
 Quiet and calm, the earth slips past below,
 as underneath a bridge still waters flow.

My turning wing inclines towards the ground;
 the ground itself glides up with graceful swing
and at the plane's far tip twirls slowly round,
 then drops from sight again beneath the wing
  to slip away serenely as before,
  a cubist-patterned carpet on the floor.

Hills gently sink and valleys gently fill.
 The flattened fields grow ludicrously small;
slowly they pass beneath and slower still
 until they hardly seem to move at all.
  Then suddenly they disappear from sight,
  hidden by fleeting wisps of faded white.

The wing-tips, faint and dripping, dimly show,
 blurred by the wreaths of mist that intervene,
Weird, half-seen shadows flicker to and fro
 across the pallid fogbank's blinding screen.
  At last the choking mists release their hold,
  and all the world is silver, blue, and gold.

The air is clear, more clear than sparkling wine;
 compared with this, wine is a turgid brew.
The far horizon makes a clean-cut line
 between the silver and the depthless blue.
  Out of the snow-white level reared on high
  glittering hills surge up to meet the sky.

Outside the wind screen's shelter gales may race:
 but in the seat a cool and gentle breeze
blows steadily upon my grateful face.
 As I sit motionless and at my ease,
  contented just to loiter in the sun
  and gaze around me till the day is done.

And so I sit, half sleeping, half awake,
   dreaming a happy dream of golden days,
until at last, with a reluctant shake
    I rouse myself, and with a lingering gaze
      at all the splendour of the shining plain
      make ready to come down to earth again.

The engine stops: a pleasant silence reigns —
   silence, not broken, but intensified
by the soft, sleepy wires' insistent strains,
    that rise and fall, as with a sweeping glide
      I slither down the well-oiled sides of space,
      towards a lower, less enchanted place.

The clouds draw nearer, changing as they come.
   Now, like a flash, fog grips me by the throat.
Down goes the nose: at once the wires' low hum
    begins to rise in volume and in note,
      till, as I hurtle from the choking cloud
      it swells into a scream, high-pitched, and loud.

The scattered hues and shades of green and brown
   fashion themselves into the land I know,
turning and twisting, as I spiral down
    towards the landing-ground; till, skimming low,
      I glide with slackening speed across the ground,
      and come to rest with lightly grating sound.

JEFFERY DAY+

A Song of the Air

This is the song of the Plane —
The creaking, shrieking plane,
The throbbing, sobbing plane,
And the moaning, groaning wires: —
The engine — missing again!
One cylinder never fires!
   Hey ho! for the Plane!

This is the song of the Man —
The driving, striving man,
The chosen, frozen man: —
The pilot, the man-at-the-wheel,
Whose limit is all that he can,
And beyond, if the need is real!
   Hey ho! for the Man!

This is the song of the Gun —
The muttering, stuttering gun,
The maddening, gladdening gun: —
That chuckles with evil glee
At the last, long dive of the Hun,
With its end in eternity!
   Hey ho! for the Gun!

This is the song of the Air —
The lifting, drifting air,
The eddying, steadying air,
The wine of its limitless space: —
May it nerve us at last to dare
Even death with undaunted face!
   Hey ho! for the Air!

'OBSERVER, RFC'

The Dawn Patrol

Sometimes I fly at dawn above the sea,
Where, underneath, the restless waters flow —
   Silver, and cold, and slow.
Dim in the east there burns a new-born sun,
Whose rosy gleams along the ripples run,
   Save where the mist droops low,
Hiding the level loneliness from me.

And now appears beneath the milk-white haze
A little fleet of anchored ships, which lie
   In clustered company,

253

And seem as they are yet fast bound by sleep,
Although the day has long begun to peep,
    With red–inflamèd eye,
Along the still, deserted ocean ways.

The fresh, cold wind of dawn blows on my face
As in the sun's raw heart I swiftly fly,
    And watch the seas glide by.
Scarce human seem I, moving through the skies,
And far removed from warlike enterprise —
    Like some great gull on high
Whose white and gleaming wings bear on through space.

Then do I feel with God quite, quite alone,
High in the virgin morn, so white and still,
    And free from human ill:
My prayers transcend my feeble earth-bound plaints —
As though I sang among the happy Saints
    With many a holy thrill —
As though the glowing sun were God's bright Throne.

My flight is done. I cross the line of foam
That breaks around a town of grey and red,
    Whose streets and squares lie dead
Beneath the silent dawn — then am I proud
That England's peace to guard I am allowed;
    Then bow my humble head,
In thanks to Him Who brings me safely home.

PAUL BEWSHER

Dawn

'Machines will raid at dawn,' they say:
It's always dawn, or just before;
why choose this wretched time of day
    for making war?

From all the hours of light there are
why do they always choose the first?
Is it because they know it's far
    and far the worst?

Is it a morbid sense of fun
that makes them send us day by day
a target for the sportive Hun? —
    who knows our way,

and waits for us at dawn's first peep,
knowing full well we shall be there,
and he, when that is done, may sleep
    without a care.

And was it not Napoleon
who said (in French) these words, 'Lor' lumme!
no man can hope to fight upon
    an empty tummy'?

Yet every morn we bold bird-boys
clamber into our little buses,
and go and make a futile noise
    with bombs and cusses.

And every night the orders tell
the same monotonous old story
'machines will raid at dawn.' To hell
    with death or glory!

Why can't they let us lie in bed
and, after breakfast and a wash,
despatch us, clean and fully fed,
    to kill the Boche?

I hate the dawn, as dogs hate soap:
and on my heart, when I am done,
you'll find the words engraved, 'Dawn hope-
    less, streak of, one.'

JEFFERY DAY+

The Call of the Air

Have you ever sat in crystal space, enjoying the sensations
    of an eagle hovered high above the earth.
gazing down on man's ridiculous and infantile creations
    and judging them according to their worth?
Have you looked upon a basin small enough to wash your face in,
    with a few toy-ships collected by the shore,
and then realised with wonder that if those toys go under
    nine-tenths of Britain's navy is no more?

Have you seen a khaki maggot crawling down a thread of cotton —
    the route march of a regiment or so?
Have you seen the narrow riband, unimportant, half-forgotten,
    that tells you that the Thames is far below?
Have you glanced with smiling pity at the world's most famous city,
    a large grey smudge that barely strikes the eye?
Would you like to see things truly and appreciate them duly?
    Well then do it, damn you, do it; learn to fly!

Have you left the ground in murkiness, all clammy, grey, and soaking,
    and struggled through the dripping, dirty white?
Have you seen the blank sides closing in and felt that you were
    choking,
    and then leapt into a land of blazing light,
where the burnished sun is shining on the clouds' bright, silver lining,
    a land where none but fairy feet have trod,
where the splendour nearly blinds you and the wonder of it binds you,
    and you know you are in heaven, close to God?

Have you tumbled from the sky until your wires were shrilly
    screaming,
    and watched the earth go spinning round about?
Have you felt the hard air beat your face until your eyes were
    streaming?
    Have you turned the solar system inside out?
Have you seen earth rush to meet you and the fields spread out to
    greet you,

and flung them back to have another try?
Would it fill you with elation to be boss of all creation?
   Well then do it, damn you, do it; learn to fly!

Have you fought a dummy battle, diving, twisting, pirouetting,
   at a lightning speed that takes away your breath?
Have you been so wildly thrilled that you have found yourself
   forgetting
   that it's practice, not a battle to the death?
Have you hurtled low through narrow, tree-girt spaces like an arrow —
   seen things grow and disappear like pricked balloons?
Would you feel the breathless joys of it and hear the thrilling noise of
   it,
   the swish, the roar, the ever-changing tunes?

Have you chased a golden sunbeam down a gold and silver alley,
   with pink and orange jewels on the floor?
Have you raced a baby rainbow round a blue and silver valley,
   where purple caves throw back the engine's roar?
Have you seen the lights that smoulder on a cloud's resplendent
   shoulder
   standing out before a saffron-coloured sky?
Would you be in splendid places and illimitable spaces?
   Well then do it, damn you, do it; learn to fly!

JEFFERY DAY+

The Flight to Flanders

Does he know the road to Flanders, does he know the criss-cross
   tracks
With the row of sturdy hangars at the end?
Does he know that shady corner where, the job done, we relax
To the music of the engines round the bend?
   It is here that he is coming with his gun and battle 'plane
   To the little aerodrome at — well, you know!
   To a wooden hut abutting on a quiet country lane,
   For he's ordered overseas and he must go.

257

Has he seen those leagues of trenches, the traverses steep and stark,
High over which the British pilots ride?
Does he know the fear of flying miles to east-ward of his mark
When his only map has vanished over-side?
    It is there that he is going, and it takes a deal of doing,
    There are many things he really ought to know;
    And there isn't time to swot 'em if a Fokker he's pursuing,
    For he's ordered overseas and he must go.

Does he know that ruined town, that old — of renown?
Has he heard the crack of Archie* bursting near?
Has he known that ghastly moment when your engine lets you down?
Has he ever had that feeling known as fear?
    It's to Flanders he is going with a brand-new aeroplane
    To take the place of one that's dropped below,
    To fly and fight and photo mid the storms of wind and rain,
    For he's ordered overseas and he must go.

Then the hangar door flies open and the engine starts its roar,
And the pilot gives the signal with his hand;
As he rises over England he looks back upon the shore,
For the Lord alone knows where he's going to land.
    Now the plane begins to gather speed, completing lap on lap,
    Till, after diving down and skimming low,
    They're off to shattered Flanders, by the compass and the map —
    They were ordered overseas and had to go.

LESSEL HUTCHEON

---

* Anti-aircraft fire. 'Archie' derives from a popular song of the time — as the shells burst near
their aircraft, British pilots would shout 'Archibald — certainly not!'

258

A Revised Version
To the Editor of *The New Witness*

SIR,

[*From The Times*, January 5, 1915.]

Hymn for Airmen
(Set to Music by Sir Hubert Parry.)

Lord, guard and guide the men who fly
Through the great spaces of the sky,
Be with them traversing the air
In darkening storm or sunshine fair.

Thou who dost keep with tender might
The balanced birds in all their flight,
Thou of the tempered winds be near,
That, having Thee, they know no fear.

Control their minds, with instinct fit
What time, adventuring, they quit
The firm security of land:
Grant steadfast eye and skilful hand.

Aloft in solitudes of space
Uphold them with Thy saving Grace.
O God, protect the men who fly
Through lonely ways beneath the sky.

M. C. D. H.

The above-quoted Hymn, though admirably suited for performance (if that is the right word) in time of peace, seems hardly suitable at the present juncture; and if the petitions it contains were accorded without exception, the result might be most unfortunate.

With a view of averting this danger,
and in order to bring the work into
harmony with existing conditions, I
venture to suggest the addition of the
following stanzas:—

This prayer, O Lord, of course applies
Only to us and our Allies;
The men upon the other side
Do *not* 'uphold', or 'guard', or 'guide',

It is not hard, O Lord, to know
A 'Taube' from a 'Blériot':*
Should Zeppelins attempt a flight,
Don't keep them with thy 'tender might',

Don't prosper the aërial work
Of German, Austrian, or Turk;
But give the impious fellows fits,
And smash them into little bits.

CHARLES STRACHEY

* Primitive monoplanes. The Taube ('dove') was used by German and Austrian forces, the
Blériot, very similar to the aircraft in which Louis Blériot first flew the Channel in 1909, by
the French and British.

VII

'Poor Sally'

HOME FRONT

19 September 1914:   David Lloyd George, Liberal Chancellor of the Exchequer, who has been opposed to entry into the war until the very last moment, speaks out in favour of it.

September–December 1914:   Rumours circulate of Russian troops with 'snow on their boots' seen on passage through Britain. Myths created of German atrocities against Belgian refugees. Influx of Belgian refugees to England. Rigorous censorship imposed.

1915:   Women start to be employed for the first time in significant numbers as munition workers, and for a wide range of other jobs; this includes their being recruited into the armed forces as auxiliaries.

25 December 1915:   Address by Lloyd George fails to end strikes in Glasgow.

January 1916:   In Britain, compulsory military service is brought in for single men between the ages of eighteen and forty, with effect from February. The Military Service Act remains in force until April 1920. First limited signs of opposition to the war start to appear.

Easter Monday, 4 April 1916:   Provisional Government of the Irish Republic proclaimed from Dublin Post Office, which the rebels have captured. Republic lasts five days before British restore control, after considerable fighting. Fourteen ring-leaders are executed; the rest, including Éamonn de Valéra, are released under an amnesty in June 1917.

21 May 1916:	'Daylight Saving' (British Summer Time) introduced, although the idea has been continuously mooted since 1908 by William Willett, a Chelsea builder.
May 1916:	Compulsory military service for all introduced.
5 December 1916:	Lloyd George, by now Minister of Munitions, succeeds H.H. Asquith, also a Liberal, as Prime Minister, having collaborated with the Conservatives to overthrow a man who, they consider, lacks vigour. Lloyd George's Coalition government lasts until October 1922.
1 January 1918:	Rationing of individuals introduced in Britain, principally for sugar, tea, margarine, bacon, cheese and butter. Since June 1917 there has been a system of registering with traders for supplies of sugar, and in February 1918 a system of rationing Londoners for meat and fats is introduced. National meat rationing begins on 7 April 1918, and on 14 July coupon books for meat, fats, sugar and lard are brought in. Rationing finally ends in November 1920.
11 November 1918: Armistice Day.	It is greeted in Britain with displays ranging from the joyful to the downright riotous, which last in some places for several days. The reaction of the troops in the line, however, is markedly less demonstrative.

Siegfried Sassoon's poetry has been particularly effective in establishing an image of the home front. Sassoon wrote about ousting the 'Junkers' from the British Parliament with British Troops, about tanks opening up on the baying crowds in music-halls, about people not worrying 'a bit' when a maimed soldier was condemned to live out the rest of his life in a wheel-chair.* There is much truth in the images he thus created. Many of those left at home retained an image of the war that was sacrificial, romantic, and glamorous. It could hardly be anything else. Rigid censorship and primitive communications meant that the media reported very little hard or accurate news, while soldiers on leave were often reluctant to discuss their experiences or air their views. A communication gap wider than the Channel frequently opened up

---

* See Sassoon's poems 'Fight to a Finish', 'Blighters', and 'Does It Matter?', which can be found in most modern anthologies of Great War verse, and in his collected war poetry.

between soldiers returning from the front and those who had never seen it. It was easier for exhausted men to grunt vaguely in agreement when fathers or mothers fed them questions based on *The Times*'s image of the war, than it was for them to try and re-educate those who had never seen the peculiar awfulness of the front line. An especial target of people's hatred was the Profiteer, the man thought to have made millions out of the war, and to be feeding off the blood of the soldiers.

It is true that those left at home led relatively easy lives, at least in the physical sense. German bombing raids by Zeppelins and aircraft caused, comparatively, only a handful of casualties. Food shortages became worse as the war progressed, but bread was never rationed, and any suffering in Britain was tiny compared to that endured by the Germans. Coal and petrol were in short supply, but not disastrously so. There were many industries — and many men — who made fortunes out of the war, and it also put workers themselves in strong bargaining positions, allowing them the opportunity to earn good money because of the importance of their work for the war effort. It was a source of much bitterness in both wars that the sailors who risked their lives at sea often earned far less than the comfortable dockyard workers who built, serviced, and repaired the fighting ships and merchant vessels. Churchill made himself very popular with the Fleet for a time in 1914 by demanding that the dockyard workers frantically trying to get the two battle-cruisers ready for the Falkland Islands expedition should sail into action with the ships if the work was not completed on time. It was.

The views of poets such as Sassoon form only a part of the truth, however. Penny histories of the war tend to see it as marking the start of real liberation for women in Britain, and as something of a heaven-sent opportunity for feminism. Thus the historian's conventional reaction has been to write a discursive chapter on 'The Role of Women' or some such, and to sign off with the general view that by and large the women had a jolly good time in the war, and did pretty well by it. This is a horrendous misconception. Despite poems such as G.K. Menzies's 'The General', given below, women in munitions factories often had to work appalling hours in grim conditions at filthy and sometimes dangerous tasks. Such a woman might very well then find herself going back home to do exactly the same duties as she would have been required to do had she not been working. It was not easy for a woman to force herself into a man's world, and many suffered as a result of having to do so. Perhaps most tragic of all was the plight of women who lost husbands, fiancés or lovers in the war, and who were then often faced with families to bring up through long, lonely years, in a world where the one-parent family was regarded as being morally, socially and culturally unacceptable. History has stayed curiously silent on this particular aspect of suffering in the war. It is the blood, guts, filth and gunfire that have helped attract attention to Great War verse, but poems like May Cannan's 'Lamplight', and much of Rose Macaulay's work (pp. 67-8) show a different side of the war, and one possessing as much pathos and suffering as was found in the front line. Wilfred Owen was particularly savage about women, and even in one of his most moving poems — 'The Send-Off' — could not resist a back-handed swipe at the women who gave flowers to departing soldiers. There was little else they could give, apart from their love. One or two women who brazenly supported the war were leapt on by the media and heavily publicised, but the majority of women could do nothing to stop the war, had not asked for it to start any more than anyone else, and were left with a legacy of suffering and loss that in its own way was as appalling as anything that happened at the front. It is interesting to note how many of the most famous trench poets were unmarried. This has nothing to do with whether or not they were homosexual, but everything to do with the manner in which they wrote about the feminine side of the Great War. They lacked the perspective and knowledge to see clearly into another whole area of suffering. The poetry of the First World War has been allowed to appear as a man's world. The involvement of women in it was more passive, but no less significant.

Nor should we dismiss quite as easily as has sometimes been the case the perception of suffering found in the work of those men who stayed at home. A poem such as Owen's well-known 'S.I.W.' paints a picture of Father packing Son off to war with a cheery smile and some platitudes about fighting the Hun. The whole bias of the poem is towards the soldier, and its sympathy goes with him. It ends, as do many of the verses written by the trench poets, with the soldier's death. Some of the stay-at-home poets picked up where Owen's poem ends. One such was J.C. Squire, every bit as bitter about the loss of friends as those who served at the front, and surprisingly effective for a writer who is often seen as a right-wing Establishment figurehead.

Profiteers came in for as hard a ride from those left at home as they did from the front-line soldiers, as the poems here show. Inflation was a new concept in 1914-1918, as were shortages. The temptation was to blame profiteering for inflation, rather than the real cause, which was the Government printing paper money. In addition, those with friends and family at the front felt all the hatred and bitterness towards the profiteer as did the soldiers, for the same reasons, and expressed it.

Punch is a source for a good measure of middle-class opinion about the war. Food shortages, the quality of food, the strange things being done by women, and the lack of servants all feature strongly in the poetry which the magazine chose to publish during the war. The patronising tone of some of the poems about women suggest strongly that the battle for equality was not won in the First World War, but merely started. By and large *Punch* was scathing about pacifists, and in this area at least was considerably out of line with trench poetry, which seems to have ignored pacifism almost completely.

Lamplight

We planned to shake the world together, you and I
Being young, and very wise;
Now in the light of the green-shaded lamp
Almost I see your eyes
Light with the old gay laughter; you and I
Dreamed greatly of an Empire in those days,
Setting our feet upon laborious ways,
And all you asked of fame
Was crossed swords in the Army List,
My dear, against your name.

We planned a great Empire together, you and I,
Bound only by the sea;
Now in the quiet of a chill Winter's night
Your voice comes hushed to me
Full of forgotten memories: you and I
Dreamed great dreams of our future in those days,
Setting our feet on undiscovered ways,
And all I asked of fame
A scarlet cross on my breast, my Dear,
For the swords by your name.

We shall never shake the world together, you and I,
For you gave your life away;
And I think my heart was broken by the war,
Since on a summer day
You took the road we never spoke of: you and I

You set your feet upon the Western ways
And have no need of fame —
There's a scarlet cross on my breast, my Dear,
And a torn cross with your name.

MAY WEDDERBURN CANNAN

Hats

The hollow sound of your hard felt hat
As you clap it on your head
Is echoed over two thousand miles of trenches
By a thousand thousand guns;
And thousands and thousands of men have been killed,
And still more thousands of thousands have bled
And been maimed and have drowned
Because of that sound.

Towns battered and shattered,
Villages blasted to dust and mud,
Forests and woods stripped bare,
Rivers and streams befouled,
The earth between and beyond the lines
Ravaged and sown with steel
And churned with blood
And astink with decaying men,
Nations starving, women and children murdered,
Genius destroyed, minds deformed and twisted,
And waste, waste, waste
Of the earth's fruits, of the earth's riches, —
All in obedience to your voice;
And the sound of your hat
Is in the same gamut of void and thoughtless
And evil sounds.

O estimable man,
Keeper of the season ticket,
Walker on the pavement,

Follower of the leader writer,
Guardian of the life policy,
Insured against all harm —
Fire, burglary, servants' accidents —
Warden and ward of the church,
Wallflower of the suburbs,
Primrose of respectability,
As you go home beneath your hard felt hat
The tradesmen do you homage.
Happily, the trees do not know you.

You have scoffed at the poet,
Because you are a practical man:
And does not your house bear you out?
Have poets such houses?
It has a garden in front with a plot of grass,
And in the middle of that a flower-bed.
With a rose-tree in its midst, and other rose-trees
Against the walls, and a privet hedge,
And stocks and delphiniums, flowers in season!
The path is irregularly paved for quaintness;
There is a rustic porch, and a street door
With a polished brass letter-box and knocker,
And stained glass panels, showing a bird and flowers,
And an electric-bell push.
But you have a key, and you let yourself in
To the quiet red-tiled hall, where the doormat
Says 'Welcome,' and the stand receives your umbrella
And your coat and your hard felt hat.
A drawing room, a dining-room (because
All your fellows have them), and a kitchen
All clean and neat; and because the kitchen is comfortable
You have your tea there with your wife and child —
Only one child, for are you not practical?
On the upper floor are a bathroom and three bedrooms.
Let your furniture stand undisturbed,
I will not describe it: a hundred shops in London
Show off the like in their windows. As for your books
They are as haphazard and as futile as your pictures.

But here is your comfort and you are comfortable;
And on summer evenings and Saturday afternoons
You wander out into the garden at the back,
Which is fenced off on three sides from similar gardens,
And you potter around with garden tools and are happy.

O insured against all harm,
Waiter on the pension at sixty,
Domestic vegetable, cultivated flower,
You have laughed at the poet, the unpractical dreamer:
You have seen life as bookkeeping and accountancy;
Your arithmetic has pleased you, your compound interest
Your business, more than the earth and the heavens;
And if your brother suffered, you took no heed,
Or read a liberal newspaper, and salved your conscience.
Ant, ant oblivious of the water being poured in the cauldron!

But when the time came for your chastisement,
For the punishment of your apathy, your will-less ignorance,
When the atmospheric pressure was just equivalent
To the weight of the seventy-six centimetre column of mercury,
And the water had exactly reached the hundredth degree of
    centigrade,
You felt, though you feared it, that the time had come,
That you had something called a collective honour, some patriotism;
And those others too felt the same honourable sentiment,
And you called for the slaughter that sanctifies honour,
And the boiling water was poured on us all. Ants! Ants!

Friend and brother, you have not been killed;
Chance still allows you to wear your bowler hat,
The helmet of the warrior in its degeneracy,
The symbol of gracelessness and of the hate of beauty,
The signature of your sameness and innocuousness.
Take off your hat; let your hair grow; open your eyes;
Look at your neighbour; his suffering is your hurt.
Become dangerous; let the metaphysical beast
Whose breath poisons us all fear your understanding,

And recoil from our bodies, his prey, and fall back before you,
And shiver and quake and thirst and starve and die.

F.S. FLINT

German Prisoners

When first I saw you in the curious street,
Like some platoon of soldier ghosts in grey,
My mad impulse was all to smite and slay,
To spit upon you — tread you 'neath my feet.
But when I saw how each sad soul did greet
My gaze with no sign of defiant frown,
How from tired eyes looked spirits broken down,
How each face showed the pale flag of defeat,
And doubt, despair, and disillusionment,
And how were grievous wounds on many a head,
And on your garb red-faced was other red;
And how you stooped as men whose strength was spent,
I knew that we had suffered each as other,
And could have grasped your hand and cried,
    'My brother.'

JOSEPH LEE

Train

Will the train never start?
God, make the train start.

She cannot bear it, keeping up so long;
and he, he no more tries to laugh at her.
He is going.

She holds his two hands now.
Now, she has touch of him and sight of him.
And then he will be gone.
He will be gone.

They are so young.
She stands under the window of his carriage,
and he stands in the window.
They hold each other's hands
across the window ledge.
And look and look,
and know that they may never look again.

The great clock of the station, —
how strange it is.
Terrible that the minutes go,
terrible that the minutes never go.

They had walked the platform for so long,
up and down, and up and down —
the platform, in the rainy morning,
up and down, and up and down.

The guard came by, calling,
'Take your places, take your places.'

She stands under the window of his carriage,
and he stands in the window.

God, make the train start!
Before they cannot bear it,
make the train start!

God, make the train start!

The three children, there,
in black, with the old nurse,
standing together, and looking, and looking,
up at their father in the carriage window,
they are so forlorn and silent.

The little girl will not cry,
but her chin trembles.
She throws back her head,
with its stiff little braid,
and will not cry.

Her father leans down,
out over the ledge of the window,
and kisses her, and kisses her.

She must be like her mother,
and it must be the mother who is dead.

The nurse lifts up the smallest boy,
and his father kisses him,
leaning through the carriage window.

The big boy stands very straight,
and looks at his father,
and looks, and never takes his eyes from him.
And knows that he may never look again.

Will the train never start?
God, make the train start!

The father reaches his hand down from the window,
and grips the boy's hand,
and does not speak at all.

Will the train never start?

He lets the boy's hand go.

Will the train never start?

He takes the boy's chin in his hand,
leaning out through the window,
and lifts the face that is so young, to his.
They look and look,
and know that they may never look again.

Will the train never start?
God, make the train start!

HELEN MACKAY

A Telephone Message
(*To Whom it May Concern*)

Hello! Hello!
Are you there? Are you there?
Ah! That you? Well, —
This is just to tell you
That there's trouble in the air . . .
Trouble, —
T–R–O–U–B–L–E — Trouble!
Where?
In the air.
Trouble in the air!
Got that? . . . Right!
Then — take a word of warning,
And . . . Beware!

What trouble?
Every trouble, — everywhere,
Every wildest kind of nightmare
That has ridden you is there,
In the air.
And it's coming like a whirlwind,
Like a wild beast mad with hunger,
To rend and wrench and tear, —
To tear the world in pieces maybe,
Unless it gets its share.
Can't you see the signs and portents?
Can't you feel them in the air?
Can't you see, — you unbeliever?

Can't you see? — or don't you care, —
That the Past is gone for ever,
Past your uttermost endeavour, —
That To-day is on the scrap-heap,
And the Future — anywhere?

Where?
Ah — that's beyond me! —
But it lies with those who dare
To think of big To-morrows,
And intend to have their share.

All the things you've held and trusted
Are played-out, decayed, and rusted;
Now, in fiery circumstance,
They will all be readjusted.
If you cling to those old things,
Hoping still to hold the strings,
And, for your ungodly gains,
Life to bind with golden chains; —
Man! you're mightily mistaken!
From such dreams you'd best awaken
To the sense of what is coming,
When you hear the low, dull booming
Of the far-off tocsin drums.
— Such a day of vast upsettings,
Dire outcastings and downsettings! —
You have held the reins too long, —
Have you time to heal the wrong?

What's wrong? What's amiss?
Man alive! If you don't know that —
There's nothing more to be said!
— You ask what's amiss when your destinies
Hang by a thread in the great abyss?
What's amiss? What's amiss? —
Well, my friend, just this, —
There's a bill to pay and it's due to-day,
And before it's paid you may all be dead.
Wake up! Wake up! — or, all too late,
You will find yourselves exterminate.

What's wrong?
Listen here! —

273

Do you catch a sound like drumming? —
Far-away and distant drumming?
You hear it? What?
The wires humming?
No, my friend, it is *not!*
It's the tune the prentice-hands are thrumming, —
The tune of the dire red time that's coming, —
The far-away, pregnant, ghostly booming
Of the great red drums' dread drumming.
For they're coming, coming, coming, —
With their dread and doomful drumming,
Unless you ...
Br-r-r-r-r-r-r-r-r — click — clack!

JOHN OXENHAM

The poems which follow give a variety of views on the odd-men-out of the Great War — pacifists, conscientious objectors, and profiteers. The easiest of all approaches was to condemn the conscientious objector, and because the term 'profiteer' was universally condemned a simple condemnation consisted of lumping together conscientious objector and profiteer. Edward Davison puts the record straight with a forgotten but beautifully worked little poem, reflecting his own views and the stance he adopted in the war. Sinn Fein, another agency opposed to the war effort, came in for relatively little treatment in poetry, at least from the British side. The Reverend Rowland Hill's famous comment, echoed by Shaw, that the Devil had nearly all the good tunes, could apply in a different context to the Irish in the First World War; on the subject of Ireland, at least, the Irish had all the best poets, but that war is outside the scope of this book.

J.C. Squire's poems are interesting because they show that not all those who stayed at home waved flags and bought them on flag days. There was a huge gap in communication that opened up between the front-line soldier and those who remained at home, and because so many of the well known poets of the war were trench poets our view of those who remained behind has to some extent been coloured by the prevailing views of them held by the men who fought at the front. Yet many of those who stayed at home suffered grievous losses of friends and family, and witnessed with distaste equal to that of the soldiers the excesses of industry, politicians, and the Church in talking about the war.

The Rime of the Gentle Pacifist

I met a little Pacifist, —
    He was far from bold, he said;
He thought that he would not be missed
    Even if he were dead.

'Sisters and brothers, little man,
    How many may you be?'
He said, 'I'll tell you if I can;
    There can't be more than three.

'There's Ramsay and E.D. Morel
    And Mr. Pethick-Lawrence,
Angell and Ponsonby as well,
    The jingo's pet abhorrence.'

'But stop,' I cried, 'loquacious friend,
    Forbear my heart to rive.
If you speak truth — which God forfend! —
    There must at least be five.'

'I am,' he solemnly replied,
    'One of the I.L.P.*
Unless you think that I have lied,
    I tell you — We are *three!*

'Two of us in the Common lie,
    And two in Norfolk Street;
One, when attacked, makes no reply —
    That makes the list complete.

'There's Ramsay —' 'Yes,' I said, 'I know,
    There also is Morel;
There's Ponsonby — you told me so —'
    He answered, 'Go to hell!'

* Independent Labour Party.

'Such language,' I remarked, 'is quite
　　Unlike the I.L.P.'
He said, 'I *know* that I am right;
　　We're really only three.'

He paused, and left me ill at ease.
　　Then, from a distant hill,
I heard a voice borne on the breeze.
　　'Three cheers for Kaiser Bill!'

And often, at the close of day,
　　When work is left behind,
And morning's cares are put away,
　　That man comes to my mind;

And, in the quiet evening glow,
　　It just occurs to me
That I should rather like to know
　　Who paid the chap his fee.

　　　　　　　　　　'PONTIFF'

Conscientious Objector

His was the mastery of life
Who locked the doors on wrath,
And would not join the common strife
At the cold beck of death.

But singing in the shattered street
When it ran dim with blood,
Flung down his soul at England's feet,
And was not understood.

　　　　　　　EDWARD L. DAVISON

Sinn Fein*
'Ourselves Alone'

And is not ours a noble creed,
    With Self uplifted on the throne?
Why should we bleed for others' need?
    Our motto is 'Ourselves Alone.'

Why prate of ruined lands 'out there',
    Of churches shattered stone by stone?
We need not care how others fare,
    We care but for Ourselves Alone.

Though mothers weep with anguished eyes
    And tortured children make their moan,
Let others rise when Pity cries;
    We rise but for Ourselves Alone.

Let Justice be suppressed by Might
    And Mercy's seat be overthrown;
For Truth and Right the fools may fight,
    We fight but for Ourselves Alone.

MISS ISOBEL MARCHBANK

Judas and the Profiteer

Judas descended to this lower Hell
    To meet his only friend — the profiteer —
Who, looking fat and rubicund and well,
    Regarded him, and then said with a sneer,
'Iscariot, they did you! Fool! to sell
For silver pence the body of God's Son,
Whereas from maiming men with tank and shell
    I gain at least a golden million.'

* The Irish phrase *sinn féin* means 'we ourselves' or 'ourselves alone'.

277

But Judas answered: 'You deserve your gold;
It's not His body but His soul *you've* sold!'

OSBERT SITWELL

Profiteers

There are certain brisk people among us today
Whose patriotism makes quite a display.
But on closer inspection I fancy you'll find
The tools that they work with are axes to grind.

Apparently guiltless of personal greed,
They hasten to succour their country in need;
But private returns in their little top shelves
Show it's one for the country and two for themselves.

Unselfish devotion this struggle demands,
All helping each other whole heart and clean hands.
No quarter for humbugs; we want to be quit
Of men who are making, not doing their bit.

Jones challenges Brown, and Brown implicates Jones,
To the slur of self-interest nobody owns;
But each one must know at the back of his mind,
If his patriotism spells axes to grind.

JESSIE POPE*

The Profiteer

Metevsky said to the one side ...
Don't buy until you can get ours.
And he went over the border

---

* Miss Pope (later Mrs Babington Lenton) wrote light verse, humorous fiction, articles, books (including poetry) for children, and three volumes of war poetry. One of her poems moved Owen to write his savagely indignant 'Dulce et Decorum Est', on the earliest draft of which he wrote 'To Jessie Pope etc'.

And he said to the other side
The *other* side has more munitions. Don't buy
    until you can get ours.
And Ackers made a large profit and imported gold into England.

EZRA POUND

Homœopathy

'A great outburst of popular indignation,' — Press, *passim*, after the anti-German riots.
'Trouncing the Teuton,' — *Evening News*, headline.
'We are heartily glad that the Russians burned Memel, and we hope that the Allies
will burn a good many more German towns before this war is over,' — *Morning
Post*, leading article.

We was in the 'Blue Dragon', Sid 'Awkins and me,
When all of a sudden, 'Here, Ernie,' says he,
'There are limits to what flesh and blood can endure;
We must really protest against Prussian Kultur.

'There's an alien butcher down Wapping High Street,
The swine's gone and asked me to pay for my meat;
His father's a Frenchman, his mother's a Moor,
But he'd do with a lesson in Prussian Kultur.'

So we off like a streak, and we pulled him from bed,
And tore off his nightshirt and pummelled his head,
And rolled him along in the mud to secure
He should quite grasp the meaning of Prussian Kultur.

O the way that we bashed 'im and hooted and hissed
Was a sight Lady Bathurst ought not to have missed;
For her organ *Die Post* gives a steady and sure
Support to the tenets of Prussian Kultur.

Then we emptied the shop in a white moral heat,
I got half a bullock, my wife some pigs' feet,
And some very nice tripe which she thought ought to cure
The Kaiser's devotion to Prussian Kultur.

Yes, even the coppers themselves took a part
With a cutlet apiece from Sid 'Awkins's cart,
As a positive proof that they shared in our feeling,
And did not confuse moral protest with stealing.

Reassured by these kindly, encouraging cops,
We protested at each of the neighbouring shops,
Till at last at the end of our punitive week
They took us, *pro forma*, in front of the beak.

But he only remarked that no civilised nation
Could hope to withstand such extreme provocation.
'You're discharged, for I know that your motives were pure —
You desired to protest against Prussian Kultur!'

GRAND CHORUS

So fill up the cup and fill up the can!
A tradesman's a Hun and a copper's a man;
But O that each restaurateur were a brewer,
For a healthy great thirst has our British Kultur.

J.C. SQUIRE

The Survival of the Fittest
(*In Memoriam, L.C. and T.*)

'Those like Mr. Tompkins, of *The — —*, who say that without war the race would
degenerate.' — *Star*, March 30, 1915.

These were my friends; Tompkins, you did not know them,
 For they were simple, unaspiring men;
No ordinary wind of chance could blow them
 Within the range of your austerer ken.
They were most uninformed. They never even
 — So ignorant and godless was their youth —
Heard you expound, with reverences to Heaven,
 The elements of biologic truth.

Had they but had the privilege to cluster
   Around Gamaliel's feet, they would have known
That hate and massacre also have their lustre,
   And that man cannot live by Love alone.
But having no pillar of flame of your igniting
   To guide by night, no pillar of cloud by day,
They thought War was an evil thing, and fighting
   Filthy at best. So, thus deluded, they

Not seeing the war as a wise elimination
   Or a cleansing purge, or a wholesome exercise,
Went out with mingled loathing and elation
   Only because there towered before their eyes
England, an immemorial crusader,
   A great dream-statue, seated and serene,
Who had seen much blood, and sons who had betrayed her,
   But still shone out with hands and garments clean;

Summoning now with an imperious message
   To one last fight that Europe should be free,
Whom, though it meant a swift and bitter passage,
   They had to serve, for she served Liberty.

Romance and rhetoric! Yet with such nonsense nourished,
   They faced the guns and the dead and the rats and the rains,
And all in a month, as summer waned, they perished;
   And they had clear eyes, strong bodies, and some brains.

*

Tompkins, these died. What need is there to mention
   Anything more? What argument could give
A more conclusive proof of your contention?
   Tompkins, these died, and men like you still live.

J.C. SQUIRE

To Little Sister
From No. 16

Have you seen our Little Sister?
Officers can ne'er resist her.
She will flay and burn and blister
Someone every day.
Does she tend poor wounded wretches?
No! Their wounds she probes and stretches
Till the brandy flask she fetches
When they faint away.

Not for them the gentle touches
Of a Matron or a Duchess —
Little Sister simply BUTCHERS
Everyone she gets.
Rubber gloves her hands adorning
Give to us a daily warning
That the bone she cleans each morning
Never, never sets.

Though our misery's unending,
Though with pain our wounds she's tending,
Yet with courage still unbending
We can bear the strain.
But if once we woke and missed her
We should cry with tears that blister,
'Have you seen our Little Sister?
Send her back again!'

ANONYMOUS

Untitled

'Valueless, A Duffer!' says the Sister's face,
When I try to do her orders with my bestest grace.
'Vain And Disappointing!' says Staff Nurse's eye,
If I dare to put my cap straight while she's walking by.

'Very Active Danger', looks the angry pro.,
If I sometimes score a wee bit over her, you know.
'Virtuous And Dumpy!' that's the way I feel,
When I'm uniformed from cap strings to each wardroom heel.
'Vague And Disillusioned' that's my mood each night,
When I've tried all day to please 'em and done nothing right.

'Valiant And Determined', I arise next day,
As I tell myself it's *duty* and I must obey.
'Very Anxious Daily' I await my leave,
Which I spend with my *own* soldier, as you may believe.
'Verily A Darling' That's his name for me,
When I meet him in my uniform of VAD.*

ANONYMOUS

The Nurse

Here in the long white ward I stand,
    Pausing a little breathless space,
Touching a restless fevered hand,
    Murmuring comfort's commonplace —

Long enough pause to feel the cold
    Fingers of fear about my heart;
Just for a moment, uncontrolled,
    All the pent tears of pity start.

While here I strive, as best I may,
    Strangers' long hours of pain to ease,
Dumbly I question — *Far away*
    Lies my beloved even as these?

MISS G.M. MITCHELL
August 30, 1916

* Voluntary Aid Detachment.

To The Unknown Warrior

You whom the kings saluted; who refused not
　　The one great gesture of ignoble days,
Fame without name and glory without gossip,
　　Whom no biographer befouls with praise.

Who said of you 'Defeated'? In the darkness
　　The dug-out where the limelight never comes,
Nor the big drum of Barnum's Show can shatter
　　That vibrant stillness after all the drums.

Though the time come when every Yankee circus
　　Can use our soldiers for its sandwich-men,
When those that pay the piper call the tune,
　　You will not dance. You will not move again.

You will not march for Fatty Arbuckle,
　　Though he have yet a favourable press,
Tender as San Francisco to St. Francis,
　　Or all the Angels of Los Angeles.

They shall not storm the last unfallen fortress,
　　The lonely castle where uncowed and free
Dwells the unknown and undefeated warrior
　　That did alone defeat Publicity.

　　　　　　　　　G.K. CHESTERTON

Cha Till Maccruimein*
(Departure of the 4th Camerons)

The pipes in the streets were playing bravely,
　　The marching lads went by
With merry hearts and voices singing
　　My friends marched out to die;

---

* Gaelic, lit. 'MacCrimmon comes not'. Pibroch (from Gaelic *piobaireachd*, 'pipe music') —
'variations on a theme for bagpipe, chiefly martial'.

But I was hearing a lonely pibroch
    Out of an older war,
'Farewell, farewell, farewell, MacCrimmon,
    MacCrimmon comes no more.'

And every lad in his heart was dreaming
    Of honour and wealth to come,
And honour and noble pride were calling
    To the tune of the pipes and drum;
But I was hearing a woman singing
    On dark Dunvegan shore,
'In battle or peace, with wealth or honour,
    MacCrimmon comes no more.'

And there in front of the men were marching,
    With feet that made no mark,
The grey old ghosts of the ancient fighters
    Come back again from the dark;
And in front of them all MacCrimmon piping
    A weary tune and sore,
'On gathering day, for ever and ever,
    MacCrimmon comes no more.'

EWART ALAN MACKINTOSH

Jock, to the First Army

O Rab an' Dave an' rantin' Jim,
    The geans* were turnin' reid
When Scotland saw yer line grow dim,
    Wi' the pipers at its heid;
Noo, i' yon warld we dinna ken,
    Like strangers ye maun gang —
'We've sic a wale o' Angus men
    That we canna weary lang.'

* gean — wild cherry; wale — choice; strath — broad river valley; div — do; fecht — fight.

And little Wat — my brither Wat,
    Man, are ye aye the same?
Or is yon sma' white hoose forgot
    Doon by the strath at hame?
An' div ye mind foo aft we trod
    The Isla's banks before? —
'My place is wi' the Hosts o' God,
    But I mind me o' Strathmore.'

It's deith comes skirlin' through the sky,
    Below there's nocht but pain,
We canna see whaur deid men lie
    For the drivin' o' the rain;
Ye a' hae passed frae fear an' doot,
    Ye're far frae airthly ill —
'We're near, we're here, my wee recruit,
    And we fecht for Scotland still.'

VIOLET JACOB

War

In the little port half hidden by the headlines of Pentire,
There's a sad old dame a-sitting by the ashes of a fire;
And her hands are lying listless and her head and back are bowed,
And her eyes are looking drearily at pictures through a cloud.

She sees a baby stumble where a sodden sea boot dries,
And once again she cuddles him and smiles away his cries;
She sees a boy come home so proud of blennies* in a jar,
He doesn't mind a broken knee or breeches streaked with tar.

And then she sees a lad aboard a boat that takes the tide,
And in his gladness finds her joy, and in his strength her pride,
Until a big Bluejacket comes and hides the lad from sight,
Except within the merry eyes that laughter keeps alight.

*

* Small spiny-finned sea-fish.

The men are gathered on the Plat to hear the latest news,
They know which side is bound to win, and which is sure to lose;
They proudly talk of deeds that make the name of England ring,
They cheer the latest victory and shout 'God save the King.'

*

But a sad old dame is sitting by the ashes of a fire
With empty hands that never more may hold her heart's desire;
And drearily and wearily she murmurs in her pain,
'And I shall never see my son, my little son again.'

BERNARD MOORE

The Wife of Flanders

Low and brown barns thatched and repatched and tattered
 Where I had seven sons until to-day,
A little hill of hay your spur has scattered ...
 This is not Paris. You have lost the way.

You, staring at your sword to find it brittle,
 Surprised at the surprise that was your plan,
Who shaking and breaking barriers not a little
 Find never more the death-door of Sedan.

Must I for more than carnage call you claimant,
 Paying you a penny for each son you slay?
Man, the whole globe in gold were no repayment
 For what *you* have lost. And how shall I repay?

What is the price of that red spark that caught me
 From a kind farm that never had a name?
What is the price of that dead man they brought me?
 For other dead men do not look the same.

How should I pay for one poor graven steeple
 Whereon you shattered what you shall not know,
How should I pay you, miserable people?
 How should I pay you everything you owe?

287

Unhappy, can I give you back your honour?
  Though I forgave would any man forget?
While all the great green land has trampled on her
  The treason and terror of the night we met.

Not any more in vengeance or in pardon
  An old wife bargains for a bean that's hers.
You have no word to break: no heart to harden.
  Ride on and prosper. You have lost your spurs.

G.K. CHESTERTON

Elegy in a Country Churchyard

The men that worked for England
They have their graves at home:
And bees and birds of England
About the cross can roam.

But they that fought for England,
Following a falling star,
Alas, alas for England
They have their graves afar.

And they that rule in England,
In stately conclave met,
Alas, alas for England
They have no graves as yet.

G.K. CHESTERTON

Miners

There was a whispering in my hearth,
  A sigh of the coal,
Grown wistful of a former earth
  It might recall.

I listened for a tale of leaves
    And smothered ferns,
Frond-forests, and the low sly lives
    Before the fauns.

My fire might show steam-phantoms simmer
    From Time's old cauldron,
Before the birds made nests in summer,
    Or men had children.

But the coals were murmuring of their mine,
    And moans down there
Of boys that slept wry sleep, and men
    Writhing for air.

And I saw white bones in the cinder-shard,
    Bones without number.
Many the muscled bodies charred,
    And few remember.

I thought of all that worked dark pits
    Of war, and died
Digging the rock where Death reputes
    Peace lies indeed.

Comforted years will sit soft-chaired,
    In rooms of amber;
The years will stretch their hands, well-cheered
    By our life's ember;

The centuries will burn rich loads
    With which we groaned,
Whose warmth shall lull their dreaming lids,
    While songs are crooned;
But they will not dream of us poor lads,
    Left in the ground.

WILFRED OWEN+

The Miners' Response

'We must keep on striking, striking, striking …' — from the first speech by the Minister of Munitions.

We do: the present desperate stage
Of fighting brings us luck;
And in the higher war we wage
(For higher wage) *We struck.*

D.S. MacColl

Where are You Sleeping To-night, My Lad?

Where are you sleeping to-night, My Lad,
    Above-ground — or below?
The last we heard you were up at the front,
Holding a trench and bearing the brunt; —
    But — that was a week ago.

Ay! — that was a week ago, Dear Lad,
    And a week is a long, long time,
When a second's enough, in the thick of the strife
To sever the thread of the bravest life,
    And end it in its prime.

Oh, a week is long when so little's enough
    To send a man below.
It may be that while we named your name
The bullet sped and the quick end came, —
    And the rest we shall never know.

But this we know, Dear Lad, — all's well
    With the man who has done his best.
And whether he live, or whether he die,
He is sacred high in our memory; —
    And to God we can leave the rest.

So — wherever you're sleeping to-night, Dear Lad,
    This one thing we do know, —
When 'Last Post' sounds, and He makes His rounds.
Not one of you all will be out of bounds,
    Above ground or below.

JOHN OXENHAM

The three poems which follow give a representative sample of how *Punch* looked at the war. *Punch* had its serious moments, but its essential initiative and nature was comic, and it found comedy in the attitudes of those who remained at home, and the social changes that the war brought about. Food and servants dominate a considerable portion of *Punch*'s poetic output during the war.

The General

Last night, as I was washing up,
And just had rinsed the final cup,
All of a sudden, 'midst the steam,
I fell asleep and dreamt a dream.
I saw myself an old, old man,
Nearing the end of mortal span,
Bent, bald and toothless, lean and spare,
Hunched in an ancient beehive chair.
Before me stood a little lad
Alive with questions. 'Please, Granddad,
Did Daddy fight, and Uncle Joe,
In the Great War of long ago?'
I nodded as I made reply:
'Your Dad was in the H.L.I.,
And Uncle Joseph sailed the sea,
Commander of a T.B.D.,
And Uncle Jack was Major too —'
'And what,' he asked me, 'what were you?'
I stroked the little golden head;
'I was a General,' I said.
'Come, and I'll tell you something more

Of what I did in the Great War.'
At once the wonder-waiting eyes
Were opened in a mild surmise;
Smiling, I helped the little man
To mount my knee, and so began:
'When first the War broke out, you see,
Grandma became a V.A.D.;
Your Aunties spent laborious days
In working at Y.M.C.A.s;
The servants vanished. Cook was found
Doing the conscript baker's round;
The housemaid, Jane, in shortened skirt
(She always was a brazen flirt),
Forsook her dusters, brooms and pails
To carry on with endless mails.
The parlourmaid became a vet.,
The tweeny a conductorette,
And both the others found their missions
In manufacturing munitions.
I was a City man. I knew
No useful trade. What could I do?
Your Granddad, boy, was not the sort
To yield to fate; he was a sport.
I set to work; I rose at six,
Summer and winter; chopped the sticks,
Kindled the fire, made early tea
For Aunties and the V.A.D.
I cooked the porridge, eggs and ham,
Set out the marmalade and jam,
And packed the workers off, well fed,
Well warmed, well brushed, well valeted.
I spent the morning in a rush
With dustpan, pail and scrubbing-brush;
Then with a string-bag sallied out
To net the cabbage or the sprout,
Or in the neighbouring butcher's shop
Select the juiciest steak or chop.
So when the sun had sought the West,
And brought my toilers home to rest,

Savours more sweet than scent of roses
Greeted their eager-sniffing noses —
Savours of dishes most divine
Prepared and cooked by skill of mine.
I was a General. Now you know
How Generals helped to down the foe.'
The little chap slipped off my knee
And gazed in solemn awe at me,
Stood at attention, stiff and mute,
And gave his very best salute.*

G.K. MENZIES

The Flapper

(DR. ARTHUR SHADWELL, in the January *Nineteenth Century*, in his article on
'Ordeal by Fire,' after denouncing idlers and loafers and shirkers, falls foul 'above all' of
the young girls called flappers, 'with high heels, skirts up to their knees and blouses
open to the diaphragm, painted, powdered, self-conscious, ogling: "Allus adal-lacked
and dizened oot and a 'unting arter the men." ')

Good Dr. ARTHUR SHADWELL, who lends lustre to a name
Which DRYDEN in his satires oft endeavoured to defame,
Has lately been discussing in a high-class magazine
The trials that confront us in the year Nineteen Seventeen.

He is not a smooth-tongued prophet; no, he takes a serious view;
We must make tremendous efforts if we're going to win through;
And though he's not unhopeful of the issue of the fray
He finds abundant causes for misgiving and dismay.

Our optimistic journals his exasperation fire,
And the idlers and the loafers stimulate his righteous ire;
But it is the flapper chiefly that in his gizzard sticks,
And he's down upon her failings like a waggon-load of bricks.

* HLI – Highland Light Infantry; TBD – torpedo-boat destroyer (the original designation of
what is now called a destroyer); VAD – Voluntary Aid Detachment; tweeny – between-stairs
maid.

She's ubiquitous in theatres, in rail and 'bus and tram,
She wears her 'blouses open down to the diaphragm,'
And, instead of realising what our men are fighting for,
She's an orgiastic nuisance who in fact *enjoys* the War.

It's a strenuous indictment of our petticoated youth
And contains a large substratum of unpalatable truth;
Our women have been splendid, but the Sun himself has specks,
And the flapper can't be reckoned as a credit to her sex.

Still it needs to be remembered, to extenuate her crimes,
That these flappers have not always had the very best of times;
And the life that now she's leading, with no Mentors to restrain,
Is decidedly unhinging to an undeveloped brain.

Then again we only see her when she's out for play or meals,
And distresses the fastidious by her gestures and her squeals,
But she is not always idle or a decorative drone,
And if she wastes her wages, well, she wastes what is her own.

Still to say that she's heroic, as some scribes of late have said,
Is unkind as well as foolish, for it only swells her head;
She oughtn't to be flattered, she requires to be repressed,
Or she'll grow into a portent and a peril and a pest.

Dr. SHADWELL to the PREMIER makes an eloquent appeal
In firm and drastic fashion with this element to deal;
And 'twould be a real feather in our gifted Cambrian's cap
If he taught the peccant flapper less flamboyantly to flap.

But, in *Punch's* way of thinking, 'tis for women, kind and wise,
These neglected scattered units to enrol and mobilise,
Their vagabond activities to curb and concentrate,
And turn the skittish hoyden to a servant of the State.

She's young; her eyes are dazzled by the glamour of the streets;
She has to learn that life is not all cinemas and sweets;
But given wholesome guidance she may rise to self-control
And earn the right of entry on the Nation's golden Roll.

C.L. GRAVES

Back to the Land

The wintry days are with us still;
    The roads are deep in liquid dirt;
The rain is wet, the wind is chill,
    And both are coming through my shirt;
And yet my heart is light and gay;
    I shout aloud, I hum a snatch;
Why am I full of mirth? To-day
    I'm planting my potato patch.

The KAISER sits and bites his nails
    In Pots- (or some adjoining) dam;
He wonders why his peace talk fails
    And how to cope with Uncle Sam;
The General Staff has got the hump;
    In vain each wicked scheme they hatch;
I've handed them the final thump
    By planting my potato patch.

The U-boat creeps beneath the sea
    And puts the unarmed freighters down;
It fills the German heart with glee
    To see the helpless sailors drown;
But now and then a ship lets fly
    To show that Fritz has met his match!
She's done her bit, and so have I
    Who dig in my potato patch.

And later, when the War is won
    And each man murmers, 'Well, that's that,'
And reckons up what he has done
    To put the Germans on the mat,
I'll say, 'It took ten myriad guns
    And fighting vessels by the batch;
But we too served, we ancient ones,
    Who dug in our potato patch.'

C.L. GRAVES

The Send-Off

Down the close, darkening lanes they sang their way
To the siding shed,
And lined the train with faces grimly gay.

Their breasts were stuck all white with wreath and spray
As men's are, dead.

Dull porters watched them, and a casual tramp
Stood staring hard,
Sorry to miss them from the upland camp.
Then, unmoved, signals nodded, and a lamp
Winked to the guard.

So secretly, like wrongs hushed up, they went.
They were not ours:
We never heard to which front these were sent.

Nor there if they yet mock what women meant
Who gave them flowers.

Shall they return to beatings of great bells
In wild trainloads?
A few, a few, too few for drums and yells,
May creep back, silent, to still vintage wells
Up half-known roads.

WILFRED OWEN

The above is the 'original' version of this poem, differing from the more modern version edited by Jon Stallworthy (see Bibliography) only in relatively minor areas. Stallworthy omits the comma after 'close' in line 1, inserts a semi-colon after 'sent' in line 13, and has 'village wells' in place of 'still vintage wells' in the penultimate line. In addition, he divides the poem up into alternating three-and two-line stanzas, four of each.

VIII

'Will they remember?'

AFTER

The Second World War killed roughly five times as many people as did the First, brought untold destruction to civilian populations, and in its final throes unleashed a horror that could — and still can — wipe out life on earth. The facts, and logic, dictate that if any images dominate poetry they should be those of Hiroshima, Dachau, and Stalingrad. Certainly these images appear frequently in modern writing, but it is far easier to find the images of the Great War: the selection which follows is only a sampling of the available material. The Great War seems to exert a terrible and perhaps terrified fascination over the modern imagination, and not only in terms of poetry. The novels of the Great War, most notably *Memoirs of an Infantry Officer* and *All Quiet on the Western Front*, and non-fiction like *Goodbye to All That* and *Undertones of War*, have achieved a popularity and width of recognition denied any equivalent from the Second World War. In drama, there is nothing from later wars to match *Journey's End*. In 1975 I compiled an exhaustive bibliography of books relating to the Great War, just over a decade on, that bibliography is almost a third as long again, packed out with new material on every aspect of the war. The fascination does not stop at bookshelves: children who think Hamlet is a brand of cigar, for instance, know the meaning of 'over the top' and are familiar with at least some of the images of the Great War. I quoted at the start of this work John Terraine's comment to the effect that the First World War was unquestionably a major watershed in history. It was more than that. In ways that have never become altogether clear it created a folk-myth — not a myth in the sense of its being untrue, but a myth in the sense that the war came to symbolise and express something central to our fears and our whole concept of living and dying. Why it did so has never satis-factorily been explained. In the making of the myth some untruths have crept in. It is a shock to some people to realise that the front-line soldier might expect to spend only one week in three actually manning the line, that the highest percentage of casualties was caused

297

not by rifle or machine-gun fire, but by artillery, and that the wounded had a better chance of survival in the Great War than they had had in any previous war in history. These facts hardly matter: we see the Great War as we feel a need to see it, even if sometimes (as far as we can judge) it was not like that.

It would take a greater expert than myself to explain why the Great War had such a lasting impact on the imagination of a whole culture, and particularly on the British, and why wholly disparate authors seem to return to it as something approaching a universal symbol. Such feelings as I do have are expressed in the title of this work, taken from the poem below by Philip Larkin. We know now that war is dirty. Edwardian England had much less cause to feel it so. Despite the appalling horrors of that society's industrial slums, its gross imbalance of wealth, and its frequent hypocrisy, it went out to fight the Great War with a simple set of virtues that, in its own eyes at least, had won Britain one of the largest empires the world had ever seen, and had made it one of the greatest and most powerful nations. We can laugh and sneer now at those 'virtues'. We can see the Empire as a thin fabric of moral justification erected over a sea of capitalist lust and extortion. We can see crass ineptitude amongst some of the most honoured leaders of that society. We can understand that the glorious Empire was won by men who were effectively warlords of private enterprise, and then was lost when the early ruthlessness was replaced by public-school men of Arnold's inspiration who tried to mix morality and colonialism. We can see all this.

But did Edwardian Britain see it?

The British people may have known all this, but they were able either to hide it from themselves, or to put up against it another set of values. Whether they should have done so or not, many of them believed in themselves when they went out to fight the Kaiser, and believed in their country and their cause. They valued pluck and patriotism, and what might be termed now 'true grit'. They believed — and what a horrific belief it is in a wiser but sadder age — that they were better than the Europeans they went out to fight. They valued the cult of the amateur, and however professional they might have been in war, they took pains to disguise it, and their emotions. When their beliefs were shattered by Loos and the Somme, and the full horror of war was brought home to them, they kept on fighting. They did not desert in large numbers, stage mutinies in any significant manner, shoot their officers in droves, or take to drugs. By and large they did not rape women, wipe out villages full of innocent civilians, stage massacres, or lock their prisoners up in concentration camps, there to beat, gas, shoot, and humiliate them. When they came home they did the decent thing, refused to take Sassoon's advice and bayonet their leaders and the media, and for the most part restricted their activities to turning out year after year on Armistice Day. Some of their sons spoke up in debates and said they would rather die for their friends than for their country, but then rather spoilt the effect by doing the latter in significant numbers when 1939 came round. As for the fathers, whatever they had said and felt about the Great War, they choked the recruiting offices when another war broke out. Whatever happened in reality, these were the days when, in popular literature, villains did not turn round and empty sawn-off shotguns into the eyes of policemen, but merely said 'It's a fair cop'. In our time we are all agog to prove that Biggles had his hand in Algy's underwear, and that Bunny wore a dress to please Raffles; in an earlier age they could be let be to remain 'just good friends'. It is not only lives that were lost in the Great War, but simplicity, certainty, and faith.

The Great War fascinates us so much because, on a vast historical and human canvas, it is tragic in form — and tragedy is perhaps the most profound and central symbolisation of man's plight of any that exist. Tragedy shows a great or admirable man led to destruction partly through his own blindness, partly through vast and inexorable forces over which he has no control and which he can only dimly comprehend. It arouses vast feelings of pity and terror in us, reveals vast carnage and disruption, and shows the death of that hero, at the same time as showing how hard he can fight, and how much he can resist. At the end we feel a tremendous sense of waste, but we also understand that death for the tragic hero is a blessing and a relief from pain. Most of all, we feel that he has made a statement which, in the midst of terror, reassures us of our own strength and our own dignity, and causes us to admire the figure who can endure so much. In the place of the tragic hero put the men who went out to fight the Great War, and it seems to me that one has as good a description of that experience as any. If the Great War is indeed tragedy writ grossly large, and one which actually happened, then a part of the aim of this book is to include in that script the Porter's scene from *Macbeth*, and the scene where the Clown brings in the asps to Cleopatra. Aristotle cited terror and pity as the main ingredients of tragedy; he could hardly find them better illustrated than in the Great War. We may deride that age for its innocence, see how wrong it was, and see how that innocence actively helped to make such carnage possible. It does not stop us from envying it in a time which signally lacks both simplicity and innocence.

Finally, the selection of poetry throughout this book is a highly personal one. There is a healthy tradition in English literature of frying alive editors who make such choices, and with rare exceptions, like Wavell's magnificent anthology *Other Men's Flowers*, the usual and only defence is the towering reputation of the compiler, as was the case with W.B. Yeats. Without any such reputation, or the possibility of one, editors should beware the gathering storm. I remain an academic with a seared conscience, and one who found himself, whilst researching a doctorate, spending far, far too long poring over 'slim volumes' of Great War poetry when mightier authors demanded attention. The poems were frequently abysmally incompetent in technique, banal, and full of intellectual flatulence, unworthy of serious attention by any of the standards that apply to modern literary criticism — yet memorable in a strange way that some undoubtedly greater poems could not claim. I remember the sense of shame I felt when admitting to a charming and helpful set of oral examiners that J.C. Squire's 'To A Bulldog' moved me greatly, even though I knew it shouldn't. They gave me an understanding smile, deferred calling the men with the white coats, and went on to talk about Isaac Rosenberg. Perhaps we are told a little too often what we *ought* to read, instead of being allowed to read what we like. Owen said he did not wish to write anything to which a soldier would say 'no compris'. It may be that this selection also panders to that wish, seventy years on. If it does so, at least that simplicity is in itself an expression of something naive, honourable, and strangely admirable that we lost with the Great War.

Many of the most famous poems written in and about the Great War did not see publication or become well known until the 1930s. It was in this period that the great revulsion against the war came to full fruition. In the immediate aftermath of the conflict exhaustion, desire to forget, and the struggle to live in a peacetime world dominated much thinking. In the poems that were written up to five years or so after the Armistice it is a sense of loss — of comrades, innocence, and youth — that dominates poetry. Revulsion, as typified by Sassoon's satirical verse, is surprisingly absent from the pages of poetry magazines and anthologies published immediately after the war. It came as a shock to me to realise how quickly Sassoon's hatred seemed to evaporate after the Armistice, and an equal shock to realise how much magnificent poetry he had written post-1918, couched in an altogether softer, more elegiac mode than his harsh wartime writing. If there are to be laurels awarded for poetry written after the war but still about it, I would unhesitatingly award the chiefest to Sassoon.

Very few of the poems in this selection require an explanation, and those in the 'After' section require less than most. Above all they catalogue how we have come to see the Great War, and the indelible mark it has left on our national awareness. A modern poet can write about the Great War, using its slang and its images, and be understood now as well as any poet ever was.

Everyone Sang*

Everyone suddenly burst out singing;
And I was filled with such delight
As prisoned birds must find in freedom,
Winging wildly across the white
Orchards and dark-green fields; on — on — and out of sight.

Everyone's voice was suddenly lifted;
And beauty came like the setting sun:
My heart was shaken with tears; and horror
Drifted away ... O, but Everyone
Was a bird; and the song was wordless; the singing will never be
    done.

SIEGFRIED SASSOON

Picture-Show

And still they come and go: and this is all I know —
That from the gloom I watch an endless picture-show,
Where wild or listless faces flicker on their way,
With glad or grievous hearts I'll never understand
Because Time spins so fast, and they've no time to stay
Beyond the moment's gesture of a lifted hand.

And still, between the shadow and the blinding flame,
The brave despair of men flings onward, ever the same

---

* Sassoon had served in the Royal Welch Fusiliers, as had Robert Graves — at one time they were in the same battalion. Graves acidly remarked of this poem: 'But "everyone" did not include me.'

As in those doom-lit years that wait them, and have been ...
And life is just the picture dancing on a screen.

SIEGFRIED SASSOON

Reconciliation

When you are standing at your hero's grave,
Or near some homeless village where he died,
Remember, through your heart's rekindling pride,
The German soldiers who were loyal and brave.

Men fought like brutes; and hideous things were done;
And you have nourished hatred, harsh and blind.
But in that Golgotha perhaps you'll find
The mothers of the men who killed your son.

SIEGFRIED SASSOON
November 1918

The Halt

'Mark time in front! Rear fours cover! Company — halt!
Order arms! Stand at — ease! Stand easy.' A sudden hush:
And then the talk began with a mighty rush —
'You weren't ever in step — The sergeant. — It wasn't my fault —
Well, the Lord be praised at least for a ten minutes' halt.'
We sat on a gate and watched them easing and shifting;
Out of the distance a faint, keen breath came drifting,
From the sea behind the hills, and the hedges were salt.

Where do you halt now? Under what hedge do you lie?
Where the tall poplars are fringing the white French roads?
And smoke I have not seen discolours the foreign sky?
Is the company resting there as we rested together
Stamping its feet and readjusting its loads
And looking with wary eyes at the drooping weather?

EDWARD SHANKS

The English Graves

Were I that wandering citizen whose city is the world,
I would not weep for all that fell before the flags were furled;
I would not let one murmur mar the trumpet vollying forth
How God grew weary of the kings, and the cold hell in the north.
But we whose hearts are homing birds have heavier thoughts
    of home,
Though the great eagles burn with gold on Paris or on Rome,
Who stand beside our dead and stare, like seers at an eclipse,
At the riddle of the island tale and the twilight of the ships.

For these were simple men that loved with hands and feet and eyes,
Whose souls were humbled to the hills and narrowed to the skies,
The hundred little lands within one little land that lie,
Where Severn seeks the sunset isles or Sussex scales the sky.

And what is theirs, though banners blow on Warsaw risen again,
Or ancient laughter walks in gold through the vineyards of Lorraine,
Their dead are marked on English stones, their lives on English trees,
How little is the prize they win, how mean a coin for these —
How small a shrivelled laurel-leaf lies crumpled here and curled:
They died to save their country and they only saved the world.

G.K. CHESTERTON

Oliver Singing

Oliver's singing
Comes down to my study,
As I sit in the twilight
Poring the problem
Of this old battered planet,
This universe tragical,
Bloodily twirling.

Nearly all his small span
And through both of his birthdays
This senseless hell-fury,
This horror has hurtled,
Yet he lies in his cot,
Happy, sleepy and singing.

Thus — I muse — at the core
Of our battered old planet,
Something young and untainted,
Something gay and undaunted,
Like a bud in its whiteness,
Like a bird in its joy,
Through the foul-smelling darkness,
Through the muck and the slaughter,
Pushes steadily forward,
Singing.

ISRAEL ZANGWILL

Epitaph on an Army of Mercenaries

These, in the day when heaven was falling,
    The hour when earth's foundations fled,
Followed their mercenary calling
    And took their wages and are dead.

Their shoulders held the sky suspended;
    They stood, and earth's foundations stay;
What God abandoned, these defended,
    And saved the sum of things for pay.

A.E. HOUSMAN

Another Epitaph on an Army of Mercenaries

It is a God-damned lie to say that these
Saved, or knew, anything worth any man's pride.
They were professional murderers, and they took

Their blood money, and impious risks, and died.
In spite of all their kind, some elements of worth
Persist with difficulty here and there on earth.

HUGH McDIARMID

Macleod's Lament

Allan Ian Og Macleod of Raasay,
Treasure of mine, lies yonder dead in Loos,
His body unadorned by Highland raiment,
Trammelled for glorious hours, in Saxon trews.
Never man before of all his kindred
Went so apparelled to the burial knowe,
But with the pleated tartan for his shrouding,
The bonnet on his brow.

My grief! That Allan should depart so sadly,
When no wild mountain pipe his bosom rung,
With no one of his race beside his shoulder,
Who knew his history, or spake his tongue.
Ah! Lonely death and drear for darling Allan;
Before his ghost had taken wings and gone,
Loud would he cry in Gaelic to his gallants,
'Children of storm, press on!'

Beside him, when he fell there in his beauty,
Macleods of all the islands should have died;
Brave hearts his English! — but they could not fathom
To what old deeps the voice of Allan cried;
When in that strange French countryside war-battered,
Far from the creeks of home and hills of heath,
A boy, he kept the old tryst of his people
With the dark girl Death.

Oh, Allan Ian Og! Oh, Allan aluinn!
Sore is my heart remembering the past,
And you of Raasay's ancient gentle children
The farthest-wandered, kindliest, and last.

It should have been the brave dead of the Islands
    That heard ring o'er their tombs your battle-cry,
To shake them from their sleep again, and quicken
    Peaks of Torridon and Skye!

Gone like the mist, the brave Macleods of Raasay,
    Far forth from fortune, sundered from their lands,
And now the last grey stone of Castle Raasay,
    Lies desolate and levelled with the sands;
But pluck the old isle from its roots deep planted
    Where tides cry coronach round the Hebrides,
And it will bleed of the Macleods lamented,
    Their loves and memories!*

NEIL MUNRO

A Victory Dance

The cymbals crash,
    And the dancers walk,
With long silk stockings
    And arms of chalk,
Butterfly skirts,
    And white breasts bare,
And shadows of dead men
    Watching 'em there.

Shadows of dead men
    Stand by the wall,
Watching the fun
    Of the Victory Ball.
They do not reproach,
    Because they know,
If they're forgotten,
    It's better so.

Og — young or 'the younger'; *knowe* — hillock, mound; *aluinn* — beautiful, lovely, delightful (a pun on Allan); *coronach* — a war-cry.

Under the dancing
  Feet are the graves.
Dazzle and motley,
  In long bright waves,
Brushed by the palm-fronds
  Grapple and whirl
Ox-eyed matron,
  And slim white girl.

Fat wet bodies
  Go waddling by,
Girdled with satin,
  Though God knows why;
Gripped by satyrs
  In white and black,
With a fat wet hand
  On the fat wet back.

See, there is one child
  Fresh from school,
Learning the ropes
  As the old hands rule.
God, how the dead men
  Chuckle again,
As she begs for a dose
  Of the best cocaine.

'What did you think
  We should find,' said a shade,
'When the last shot echoed
  And peace was made?'
'Christ,' laughed the fleshless
  Jaws of his friend,
'I thought they'd be praying
  For worlds to mend,

'Making earth better,
  Or something silly,
Like whitewashing hell

Or Piccadilly.
They've a sense of humour,
   These women of ours,
These exquisite lilies,
   These fresh young flowers!'

'Pish,' said a statesman
   Standing near,
'I'm glad they can busy
   Their thoughts elsewhere!
We mustn't reproach 'em.
   They're young, you see.'
'Ah,' said the dead men,
   'So were we!'

Victory! Victory!
   On with the dance!
Back to the jungle
   The new beasts prance!
God, how the dead men
   Grin by the wall,
Watching the fun
   Of the Victory Ball.

ALFRED NOYES

In Memoriam

Do you recall the Vardar River
Flowing across the rolling plains?
Do you recall the sunset splendour,
The distant cry of the homing cranes?
Have you forgotten Salonika,
Its towers, and minarets, and fanes?

Can you yet see the hovering biplanes,
Like vultures over a flock of sheep?
Does not the tramp of the passing columns
Startle and rouse you from your sleep?

And the distant rattle of mitrailleuses*
Make your heart and pulses leap?

Do you recall how we grubbed together
Biscuits and bully beef and tea;
And watched, as we lay on the close-cut heather,
The sun dip down by the Cypress tree,
Till, like silver swords in the velvet darkness,
The searchlights swung over land and sea?

Brother in arms, do you hear me calling,
Here, in the land that you died to save?
With shattered frame I lie and wonder
Whether, beyond the far-flung wave
By the sandy bank of the Vardar River,
You lie content in your lonely grave?

The ultimate sacrifice completed,
Suffering, toil, and grief o'erpast;
Knowing no more the long night-watching,
The bullets' whine and the cannons' blast
There, where the night wind rustles the grasses
Over you, are you content at the last?

A.B.L. HODGSON

On a War-Worker, 1916

Far from their homes they lie, the men who fell
Fighting, in Flanders clay or Tigris sand:
She who lies here died for the cause as well,
Whom neither bayonet killed nor bursting shell,
But her own heart that loved its native land.

ARUNDELL ESDAILE

* French for machine-gun.

Repression of War Experience

Now light the candles; one; two; there's a moth;
What silly beggars they are to blunder in
And scorch their wings with glory, liquid flame —
No, no, not that, — it's bad to think of war,
When thoughts you've gagged all day come back to scare you;
And it's been proved that soldiers don't go mad
Unless they lose control of ugly thoughts
That drive them out to jabber among the trees.

Now light your pipe; look, what a steady hand.
Draw a deep breath; stop thinking; count fifteen,
And you're as right as rain ...
                    Why won't it rain? ...
I wish there'd be a thunder-storm to-night,
With bucketsful of water to sluice the dark,
And make the roses hang their dripping heads.
Books; what a jolly company they are,
Standing so quiet and patient on their shelves,
Dressed in dim brown, and black, and white, and green,
And every kind of colour. Which will you read?
Come on; O *do* read something; they're so wise.
I tell you all the wisdom of the world
Is waiting for you on those shelves; and yet
You sit and gnaw your nails, and let your pipe out,
And listen to the silence: on the ceiling
There's one big, dizzy moth that bumps and flutters;
And in the breathless air outside the house
The garden waits for something that delays.
There must be crowds of ghosts among the trees, —
Not people killed in battle, — they're in France, —
But horrible shapes in shrouds — old men who died
Slow, natural deaths, — old men with ugly souls,
Who wore their bodies out with nasty sins.

*

You're quiet and peaceful, summering safe at home;
You'd never think there was a bloody war on! ...
O yes, you would ... why, you can hear the guns.
Hark! Thud, thud, thud, — quite soft ... they never cease —
Those whispering guns — O Christ, I want to go out
And screech at them to stop — I'm going crazy;
I'm going stark, staring mad because of the guns.

SIEGFRIED SASSOON

Aftermath

Have you forgotten yet? ...
For the world's events have rumbled on since those gagged days,
Like traffic checked while at the crossing of city-ways:
And the haunted gap in your mind has filled with thoughts that flow
Like clouds in the lit heaven of life; and you're a man reprieved to go,
Taking your peaceful share of Time, with joy to spare.
But the past is just the same — and War's a bloody game ...
Have you forgotten yet? ...
Look down, and swear by the slain of the War that you'll never forget.

Do you remember the dark months you held the sector at Mametz —
The nights you watched and wired and dug and piled sandbags
      on parapets?
Do you remember the rats; and the stench
Of corpses rotting in front of the front-line trench —
And dawn coming, dirty-white, and chill with a hopeless rain?
Do you ever stop and ask, 'Is it all going to happen again?'

Do you remember that hour of din before the attack —
And the anger, the blind compassion that seized and shook you then
As you peered at the doomed and haggard faces of your men?
Do you remember the stretcher-cases lurching back
With dying eyes and lolling heads — those ashen-grey
Masks of the lads who once were keen and kind and gay?

Have you forgotten yet? . . .
Look up, and swear by the green of the spring that you'll never
forget.

SIEGFRIED SASSOON
March 1919

A Lament

We who are left, how shall we look again
Happily on the sun or feel the rain,
Without remembering how they who went
Ungrudgingly and spent
Their all for us loved, too, the sun and rain?

A bird among the rain-wet lilac sings —
But we, how shall we turn to little things
And listen to the birds and winds and streams
Made holy by their dreams,
Nor feel the heart-break in the heart of things?

WILFRID WILSON GIBSON

To One Who Was With Me in the War

It was too long ago — that Company which we served with . . .
We call it back in visual fragments, you and I,
Who seem, ourselves, like relics casually preserved with
Our mindfulness of old bombardments when the sky
With blundering din blinked cavernous,
                Yet a sense of power
Invaded us when, recapturing an ungodly hour
Of ante-zero crisis, in one thought we've met
To stand in some redoubt of Time — to share again
All but the actual witness of the flare-lit rain,
All but the living presences who haunt us yet
With gloom-patrolling eyes.
            Remembering, we forget

312

Much that was monstrous, much that clogged our souls with clay
When hours were guides who led us by the longest way —
And when the worst had been endured could still disclose
Another worst to thwart us ...
                    We forget our fear ...
And, while the uncouth Event begins to lour less near,
Discern the mad magnificence whose storm-light throws
Wild shadows on these after-thoughts that send your brain

Back beyond Peace, exploring sunken ruinous roads.
Your brain, with files of flitting forms hump-backed with loads,
On its own helmet hears the tinkling drops of rain, —
Follows to an end some night-relief, and strangely sees
The quiet no-man's-land of daybreak, jagg'd with trees
That loom like giant Germans ...
                    I'll go with you, then,
Since you must play this game of ghosts. At listening–posts
We'll peer across dim craters; joke with jaded men
Whose names we've long forgotten. (Stoop low there; it's the place
The sniper enfilades.) Round the next bay you'll meet
A drenched platoon-commander; chilled he drums his feet
On squelching duck-boards; winds his wrist watch; turns his head,
And shows you how you looked — your ten–years–vanished face,
Hoping the War will end next week ...
                              What's that you said?

SIEGFRIED SASSOON

From 'The Song of Tiadatha'

In this war the Hun has brought us,
Some have learnt to make returns out,
Some have learnt to write out orders.
Some have learnt the way to kill Huns,
Some to lead the men that kill them,
Some have learnt to cope with bully,
Learnt to shave with army razors,
Learnt to make the best of blizzards,
Mud and slush and blazing sunshine,

Learnt to coax a little comfort
Out of bivvies, barns and dug-outs,
Learnt of things they never dreamed of
In July of 1914.

And they all have learnt this lesson,
Learnt as well this common lesson,
Learnt to hold a little dearer
All the things they took for granted
In July of 1914 —
Whether it be Scottish Highlands,
Hills of Wales or banks of Ireland,
Or the swelling downs of Dudshire,
Or the pavement of St. James's —
Even so my Tiadatha.

So I leave him and salute him
Back in his beloved London,
Knowing that the war has one thing
(If no others) to its credit —
It has made a nut a soldier,
Made a silk purse from a sow's ear,
Made a man of Tiadatha
And made men of hundreds like him.

And the world has cause to thank us
For that band of so-called filberts,*
For those products of St. James's,
Light of heart and much enduring,
Straight and debonair and dauntless,
Grousing at their small discomforts,
Smiling in the face of danger.
Who have faced their great adventure,
Crossed through No Man's Land to meet it,
Lightly as they'd cross St. James's.
Eyes and heart still full of laughter,

---

* Slang for a showy young man or dandy, derived from 'nut' by way of the then popular song
'Gilbert the Filbert, Colonel of the Nuts'.

Till the world had cause to wonder,
Till the world had cause to thank us
For the likes of Tiadatha.

MAJOR OWEN RUTTER
Cendresselles, September 1918

From a Full Heart

In days of peace my fellow-men
    Rightly regarded me as more like
A Bishop than a Major-Gen.,
    And nothing since has made me warlike;
But when this age-long struggle ends
    And I have seen the Allies dish up
The goose of HINDENBURG — oh, friends!
    I shall out-bish the mildest Bishop.

When the War is over and the KAISER's out of print,
I'm going to buy some tortoises and watch the beggars sprint;
When the War is over and the sword at last we sheathe,
I'm going to keep a jelly-fish and listen to it breathe.

I never really longed for gore,
    And any taste for red corpuscles
That lingered with me left before
    The German troops had entered Brussels.
In early days the Colonel's "Shun!'
    Froze me; and, as the War grew older,
The noise of someone else's gun
    Left me considerably colder.

When the War is over and the battle has been won,
I'm going to buy a barnacle and take it for a run;
When the War is over and the German Fleet we sink,
I'm going to keep a silk-worm's egg and listen to it think.

The Captains and the Kings depart —*
    It may be so, but not lieutenants;

*A line from Kipling's 'Recessional'.

Dawn after weary dawn I start
    The never-ending round of penance;
One rock amid the welter stands
    On which my gaze is fixed intently —
An after-life in quiet hands
    Lived very lazily and gently.

When the War is over and we've done the Belgians proud,
I'm going to keep a chrysalis and read to it aloud;
When the War is over and we've finished up the show,
I'm going to plant a lemon-pip and listen to it grow.

Oh, I'm tired of the noise and the turmoil of battle,
And I'm even upset by the lowing of cattle,
And the clang of the bluebells is death to my liver
And the roar of the dandelion gives me a shiver,
And a glacier, in movement, is much too exciting
And I'm nervous, when standing on one, of alighting —
Give me Peace; that is all, that is all that I seek ...
    Say, starting on Saturday week.

A.A. MILNE

I Vow To Thee, My Country

I vow to thee, my country — all earthly things above —
Entire and whole and perfect, the service of my love,
The love that asks no questions: the love that stands the test,
That lays upon the altar the dearest and the best:
The love that never falters, the love that pays the price,
The love that makes undaunted the final sacrifice.

And there's another country, I've heard of long ago —
Most dear to them that love her, most great to them that know —
We may not count her armies: we may not see her king —
Her fortress is a faithful heart, her pride is suffering —
And soul by soul and silently her shining bounds increase,
And her ways are ways of gentleness and all her paths are peace.

CECIL SPRING-RICE

MCMXIV

Those long uneven lines
Standing as patiently
As if they were stretched outside
The Oval or Villa Park,
The crowns of hats, the sun
On moustached archaic faces
Grinning as if it were all
An August Bank Holiday lark;

And the shut shops, the bleached
Established names on the sunblinds,
The farthings and sovereigns,
And dark-clothed children at play
Called after kings and queens,
The tin advertisements
For cocoa and twist, and the pubs
Wide open all day-

And the countryside not caring:
The place names all hazed over
With flowering grasses, and fields
Shadowing Domesday lines
Under wheat's restless silence;
The differently-dressed servants
With tiny rooms in huge houses,
The dust behind limousines;

Never such innocence,
Never before or since,
As changed itself to past
Without a word — the men
Leaving the gardens tidy,
The thousands of marriages,
Lasting a little while longer:
Never such innocence again.

PHILIP LARKIN

A Square Dance

In Flanders fields in Northern France
They're all doing a brand new dance
It makes you happy and out of breath
And it's called the Dance of Death

Everybody stands in line
Everybody's feeling fine
We're all going to a hop
1 — 2 — 3 and over the top

It's the dance designed to thrill
It's the mustard gas quadrille
A dance for men — girls have no say in it
For your partner is a bayonet.

See how the dancers sway and run
To the rhythm of the gun
Swing your partner dos-y-doed
All around the shells explode

Honour your partner form a square
Smell the burning in the air
Over the barbed wire kicking high
Men like shirts hung out to dry

If you fall that's no disgrace
Someone else will take your place
'Old soldiers never die …'
                    … Only young ones

In Flanders fields where mortars blaze
They're all going the latest craze
Khaki dancers out of breath
Doing the glorious Dance of Death
Doing the glorious (*clap, clap*) Dance of Death.

ROGER MCGOUGH

318

A Grand Night

When the film *Tell England** came
To Leamington, my father said,
'That's about Gallipoli — I was there
I'll call and see the manager …'

Before the first showing, the manager
Announced that 'a local resident …' etc.
And there was my father on the stage
With a message to the troops from Sir Somebody
Exhorting, condoling or congratulating.
But he was shy, so the manager
Read it out, while he fidgeted.
Then the lights went off, and I thought
I'd lost my father.
The Expedition's casualty rate was 50%.

But it was a grand night,
With free tickets for the two of us.

                                    D.J. ENRIGHT

The Great War

Whenever war is spoken of
I find
The war that was called Great invades the mind:
The grey militia marches over land
A darker mood of grey
Where fractured tree-trunks stand
And shells, exploding, open sudden fans
Of smoke and earth.
Blind murders scythe

---

* A sentimental novel by Ernest Raymond, about a British officer in the Gallipoli campaign, which enjoyed tremendous popularity when it was published in 1922. The film was made in the 1930s.

The deathscape where the iron brambles writhe;
The sky at night
Is honoured with rosettes of fire,
Flares that define the corpses on the wire
As terror ticks on wrists at zero hour.
These things I see,
But they are only part
Of what it is that slyly probes the heart:
Less vivid images and words excite
The sensuous memory
And, even as I write,
Fear and a kind of love collaborate
To call each simple conscript up
For quick inspection:
Trenches' parapets
Paunchy with sandbags; bandoliers, tin-hats.
Candles in dug-outs,
Duckboards, mud and rats.
Then, like patrols, tunes creep into the mind:
A long, long trail, The Rose of No-Man's Land,
Home Fire and *Tipperary*:
And through the misty keening of a band
Of Scottish pipes the proper names are heard
Like fateful commentary of distant guns:
Passchendaele, Bapaume, and Loos, and Mons.
And now,
Whenever the November sky
Quivers with a bugle's hoarse, sweet cry,
The reason darkens; in its evening gleam
Crosses and flares, tormented wire, grey earth
Splattered with crimson flowers,
And I remember,
Not the war I fought in
But the one called Great
Which ended in a sepia November
Four years before my birth.

VERNON SCANNELL

Six Young Men

The celluloid of a photograph holds them well —
Six young men, familiar to their friends.
Four decades that have faded and ochre-tinged
This photograph have not wrinkled the faces or the hands.
Though their cocked hats are not now fashionable,
Their shoes shine. One imparts an intimate smile,
One chews a grass, one lowers his eyes, bashful,
One is ridiculous with cocky pride —
Six months after this picture they all were dead.

All are trimmed for a Sunday jaunt. I know
That bilberried bank, that thick tree, that black wall,
Which are there yet and not changed. From where these sit
You hear the water of seven streams fall
To the roarer in the bottom, and through all
The leafy valley a rumouring of air go.
Pictured here, their expressions listen yet,
And still that valley has not changed in sound
Though their faces are four decades under the ground.

This one was shot in an attack and lay
Calling in the wire, then this one, his best friend,
Went out to bring him in and was shot too;
And this one, the very moment he was warned
From potting at tin-cans in no-man's land,
Fell back dead with his rifle-sights shot away,
The rest, nobody knows what they came to,
But come to the worst they must have done, and held it
Closer than their hope; all were killed.

Here, see a man's photograph,
The locket of a smile, turned overnight
Into the hospital of his mangled last
Agony and hours; see bundled in it
His mightier-than-man dead bulk and weight:

And on this one place which keeps him alive
(In his Sunday best) see fall war's worst
Thinkable flash and rending, onto his smile
Forty years rotting into soil.

That man's not more alive whom you confront
And shake by the hand, see hale, hear speak loud,
Than any of these six celluloid smiles are,
Nor prehistoric or fabulous beast more dead;
No thought so vivid as their smoking blood:
To regard this photograph might well dement,
Such contradictory permanent horrors here
Smile from the single exposure and shoulder out
One's own body from its instant and heat.

TED HUGHES

'We Shall Drink to Them that Sleep'
CAMPBELL*

Yes, you will do it, silently of course;
For after many a toast and much applause,
One is in love with silence, being hoarse,
— Such more than sorrow is your quiet's cause.

Yes, I can see you at it, in a room
Well-lit and warm, high-roofed and soft to the tread,
Satiate and briefly mindful of the tomb
With its poor victim of Teutonic lead.

Some unknown notability will rise,
Ridiculously solemn, glass abrim,
And say, 'To our dear brethren in the skies,' —
Dim are all eyes, all glasses still more dim.

Your pledge of sorrow but a cup of cheer,
Your sole remark some witless platitude,

* Thomas Campbell (1777-1844), Scottish poet, and the originator of the expression 'Now
Barabbas was a publisher', often attributed to Byron.

Such as, 'Although it does not yet appear,
To suffer is the sole beatitude.

'Life has, of course, good moments such as this
(A glass of sherry we should never spurn),
But where our brethren are, 'tis perfect bliss;
Still, we are glad our lot was, — to return.'

Yes, I can see you and can see the dead,
Keen-eyed at last for Truth, with gentle mirth
Intent. And having heard, smiling they said:
'Strange are our little comrades of the earth.'

CORPORAL ALEXANDER ROBERTSON+

The Next War

The long war had ended.
Its miseries had grown faded.
Deaf men became difficult to talk to,
Heroes became bores.
Those alchemists
Who had converted blood into gold
Had grown elderly.
But they held a meeting,
Saying,
'We think perhaps we ought
To put up tombs
Or erect altars
To those brave lads
Who were so willingly burnt,
Or blinded,
Or maimed,
Who lost all likeness to a living thing,
Or were blown to bleeding patches of flesh
For our sakes.
It would look well.
Or we might even educate the children.'
But the richest of these wizards

Coughed gently;
And he said:
   'I have always been to the front
   — In private enterprise —,
   I yield in public spirit
   To no man.
   I think yours is a very good idea
   — A capital idea —
   And not too costly ...
   But it seems to me
   That the cause for which we fought
   Is again endangered.
   What more fitting memorial for the fallen
   Than that their children
   Should fall for the same cause?'
Rushing eagerly into the street,
The kindly old gentlemen cried
To the young:
   'Will you sacrifice
   Through your lethargy
   What your fathers died to gain?
   The world *must* be made safe for the young!'

*

And the children
Went ...

OSBERT SITWELL
November 1918

Repetition
(First War graves at Ypres)

Dirty grey of the day at a Flanders dawn
Breaks down on the graves where old Englishmen born
For the earth of old England store up their infinite days
Never knowing their sons in similar ways
   Will shatter themselves, their marrow and crust
    In search of a similar dust.

The shadowed turf and the mouldering granite cross
The wind on the wold, and the smarting sense of a loss
That breaks into perpetual step with the regular dawn:
So, confirmed in my mind by such things, incredulity shorn
 Of its questioning, wondering, damnable doubt —
  Will I too be snuffed out?

ANTHONY RHODES
France, Christmas 1939

To a Conscript of 1940

Qui n'a pas une fois désespéré de l'honneur, ne sera jamais un héros.
Georges Bernanos

A soldier passed me in the freshly fallen snow,
His footsteps muffled, his face unearthly grey;
And my heart gave a sudden leap
As I gazed on a ghost of five-and-twenty years ago.

I shouted Halt! and my voice had the old accustom'd ring
And he obeyed it as it was obeyed
In the shrouded days when I too was one
Of an army of young men marching

Into the unknown. He turned towards me and I said:
'I am one of those who went before you
Five-and-twenty years ago: one of the many who never returned,
Of the many who returned and yet were dead.

We went where you are going, into the rain and the mud;
We fought as you will fight
With death and darkness and despair;
We gave what you will give — our brains and our blood.

We think we gave in vain. The world was not renewed.
There was hope in the homestead and anger in the streets,
But the old world was restored and we returned
To the dreary field and workshop, and the immemorial feud

Of rich and poor. Our victory was our defeat.
Power was retained where power had been misused
And youth was left to sweep away
The ashes that the fires had strewn beneath our feet.

But one thing we learned: there is no glory in the dead
Until the soldier wears a badge of tarnish'd braid;
There are heroes who have heard the rally and have seen
The glitter of a garland round their head.

Theirs is the hollow victory. They are deceived.
But you, my brother and my ghost, if you can go
Knowing that there is no reward, no certain use
In all your sacrifice, then honour is reprieved.

To fight without hope is to fight with grace,
The self reconstructed, the false heart repaired.'
Then I turned with a smile, and he answered my salute
As he stood against the fretted hedge, which was like white lace.

HERBERT READ

Afterwards

'My King and Country needed me,' to fight
   The Prussian's tyranny.
I went and fought, till our assembled might
With a wan triumph had dispersed in flight
   At least the initial P.

I came back. In a crowded basement now
   I scratch, a junior clerk.
Each day my tried experience must bow
Before the callow boy, whose shameless brow
   Usurps my oldtime work.

I had not cared — but that my toil was vain,
   But that still rage the strong:

I had not cared — did any good remain.
But now I scratch, and wait for War again,
   Nor shall I need to wait long.

H.B.K. ALLPASS[+]

High Wood

Ladies and gentlemen, this is High Wood,
Called by the French, Bois des Fourneaux,
The famous spot which in Nineteen-Sixteen,
July, August and September was the scene
Of long and bitterly contested strife,
By reason of its High commanding site.
Observe the effect of shell-fire in the trees
Standing and fallen; here is wire; this trench
For months inhabited, twelve times changed hands;
(They soon fall in), used later as a grave.
It has been said on good authority
That in the fighting for this patch of wood
Were killed somewhere above eight thousand men,
Of whom the greater part were buried here
This mound on which you stand being . . .

                  Madame, please,
You are requested kindly not to touch
Or take away the Company's property
As souvenirs: you'll find we have on sale
A large variety, all guaranteed.
As I was saying, all is as it was,
This is an unknown British officer,
The tunic having lately rotted off.
Please follow me — this way . . .

                the *path*, sir, *please,*

The ground which was secured at great expense
The Company keeps absolutely untouched,
And in that dug-out (genuine) we provide
Refreshments at a reasonable rate.
You are requested not to leave about
Paper, or ginger-beer bottles, or orange-peel,
There are waste-paper baskets at the gate.

PHILIP JOHNSTONE
1918

INDEX OF POETS AND SELECT BIBLIOGRAPHY

This bibliographical and biographical section is not exhaustive, but it is intended to give an indication of the sources from which were drawn the poems printed in this book. It also serves as an index of poets, giving page references for their verses printed in this collection. In the case of certain major poets, I have also given details of modern and revised editions. These will be found under the poets in question.

I have done my best to provide biographical details, or at least the dates of birth and death and the names of published works, of the writers represented here; sadly, however, a number of the poets are now nearly completely untraceable. It is also true that the anthologies listed below, and most of the original editions of the poets' work, can now be found only through second-hand booksellers or specialist dealers. The majority of such books, however, are unobtainable, except by luck or accident.

The expression '"Georgian" poet' in biographical details does not necessarily mean that a writer belonged to or was typical of the Georgian movement. It is used here to show that a poet's work appeared in one or other of the *Georgian Poetry* anthologies. There were five of these, published between 1912 and 1922, and all edited by Edward Marsh and published by Harold Monro's Poetry Bookshop, London. A modern selection, *Georgian Poetry*, edited and introduced by James Reeves (Penguin, 1961, and subsequent editions), is readily available, and contains the work of nineteen Georgian poets, some of which was published in the original editions. Timothy Rogers's *Georgian Poetry 1911-1922* (London, Routledge & Kegan Paul, 'Critical Heritage' series, 1977) is also an excellent work.

The biographical details also list a poet's verse in this book with a page reference; there is also a separate Index of Titles and First Lines.

Anthologies

The list below is a small selection from the many anthologies published during and after the Great War, but before the Second World War.

Andrews, Lieutenant Clarence Edward (ed.), *From the Front*, New York, Appleton, 1918
Brereton, Frederick (ed.), *Anthology of War Poems*, London, Collins, 1930
Clarke, George Herbert (ed.), *A Treasury of War Poetry: British and American*

Poems of the World War, 1914-1919, London, Hodder & Stoughton, 1919; Boston, Mass., Houghton Mifflin, 1919

Cunliffe, John William (ed.), *Poems of the Great War* ('Selected on behalf of the Belgian Scholarship Committee'), New York, Macmillan, 1916

Kyle, Galloway (ed.), *Soldier Poets: Songs of the Fighting Men*, London, Erskine Macdonald, 1916

—— (ed.), *Soldier Poets: More Songs by the Fighting Men*, London, Erskine Macdonald, 1917

Lest We Forget: A War Anthology, London, Jarrolds, 1915

Lowell, Amy (ed.), *Some Imagist Poets, 1916: An Annual Anthology*, Boston, Mass., Houghton Mifflin, 1916

—— (ed.), *Some Imagist Poets, 1917: An Annual Anthology*, Boston, Mass., Houghton Mifflin, 1917

Osborn, Edward Bolland (ed.), *The Muse in Arms: A Collection of war poems, for the most part written in the field of action, by seamen, soldiers, and flying men who are serving or who have served, in the Great War*, London, Murray, 1917

Punch, or the London Charivari (founded 1841), weekly humorous periodical. Issues from August 1914 to December 1918

—— *Poems from Punch*, 1909-1920, London, Macmillan, 1922

Trotter, Jacqueline Theodora (ed.), *Valour and Vision: Poems of the War, 1914-1918*, London, Longman, Green & Co., 1920

Other anthologies will be found under individual poets' entries.

Individual Poets

Abercrombie, Lascelles (1881-1938)
Extract from 'The Sale of Saint Thomas', 28
'Georgian' poet and critic, friend of Rupert Brooke (qv). Chief published works: poetry — *Interludes and Poems* (1908), *Emblems of Love* (1912) and *Deborah* (1912); criticism — *Thomas Hardy, A Critical Study* (1912), *The Epic* (1914), and *Theory of Art* (1922). His *Collected Poems* was published in 1930. Co-beneficiary with Gibson (qv) and Walter de la Mare of Brooke's will. This poem was first published privately by the author in 1911.

Alchin, Captain (later His Honour Judge) Gordon, AFC (pseudonym, 'Observer RFC', d. 1947)
'A Song of the Air', 252
Born in Kent, educated Tonbridge School and Brasenose College, Oxford; Junior Hulme Scholar, Brasenose, 1913. Commissioned into the Royal Field Artillery, August 1914, and served in

Flanders 1914-15. Transferred to Royal Flying Corps and served in Flanders, 1915-17; awarded the Air Force Cross. Returned to Oxford after the war, Senior Hulme Scholar, 1920; Eldon Scholar; called to the Bar, 1922, and practised until 1940, when he was apointed a County Court Judge. Wrote verse, short stories and legal manuals; this poem appeared in his *Oxford and Flanders* (Oxford, Blackwell, 1916) and also in Andrews (ed.), *From the Front* (1918).

Allpass, H.B.K. (k.i.a. 1916)
'Afterwards', 326
This poem was written in January 1915.

'B.', Major 'H.D'A.',
'Givenchy Field', 100, 'No-Man's-Land', 104
A major with 55th Division of the BEF in France. Poems appear in Kyle (ed.), *Soldier Poets: Songs of the Fighting Man* (1916)

Beckh, 2nd Lieutenant Harold
(k.i.a. 1916)
'The Soldier's Cigarette', 64
Commissioned into the East Yorkshire
Regiment; killed in action 15 August 1916.
His collection *Swallows in Storm and Sunlight*
was published in 1917 (London, Chapman &
Hall).

Begbie, Harold (1871-1929)
'Fall In', 71
This poem appeared in his *Fighting Lines and
Various Reinforcements* (London, Constable,
1914).

Begbie, Janet
Untitled poem, 115
This poem appeared in her *Morning Mist*
(London, Mills & Boon, 1916).

Berry, H.W.
'Somewhere East of Suez', 201
This poem appeared in *Punch*, July 1918.

Bewsher, Paul, DSC (1894-1966)
'The Dawn Patrol', 253
Educated Colet Court (where his father was
Headmaster) and St Paul's School. With the
Port of London Authority, 1912-14; joined
Advertisers' Weekly, 1914. Served in Royal
Naval Air Service, 1915-18 (was shot down
once and awarded the DSC), and the RAF,
1918-19. Worked on *Modern Transport*
magazine, 1919; lectured in the USA and
Britain, 1920; joined staff of *Daily Mail*, 1920,
and worked there for the rest of his life. This
poem comes from *The Dawn Patrol and Other
Poems of an Aviator* (London, Hodder &
Stoughton, 1917); also wrote two other
books about war flying.

Binyon, Laurence, CH (1869-1943)
'The Unreturning Spring', 184
Prolific poet and writer, an official of the
British Museum from 1893-1933, expert on
many forms of art, especially Oriental art.
Born in Lancashire, educated St Paul's
School and Trinity College, Oxford (where
he won the Newdigate Prize for Poetry). His
last post at the British Museum was Keeper
of Prints and Drawings; lectured in USA
1912, 1914, 1926; in Japan, 1929; Norton
Professor of Poetry, Harvard University,
1933-4; Byron Professor, University of
Athens, 1940. Published many collections of
his own verse, plays (of which six were

performed), and books on art and allied
subjects; he also, between 1933 and 1943,
published a translation of the three volumes
of Dante's *Divina Commedia*. Companion of
Honour, 1932. Joined the Red Cross in 1914,
and visited the Front in 1916. The poem
printed here is from *The Four Years* (London,
Elkin Matthews, 1919), but Binyon is best
remembered for the four lines from 'For The
Fallen' which are read every year at most
Armistice Day ceremonies in Britain.
Contrary to common belief, 'For The Fallen'
was written in 1914, and not at the end of
the war. Binyon's war poems are among his
best work.

Blackall, Captain C.W.
'From the Front', 63
Quoted in Andrews (ed.), *From the Front*
(1918); Blackall also produced a collection,
Songs from the Trenches, (London, Bodley
Head, 1915).

**Blunden, Edmund Charles, CBE,
MC, FRSL** (1896-1974)
'Concert Party: Busseboom', 117; 'Escape',
118; 'The Guard's Mistake', 172
Poet, critic, scholar and teacher, educated at
Christ's Hospital and Queen's College,
Oxford. Commissioned into the Royal
Sussex Regiment, 1915, and served in France
and Belgium until 1919, fighting on the
Somme and at Ypres. Lifelong friend of
Siegfried Sassoon (qv), and knew many of the
other war poets well. Won the Hawthornden
Prize, 1922, Queen's Gold Medal for Poetry,
1956, and the Royal Society of Literature's
Benson Medal. Professor of English
Literature, Imperial University, Tokyo,
1924-7 (succeeding Robert Nichols [qv]);
Fellow and Tutor in English Literature,
Merton College, Oxford, 1931-43; with UK
Liaison Mission, Tokyo, 1948-50; Emeritus
Professor of English Literature, University of
Hong Kong; Professor of Poetry, University
of Oxford, 1966-8. His memoir *Undertones of
War*, in which these poems appear (Oxford,
Oxford University Press, 1928) ranks with
Graves's *Goodbye To All That* (1929, revised
1957) and Sassoon's *Memoirs of George
Sherston* (1928, 1930, 1936) as among the
finest prose works by a Great War poet.
Poems 1914-30 (1930), *Poems 1930-40* (1940),
among other collections; prose works
include important studies of Leigh Hunt,
Shelley, Hardy, Charles Lamb, with books on

poetry, England, and cricket. Edited works by, among others, Keats, Shelley, Wilfred Owen (qv), Ivor Gurney (qv) and John Clare — Blunden discovered and brought before the public Clare's hitherto unpublished poems.

Bottomley, Gordon (1874–1948)
Extract from 'King Lear's Wife', 29
'Georgian' poet and author of verse plays and plays, friend of many of the Georgians. Published more than 20 works, many with a Scots or Gaelic basis. Fellow of the Royal Society of Literature. His *Poems of Thirty Years* (London, Macmillan) were published in 1925. 'King Lear's Wife' first appeared in Marsh, Edward (ed.), *Georgian Poetry 1913–15* (London, The Poetry Bookshop, 1915).

Brett Young, Major Francis (1884–1954)
'The Gift', 200
'Georgian' poet, friend of Marsh; educated Epsom College and University of Birmingham, where he qualified as a doctor. Served with the Royal Army Medical Corps in East Africa in the campaign against von Lettow-Vorbeck; invalided home sick in 1918. His book *Marching on Tanga* covers his experiences. Wrote novels, travel books, a study of Robert Bridges (1913), as well as poetry; his novel *Portrait of Clare* (1927) won the James Tait Black Memorial Prize. Also wrote two plays, including *Captain Swing* (1919); his *Poems 1916–18* (London, Collins), in which this verse appeared, was published in 1919.

Brooke, Rupert Chawner (1887–1915)
Extract from 'Death of John Rump', 23; 'Heaven', 26; two 'Fragments', 27, 28; 'The Soldier', 68
'Georgian' poet, educated at Rugby and King's College, Cambridge, first volume of verse published 1911. Travelled in America and the South Seas, 1913–14. Commissioned into the Royal Naval Division, 1914, and took part in the unsuccessful defence of Antwerp in October. Sent to Gallipoli early in 1915, but died of blood poisoning on the way, and is buried on Skyros. His '1914' sonnets (published 1915) include 'The Dead' and 'The Soldier'; *Letters From America* was published in 1916 with an introduction by Henry James, and his *Collected Poems* in 1918. Other famous poems include 'The Old Vicarage, Grantchester', 'Peace', and 'The

Little Dog's Day'. *Rupert Brooke: a Reappraisal and Selection*, by Timothy Rogers (London, Routledge & Kegan Paul, 1971); *The Poems of Rupert Brooke: A Centenary Edition*, edited and introduced by Timothy Rogers (London, Black Swan, 1987).

Brown, Sergeant Frank S.
'The Veteran', 109
This poem appears in Andrews (ed.), *From The Front* (1918).

Buchan, John (1st Baron Tweedsmuir of Elsfield, GCMG, GCVO, CH, PC, 1875–1940)
'The Kirk Bell', 145; 'On Leave', 148
Journalist, barrister, politician, soldier, scholar, novelist, historian, biographer, essayist and critic. Born the son of a Free Kirk minister, educated Hutcheson's Grammar School, Glasgow; University of Glasgow; Brasenose College, Oxford. Took First in Greats, Newdigate Prize (for his poem *The Pilgrim Fathers*), President of the Union etc. Friend of Raymond Asquith, Hilaire Belloc, Aubrey Herbert etc. Served on Lord Milner's staff, South Africa, 1901–2. Worked at the law and journalism (*Spectator, Sunday Times* etc.) in London until 1906, when he joined Nelson's, the publishers, as a partner (resigned 1929). At the outbreak of war, tried to join up, but rejected on grounds of health (plagued by severe ulcers from 1912 to his death); correspondent for *The Times* at the Front, 1915; commissioned into Intelligence Corps, 1916, and joined Haig's staff; appointed Director of Information, 1917, and Director of Intelligence, Ministry of Information, 1918. MP for Scottish Universities, 1927–35; High Commissioner to the General Assembly of the Church of Scotland, 1933 and 1934; created Lord Tweedsmuir, 1935, on his appointment as Governor-General of Canada, which post he held to his death in office in 1940. Author of more than 80 books (the first published in 1894, when he was 19), of which his 'shockers' are best-remembered: notably *The Thirty-Nine Steps* (1915), *Greenmantle* (1916), *Huntingtower* (1922), *The Three Hostages* (1924) etc.; wrote lives of Scott, Cromwell, Montrose, Augustus etc. These verses appear in *Poems Scots and English* (London, Nelson, 1917); also wrote *Nelson's History of the War* during the Great War, which runs to more than a million words.

Cameron Wilson, Captain T.P.
(k.i.a. 23 March 1918)
'Magpies in Picardy', 184
A schoolmaster, served in France with the
Sherwood Foresters, and was killed on the
Somme during the Ludendorff Offensive.
Magpies in Picardy, and Other War Verse was
published by Harold Monro's (qv) Poetry
Bookshop; this poem had first appeared in
The Westminster Gazette, but Monro's
printing omitted the last two verses. General
Sir Archibald (later Field-Marshal Lord)
Wavell, whose vast and accurate memory for
poetry was legendary, remembered the two
missing verses, and printed them with the
rest of the poem in his famous anthology
Other Men's Flowers (London, Cape, 1944),
assuring 'Magpies in Picardy' a place for ever
among the best-loved Great War poems.

Cannan, May Wedderburn
'Lamplight', 265
Served in the Voluntary Aid Detachment.
Her *In War Time: Poems* (Oxford, Blackwell)
was published in 1917.

Chesterton, Gilbert Keith (1874–1936)
'To the Unknown Warrior', 284; 'The Wife
of Flanders', 287; 'Elegy in a Country
Churchyard', 288; 'The English Graves', 303
Poet, essayist, novelist, short-story writer and
critic, lifelong friend of Hilaire Belloc.
Educated at St Paul's School, where his
drawing was so good that he went on to the
Slade School of Art, while continuing to
study English Literature at the University of
London. It soon became clear that writing,
not drawing, was his main talent and, after
working for two publishing houses, he
drifted into journalism, which he later
claimed as his sole profession. Published his
first two books – both verse – in 1900, and
The Napoleon of Notting Hill in 1904; 17 more
books (including the autobiographical
Orthodoxy) followed between then and 1910,
by which time his reputation was firmly
established. He conducted well-publicised
controversies with, among others, Shaw,
Wells and Kipling, all of which reflected his
concern for religion, politics, philosophy and
social conditions, but which nonetheless
demonstrated his supreme ability both as a
thinker and a humorist. He was desperately
ill for months during the Great War, but
recovered. In 1922 he was received into the
Roman Catholic faith. The magazine *The*

New Witness had been started by his brother
Cecil and Belloc in 1911, and Chesterton
took over its editorship in 1916, and
continued to edit it until 1923, when the
paper folded. It was revived in 1925 as *G.K.'s
Weekly*, and Chesterton edited it until his
death; it too folded in 1938. Besides his
poems, Chesterton is probably best
remembered for the *Father Brown* stories; he
also wrote novels, including *The Man Who
Was Thursday*, and studies of saints, painters,
writers, social reformers, as well as *A Short
History of England*. These poems are from the
New Witness; his *Collected Poems of G K.
Chesterton* appeared in 1933.

Clarke, E.F.
'The Infantryman', 133
This poem appeared in *Punch*, 1917.

Cleveland, Reginald McIntosh
'Destroyers Off Jutland', 233
This poem appeared in Clarke (ed.), *A
Treasury of War Poetry: British and American
Poems of the World War, 1914-1919* (1919).

**Corbett, Lieutenant-Commander
Noel Marcus Francis, RN**
'The Sailing of the Fleet', 231
This poem appeared in Andrews (ed.), *From
The Front* (1918). Corbett's work also
appeared in a book of his own, *A Naval
Motley: Verses Written at Sea during the War and
before it* (London, Methuen, 1916).

Cox, Rifleman S. Donald
'To My Mother – 1916', 69-70; 'The Song of
the Happy Warrior', 70
Served in the London Rifle Brigade. Some of
his verse appeared in Foxcroft (ed.), *War
Verse* (1918), and Kyle (ed.), *Soldier Poets: Songs
of the Fighting Men* (1916) and *Soldier Poets:
More Songs by the Fighting Men* (1917).

Crewe, Lord (Robert Offley Ashburton
Crewe-Milnes, 1st Marquess of Crewe, KG,
PC, JP, 1858-1945)
'Harrow and Flanders', 108
Liberal politician, son of 1st Baron
Houghton, educated Harrow and Trinity
College, Cambridge; married, after his first
wife's death, the younger daughter of Lord
Rosebery. Lord Lieutenant of Ireland, 1892-
5; Lord President of the Council, 1905-8,
and 1915-16; Lord Privy Seal, 1908 and
1912-15; Secretary of State for the Colonies,

1908-10; Secretary of State for India, 1910-15; President, Board of Education, 1916; Chairman, LCC, 1917; HM Ambassador, Paris, 1922-8; Secretary of State for War, 1931. Created Earl of Crewe, 1895, and Marquess, 1911; died without heirs. This poem appeared in the school magazine *The Harrovian* in 1915; Lord Crewe also published *Stray Verses 1889-90*, and a life of Lord Rosebery (1931). His work appears in Cunliffe (ed.), *Poems of the Great War* (1916); Edwards and Booth (eds), *The Fiery Cross: An Anthology* (1915); Holman (ed.) *In The Day of Battle: Poems of the Great War* (1916), and Knight (ed.), *Pro Patria et Rege: Poems on War, its Characteristics and Results* (1915), among other anthologies.

Davies, William Henry (1871-1940)
'A Fleeting Passion', 30; 'The Bird of Paradise', 31; 'The Heap of Rags', 32; 'The Birds Of Steel', 186
'Georgian' poet and author, wrote in his *Who's Who* entry 'became a poet at 34 years of age, been one ever since'. Travelled as a tramp in America for six years from 1893, where he lost a foot in an accident involving a train. Returned to England and continued a vagrant life, publishing his first book of poems in 1907. In 1911 he was granted a Civil List pension. Published more than 20 other books of verse and prose, but is best remembered for his *Autobiography of a Super-tramp* (1907). His complete *Collected Poems* were published in 1943. These poems are from *The Bird of Paradise* (London, Methuen, 1914).

Davison, Edward Lewis
'A Minesweeper Sunk', 245; 'Conscientious Objector', 276
These verses appeared in his *Poems* (London, Bell, 1920).

Day, Jeffery, DSC (1896-1918)
'North Sea', 238; 'On the Wings of the Morning', 250; 'The Call of the Air', 256
Educated at Repton; joined the Royal Naval Air Service on the outbreak of war, and served as a pilot until his death. A brave and daring pilot, he was awarded a posthumous DSC. He was apparently killed in action against six German aircraft on 27 February 1918, although one version holds that he was lost at sea after his aircraft ditched. His *Poems and Rhymes* (London, Sidgwick & Jackson) was published in 1919.

Dearmer, Geoffrey (b. 1893)
'The Turkish Trench Dog', 204
Educated at Westminster and Christ Church College, Oxford; fought at Gallipoli and in France, including on the Somme. Wrote novels and plays as well as verse; Examiner of Plays to the Lord Chamberlain, 1936-58; Editor, BBC *Children's Hour*, 1939-59. His *Poems* (London, Heinemann) were published in 1918. Also wrote words for carols.

Enright, Dennis Joseph (b. 1920)
'A Grand Night', 319
Poet, novelist, critic and essayist. Born in Leamington Spa, educated Leamington College and Downing College, Cambridge; taught in universities in Alexandria, Birmingham, Japan, Berlin, Bangkok and Singapore, 1947-70; Hon. Professor of English, University of Warwick, 1975-80; Co-Editor, *Encounter*, 1970-2; Director of the publishing house Chatto & Windus, 1974-82. Fellow of the Royal Society of Literature, 1961; Cholmondeley Poetry Award, 1974; Queen's Gold Medal for Poetry, 1981. Has published 13 collections of his verse; his *Collected Poems* (Oxford, Oxford University Press) came out in 1981, and a revised and enlarged edition in 1987. Has also written four novels, three children's books, two travel books, and a number of volumes of essays and criticism; edited *The Oxford Book of Contemporary Verse 1945-1980* (1980), and compiled *The Oxford Book of Death* (1983). This poem is from *The Terrible Shears* (London, Chatto & Windus, 1973).

Esdaile, Arundell James Kennedy, CBE (1880-1956)
'On a War-Worker, 1916', 309
Writer, poet, librarian and expert in bibliography. Educated Lancing School and Magdelene College, Cambridge; joined British Museum, 1903, and was Secretary 1926-1940. Lectured in Bibliography at both London and Cambridge Universities; President of the Library Association, 1939-45, among other posts and editorships. Most of his works are in the fields of librarianship and bibliography, but also wrote on the sources of English literature, and published essays as well as poetry. His poems can be found in his collections *Poems and Translations* (1906), *Moments* (1932, in which this poem appeared), *Autolycus' Pack* (1940), and *Wise Men From the West* (1949).

Ewer, William Norman (1885-1976)
'Five Souls', 205
This poem appeared in *Five Souls and Other War Time Verses*, published by *The Herald* in 1917.
Ewer's best known work now is:

How odd
Of God
To choose
The Jews.

To which Cecil Browne replied:

But not so odd
As those who choose
A Jewish God
But spurn the Jews.

Fairfax, Captain James Griffyth (1886-1976)
'The Forest of the Dead', 195
Born in Sydney, educated Winchester and New College, Oxford; called to the Bar, 1912. Served with the Army Service Corps in Mesopotamia and was Mentioned in Despatches four times. Practised law in Australia after the war, returned to England and was Conservative MP for Norwich, 1924-9. Lived the last years of his life in the South of France. First book of poems published 1908; his war poems, including this one, mostly appeared in *Mesopotamia* (London, Murray, 1919); published four other collections, and much journalism.

Flecker, (Herman) James Elroy (1884-1915)
'God Save the King', 53
'Georgian' poet. Educated at Uppingham and Trinity College, Oxford; joined Consular Service and was posted to Constantinople (Istanbul) and then Beirut, but his health broke and he died of consumption in Switzerland. Four collections published in his lifetime, including *The Golden Journey to Samarkand*; otherwise best remembered for his verse play *Hassan* (1922). *The Collected Poems of James Elroy Flecker*, edited and with an introduction by J.C. Squire (London, Martin Secker), was first published in 1916.

Flint, Frank Stewart (1885-1960)
'Hats', 266
Imagist poet. Served in the Army for 11 months of the Great War, based in England. His collection *Otherworld: Cadences* was published by Monro's (qv) Poetry Bookshop in 1920, and contained this poem.

Foulis, Hugh (*see* Munro, Neil)

Frankau, Captain Gilbert (1884-1952)
'Headquarters', 79; 'Eyes in the Air', 236
Educated at Eton, started writing in 1910, travelled round the world, 1912-14. Commissioned into East Surrey Regiment 1914, transferred to Royal Field Artillery, fought at Loos, Ypres, on the Somme and in Italy; invalided from the service, February 1918. Re-commissioned into the RAF Volunteer Reserve, August 1939, promoted Squadron Leader, invalided from the service February 1941. Author of many books — verse, novels and non-fiction. Fellow of the Royal Society of Literature. 'Headquarters' appeared in his collection *City of Fear* (London, Chatto & Windus, 1917); 'Eyes in the Air' in *The Judgement of Valhalla* (Chatto, 1918).

Frost, Robert Lee (1875-1963)
'A Soldier', 154
American (and, supremely, New England) poet, born in San Franscisco of a New England father and Scots mother. Family moved to New England, 1885, and Frost was educated at Dartmouth College and Harvard University, leaving the latter first to teach English, 1905-11, and then psychology, 1912, and to write poetry. Lived and farmed in England, 1912-15, where he became a friend of Edward Thomas (qv) and encouraged him to take up writing poetry; Frost also published his first two collections of poetry in England. Returned to New England to farm and write verse, supporting himself by teaching; Professor of English, Amherst College, 1916-1920 and 1923-5. Poet in Residence, University of Michigan, 1920-3; latterly Fellow in Humanities, Dartmouth College. Won Pulitzer Prizes for his poetry 1924, 1931, 1937, 1943. Was, and remains, one of the most popular American poets; ten volumes of his poetry were collected in 1949, and his last volume of lyrics, *In The Clearing*, appeared in 1962. This poem first appeared his collection *West Running Brook*, published in America in 1929; see *The Poetry of Robert Frost* (London, Jonathan Cape, 1971).

Galsworthy, John, OM (1867-1933)
'Youth's Own', 116
Novelist and playwright, educated at Harrow and New College, Oxford. Called to

335

the Bar, 1890, but decided instead to devote his life to literature. Galsworthy's reputation rests upon his long series of novels known collectively as *The Forsyte Saga*, but he also wrote plays, often successful in their day, and poetry. Apart from *The Forsyte Saga*, his best-known novels include *The Island of Pharisees*, *The Country House*, *Fraternity* and *The Patrician*; his best-known plays include *The Silver Box, Strife, Justice, The Skin Game* and *Loyalties*. He was awarded the Nobel Prize for Literature in 1932. Also wrote verse, essays, short stories, and a wartime commentary. His *Collected Poems* was published, after his death, in 1934.

Garstin, Crosbie (1887-1930)
'Chemin Des Dames', 180
Born in England and educated there and in Germany; worked in USA and Canada, returning on outbreak of war to join 1st King Edward's Horse. Commissioned in the field, 1915. This poem first appeared in *Punch*, 1917, and was written in the trenches while the author was waiting to go into action. After the war Garstin published novels and sea stories.

Garston, Lieutenant Edward John Langford (b. 1893)
'To the Rats', 120
Served in France with the 12th Battalion, Middlesex Regiment. Poem quoted in Kyle (ed.), *Soldier Poets: Songs of the Fighting Men* (1916).

Gibson, Wilfrid Wilson (1878-1962)
'Geraniums', 33; 'Troopship: mid-Atlantic', 72; 'Ambulance Train' 127; 'The Question' 179; 'Retreat', 183; 'A Lament', 312
'Georgian' poet and friend of Rupert Brooke (qv) (who called him 'Wibson'); joint beneficiary of Brooke's will, with Abercrombie (qv) and Walter de la Mare. Published a number of books of verse and some plays from 1905; these poems appear in his *Collected Poems 1905-1925* (London, Macmillan), published in 1926. Served in the Army in the ranks from 1914, although was not at the Front for any length of time. The rest of his life was devoted to his poetry, of which there is much.

Gilbert, Bernard (b. 1882)
'If The War Keeps On', 174
Poem from *Gone to the War and other poems in*

the Lincolnshire Dialect (Lincoln, Ruddock, 1915); his other collections are *War Workers, and other verses* (London, Erskine Macdonald, 1916); *Rebel Verses* (Oxford, Blackwell, 1918).

Graves, Charles Larcom (1856-1944)
'The Flapper', 293; 'Back to the Land', 294
Born the fourth son of the Bishop of Limerick, educated Marlborough College and Christ Church College, Oxford. Assistant Editor, *Spectator*, 1899-1917; member of the *Punch* staff, 1902-36; Assistant Editor, *Punch*, 1928-36. Published many books and collections, including humorous novels, verse and light verse, books on music, a translation (with Kipling [qv]) of Book V of Horace's *Odes*, and a two-volume life of Sir Hubert Parry. These poems appeared in *Punch*, 1917; two of his collections, *War's Surprises and Other Verses* (London, Sidgwick & Jackson, 1917) and *Lauds and Libels* (Sidgwick, 1918) also contain poetry about the Great War. His son, Captain Sir Cecil Graves, KCMG, MC, fought in the Great War, and was Joint Director-General of the BBC, 1942-3.

Grieve, Christopher Murray, JP
(pseudonym, Hugh McDiarmid, 1892-1980)
'Another Epitaph on an Army of Mercenaries', 304
Author and journalist, born in Dumfriesshire, educated Langholm Academy and Edinburgh University. Was at once a Communist, a founder and leader of the Scottish Nationalist movement, founder of the Scottish Centre of P.E.N., editor of the quarterly *Voice of Scotland*, and a Justice of the Peace for Angus; President of the Poetry Society, 1976, Professor of Literature to the Royal Scottish Academy, 1974, among other honours. This poem first appeared in his *Second Hymn to Lenin and Other Poems* (1935). Wrote, besides his verse and much journalism, novels, essays, studies of writers, and autobiography, as well as topographical, historical and literary works on Scotland. Much of his work is in Scots. Listed his recreation as 'anglophobia'. *Collected Poems* published 1962; this poem can be found in *Hugh McDiarmid: Selected Poems*, edited with an introduction by David Craig (London, Penguin, 1970). See also *The Complete Poems of Hugh McDiarmid* (London, Martin Brian & O'Keeffe, 1977).

Gurney, Ivor Bertie (1890-1937)
'Crucifix Corner', 128; 'I Saw French Once',
134
Poet and composer, born and raised in
Gloucestershire, friend of Edward (qv) and
Helen Thomas, Herbert Howells, Walter de
la Mare, J.C. Squire (qv), among others. In
1911 gained a scholarship to the Royal
College of Music, which he attended before
and after the war. There under the tutelage
of Sir Hubert Parry, Sir Charles Stanford
and, later, (Sir) Ralph Vaughan Williams, he
distinguished himself, especially for his song
settings. He volunteered unsuccessfully on
declaration of war, but in February 1915
succeeded in enlisting in the 2/5th Battalion,
the Gloucestershire Regiment, and served in
France as a private from 1916 to September
1917. He was wounded in the arm in April
1917 and spent six weeks in hospital at
Rouen, and in June transferred to the
Machine Gun Corps, although still attached
to the 2/5th Glosters. In September he was
gassed at St Julien, in the Ypres sector, and
spent the rest of the war either in hospital or
training in Britain. He suffered a severe
breakdown in June 1918, and in October was
discharged from the Army with 'deferred
shell-shock'. For four years Gurney worked
at various jobs and continued his studies in
music, but his war experiences contributed
to the final breakdown of the balance of his
mind, and the rest of his life from 1922 was
spent in a mental asylum, where he died on
Boxing Day 1937. Even during his
confinement he continued writing music
and verse, and was a prolific letter-writer,
until 1933, when his condition worsened
considerably. Among his most famous works
are song-cycles of Edward Thomas's *Lights
Out*, five of Rupert Brooke's (qv) poems, and
two of Housman's (qv) works, *Ludlow and
Teme* and *The Western Playland*, and he also
set traditional English songs, as well as
poems by, among others, Masefield, Yeats,
Hardy, Belloc and himself. His verse has
taken longer to achieve recognition than his
music, and it is true that much of his very
large output is flawed by the tragic mental
state which overtook him, but his place as
Great War poet has now come to be
recognised. His poetry collections are *Severn
and Somme* (London, Sidgwick & Jackson,
1917) and *War's Embers* (Sidgwick, 1919);
another collection, *Rewards of Wonder*, was
rejected by Sidgwick in the same year. *Poems
by Ivor Gurney*, edited and with a memoir by
Edmund Blunden (qv), London, Hutchinson,
1954; *Poems of Ivor Gurney* with an
Introduction by Edmund Blunden, selected
and with a Bibliographical Note by Leonard
Clark, London, Chatto & Windus, 1973;
Collected Poems of Ivor Gurney, chosen, edited
and with an introduction by P.J. Kavanagh,
Oxford, Oxford University Press, 1982. See
also *The Ordeal of Ivor Gurney* by Michael
Hurd, Oxford, OUP, 1978.

**Halliday, Private (later Lieutenant)
Wilfrid Joseph**
'The Grave', 59
Served in the West Yorkshire Regiment.
This poem appeared in Kyle (ed.), *Soldier
Poets: Songs of the Fighting Men* (1916);
Halliday also published a collection, *Refining
Fires* (London, Erskine Macdonald, 1917).

Head, Sir Henry (1861-1940)
'Destroyers', 233
Educated at Charterhouse, University of
Halle-am-See, Trinity College, Cambridge,
German University of Prague; became a
distinguished physician, knighted 1927. This
poem is from his *Destroyers, and other Verses*
(London, Milford, 1919); the rest of his
published work was in the field of medicine.

Herbert, Sir Alan Patrick (1890-1971)
'The German Graves', 122; 'The Cookers',
123; 'Dead-Mule Tree', 124; Untitled
(attrib.), 136; 'After the Battle', 137
Educated Winchester and New College,
Oxford, taking a First in Jurisprudence.
Served with the Hawke Battalion, Royal
Naval Division, 1914-17, first at Gallipoli
(Mentioned in Despatches), and later in
France. Wounded, 1917, and invalided from
the Service. Called to the Bar, 1918, but
never practised. Had started writing for
Punch, 1910, and many of his poems
appeared there; in 1924 joined the
magazine's staff. Independent MP for
Oxford University, 1935-50; knighted 1945.
Best remembered for his many books —
especially the *Misleading Cases* series — and
his musicals, as well as verse, essays and
novels. Was all his life the champion of
common sense in the law and in
bureaucracy, and did much to reduce the
spurious mystique of both; he was also an
early crusader for royalties to be paid to
authors on borrowings from public libraries.

His war verse is principally found in collections like *Half-Hours at Helles* (Oxford, Blackwell, 1916) and *The Bomber Gypsy* (London, Methuen, 1919); his novel *The Secret Battle* detailed his Great War experiences. All the poems printed here were published in *Punch*, except 'Untitled', which is attributed to Herbert in Lyn Macdonald's *Somme* (London, Michael Joseph, 1983)

Hodgkinson, T.
'The Sand of Palestine', 200
This poem appeared in *Punch*, 1918.

Hodgson, A.B.L.
'In Memoriam', 308
This poem appeared in the *New Witness*, 1 February 1917.

Hodgson, Ralph (1871-1962)
Extract from 'The Bull', 34
'Georgian' poet, won the Polignac Prize in 1914. Lecturer in English Studies, Imperial University, Sendai, Japan, from 1924-1938; Order of the Rising Sun, 1938, Queen's Gold Medal for Poetry, 1954. Collections include *Flying Fame*, (London, Poetry Bookshop, 1914), *Last Blackbird and Other Lines* (London Allen & Unwin, 1907), *Poems* (which includes 'The Bull'; London, Macmillan, 1917), *The Skylark and Other Poems* (London, Macmillan, 1958). His *Collected Poems* was also published by Macmillan in 1961.

Hopwood, Captain (later Admiral) Ronald Arthur, CB, RN (1868-1949)
'The Mystery Ships', 241
Educated Cheam School, specialised in Gunnery in the Navy. This poem is from *Punch*, 6 March 1918; also wrote three books, all with the Navy as their theme.

Housman, Alfred Edward (1859-1936)
'Epitaph on an Army of Mercenaries', 304
Poet and classical scholar. Born in Worcestershire, educated at Bromsgrove School and St John's College, Oxford, where he obtained a First in Classical Mods but not, to his contemporaries' surprise, in Greats. Worked for a time as a Higher Division Clerk in the Patent Office, then Professor of Latin, University College, London, 1892-1911, and, from 1911 to the end of his life, Professor of Latin at Cambridge University. Published translations of five books of Manilius, and edited Juvenal and Lucan; also

wrote many papers for philological and classical journals. Despite his opting for Latin, was as great a master of Greek. His chief fame rests on his two collections of poems, *The Shropshire Lad* (New York, Henry Holt Inc., 1896) and *Last Poems* (New York, Holt, 1922) (in which this poem appeared); his brother Laurence (prolific writer and critic, author of *Victoria Regina*, 1865-1959) published forty-eight more of A.E. Housman's poems under the title *More Poems* (1936). A.E. Housman's *Collected Poems* was first published in 1939 (London, Cape).

Hughes, Ted, OBE (b. 1930)
'Six Young Men', 321
Poet Laureate since December 1984. Educated at Pembroke College, Cambridge; was married, until her death in 1963, to the poet and writer Sylvia Plath. Awards include John Simon Guggenheim Fellow. 1959-60; Somerset Maugham Award, 1960; Hawthornden Prize, 1961; Queen's Gold Medal for Poetry, 1974. A prolific author, has published many books of poetry, including *The Hawk in the Rain* (in which this poem appears; London, Faber, 1957), *Lupercal* (1960), *Wodwo* (1967), *Crow* (1970), *Moortown* (1979), *River* (1983) etc. (all Faber); *Selected Poems 1957-81* (Faber) published in 1982. Also many books of verse for children, and edited works by, among others, Keith Douglas, Emily Dickinson, Sylvia Plath, Shakespeare; adapted Seneca's *Oedipus*; edited (with Seamus Heaney) *The Rattle Bag* (Faber, 1982); published a tribute to Henry Williamson (1979). Succeeded Sir John Betjeman, CBE (1906-84) as Poet Laureate.

Hunt, Sergeant S.S. (pseudonym, Bernard Moore)
'War', 286
Served in the Middlesex Regiment. This poem appeared in the *New Witness*, 17 June 1915; also published *A Cornish Haul by Bernard Moore* (London, Stockwell, 1917), *A Cornish Chorus by Bernard Moore* (1919), and *A Cornish Collection* (1933).

Hussey, Dyneley (1893-1972)
'The Kingfisher', 179
Educated King's School, Canterbury, Christ Church College, Oxford; commissioned into the Lancashire Fusiliers, 1914, and served with them until 1917; Assistant to the Assistant Secretary, Finance, Admiralty,

1917-22. Music critic: of *The Times*, 1923-46; of *Saturday Review, Week-End Review* and *Spectator*, successively, 1924-46; of the *Listener*, 1946-60. Held an administrative post at the Admiralty, 1939-45. Published books on Mozart (1928), Verdi (1940, 1963 revised), and *Some Composers of Opera* (1952); this poem appeared in his collection *Fleur de Lys: Poems of 1915* (London, Erskine Macdonald, 1916).

Hutcheon, Lieutenant Lessel
'The Flight to Flanders', 257
Served as a Lieutenant in the Royal Flying Corps. This poem appeared in Osborn (ed.), *The Muse in Arms* (1917).

I.C.
'Battle of the Falkland Isles', 228
This poem was published in Osborn (ed.), *The Muse in Arms* (1917).

Jacob, Violet (Mrs Arthur Jacob, d. 1947)
'Jock, to the First Army', 285
Born Violet Kennedy-Erskine, in Scotland, married Major Arthur Jacob of the 20th Hussars. Between 1910 and 1944 published thirteen books, mostly based on Scottish folk history: some fiction, some for children, and some being collections of songs and poetry, as well as books of her own verse. This poem is from *The Scottish Poems of Violet Jacob* (Edinburgh, Oliver & Boyd, 1944).

Johnstone, Philip
'High Wood', 327
This poem was published in *The Nation*, 16 February 1918. Re-published in Guy Chapman (OBE, MC, 1889-1972) (ed.), *Vain Glory* (London, Cassell, 1937), and in Brian Gardner (ed.) *Up the Line to Death: The War Poets 1914-18* (1964, many subsequent printings).

Kipling, (Joseph) Rudyard (1865-1936)
'For All We Have and Are', 59; 'A Drifter Off Tarentum', 245
Born in Bombay, son of John Lockwood Kipling (who illustrated some of Rudyard's books), and a relative of Stanley Baldwin and Sir Edward Burne-Jones, educated at the Imperial Services College (now Haileybury) in England. Journalist in India, 1882 to 1889; also travelled in China, Japan, Africa, Australasia and America, where he lived for a time. Nobel Prize for Literature, 1907; Gold

Medal of Royal Society of Literature, 1926; refused post of Poet Laureate three times. Champion of the ordinary serviceman, of whatever colour and creed, and also (though not uncritically) of the imperial ideal. Wrote his bitter 'Epitaphs of the War' (of which 'A Drifter Off Tarentum' is one) after his only son was killed in 1915; contributed for years to cost of 'Last Post' to be sounded each night at Menin Gate Memorial, Ypres. Apart from his verse, is best remembered for his short stories, many set in India; the two *Jungle Books* and his *Just-So Stories* for children; and his novel *Kim*; his poem *If* has probably been learned by more schoolchildren than any other single verse. His reputation declined after his death, as his verse fell out of fashion, but has been to a great extent restored by the efforts of, among others, T.S. Eliot. *Rudyard Kipling's Verse: Definitive Edition* (London, Hodder & Stoughton, 1940); *A Choice of Kipling's Verse*, made by T.S. Eliot with an essay on Rudyard Kipling (London, Faber, 1941).

'Klaxon' (pseudonym of Commander John Graham Bower, DSO, RN, 1886-1940)
'Destroyers', 235; 'Submarines', 236
Son of the Colonial Secretary for Mauritius, served in the Navy throughout the Great War (DSO, Mentioned in Despatches). These poems are from *On Patrol* (Edinburgh and London, Blackwood, 1918); also wrote *Songs of the Submarine* (1917) and *H.M.S.* (1918).

Larkin, Philip Arthur, CBE
(1922-1985)
'MCMXIV', 317
Poet and novelist, critic, and jazz correspondent of the *Daily Telegraph* 1961-71. Educated at King Henry VIII School, Coventry and St John's College, Oxford; held posts in different university libraries — latterly University of Hull — from 1943 to his death. Visiting Fellow, All Souls College, Oxford, 1970-1; Member, Literature Panel of the Arts Council, 1980-2; Chairman, Board of Management, Poetry Book Society from 1981; Fellow of the Royal Society of Literature and Companion of Literature 1978; awarded Queen's Gold Medal for Poetry, 1965, among other honours. His verse collections are: *The North Ship* (1945), *The Less Deceived* (1955), *The Whitsun Weddings* (1964, in which this poem

appeared), and *High Windows* (1974) (all London, Faber); he also edited *The Oxford Book of Twentieth Century English Verse* (1973), and published two novels and two books of essays. Larkin was the model for Jim Dixon in Kingsley Amis's novel *Lucky Jim* (1954), he and Amis having both read English at St John's.

Lawrence, David Herbert (1885-1930)
'Service of All The Dead', 34
'Georgian' poet. Best remembered as one of the great English novelists of this century, Lawrence was born the son of a miner, became a schoolmaster, and then a professional writer. Lived most of his life abroad, but was in England during the Great War. Novels include *Sons and Lovers* (1913), *The Rainbow* (1915), *Women in Love* (1920), *The Plumed Serpent* (1926) and *Lady Chatterley's Lover* (1928 expurgated, 1960 first full uncut British edition), and he also wrote many short stories. Published several volumes of verse, his *Collected Poems* first appearing in 1928 (London, Martin Secker), and was published in *Georgian Poetry*; a collected edition of his poems appeared in 1928. This poem first appeared in the *New Statesman*, 15 November 1913, and then in *Georgian Poetry 1913-15* (London, The Poetry Bookshop, 1915). Lawrence altered the poem later, and changed the title to 'Giorno dei Morti'.

Lee, Joseph Johnston (1876-1954)
'German Prisoners', 269
Author and artist. Born in Dundee, studied art at Heatherley's and the Slade. Served in the war as a private, lance-corporal, corporal and sergeant in the Black Watch, and as a lieutenant in the King's Royal Rifle Corps (60th Rifles). Captured later in the war and imprisoned in Germany, the experience of which is detailed in his *Captive at Carlsruhe* (1920). Wrote four other books, one of which is on Fra Lippo Lippi, and two of which are collections of verse — *Ballads of Battle* (London, Murray, 1916), and *Work-a-Day Warriors* (Murray, 1917), from which this poem is taken.

Macaulay, Dame Rose, DBE (1881-1958)
'Many Sisters to Many Brothers', 67
Descendant of the historian, Thomas Babington (Lord) Macaulay, wrote novels, verse, travel books, studies in literature and biography, essays, articles, and two books of poetry (1914, 1919); this poem appeared in her *Poems of Today* (London, Sidgwick & Jackson, 1919). Probably best-known for her novel *The Towers of Trebizond* (1956); others works include *Potterism* (1920), *Told by an Idiot* (1923), *Orphan Island* (1924), *Going Abroad* (1934), *The World My Wilderness*, (1950) and a study of Milton (1933).

MacColl, Dugald Sutherland (1859-1948)
'The Miners' Response', 290
Born in Glasgow, educated Glasgow Academy, University College School and College, London, Lincoln College, Oxford, where he won the Newdigate Prize for Poetry. Successively art critic of the *Spectator*, *Saturday Review* and *Week-End Review*; editor of the *Architectural Review* and of *Artwork*; Lecturer on the History of Art at University College, London. Then Keeper of the Tate Gallery, 1906-11; Keeper of the Wallace Collection 1911-24; Trustee of the Tate Gallery, 1917-27; Member of the Royal Fine Arts Commission, 1925-9. Published eight books, mostly on art and including a life of P. Wilson Steer; also wrote memoirs, and on English verse, prose and speech. This poem appeared in his collection *'Bull' and other War Verses* (London, Constable, 1919); his *Poems* appeared in 1940.

McDiarmid, Hugh (see Grieve, C.M.)

MacGill, Patrick (b. 1890)
'Matey', 77; 'The Star-Shell', 85; 'Marching', 86
Born in Donegal, joined editorial staff of *Daily Express*, 1911, enlisted at the outbreak of war, and became a sergeant in the London Irish Rifles; wounded at Loos, 1915. These three poems appear in his *Soldier Songs* (London, Herbert Jenkins). Between the ages of 12 and 19 worked as 'farm-servant, byre-man, drainer, potato-digger, surface-man, navvy etc'; worked on ancient manuscripts in Chapter Library, Windsor Castle, 1912-14; published many books, including verse, novels and plays.

McGough, Roger (b. 1937)
'A Square Dance', 318
'Liverpool' poet. Educated St Mary's College, Crosby, Liverpool, and the University of

Hull; Fellow of Poetry, University of Loughborough, 1973-5. Has published thirteen collections of his poetry from 1961-83; contributed to *The Oxford Book of Twentieth Century English Verse; Penguin Modern Poets* No. 10; *Mersey Sound*; and edited *Strictly Private* (1981).

Mackay, Helen
'Train' 269
This poem appeared in her collection *London, One November* (London, Andrew Melrose, 1915).

Mackintosh, Ewart Alan (1893-1917)
'Farewell', 76; 'Cha Till Maccruimein', 284
A collection, *War The Liberator*, in which these poems appear, was published in 1918 (London, John Lane).

Manning, Frederic (1882-1935)
'The Face (Guillemont)', 99; 'The Trenches', 99
Born and educated in Australia, sent to England and worked as a writer and critic; first book of poems published 1907. His remarkable essays *Scenes and Portraits* appeared in 1909, two more verse collections in 1910 and 1917, and a life of Sir William White in 1923. Enlisted, 1914, in the King's Shropshire Light Infantry, refused a commission, and served with 7th Battalion from the Somme (July 1916) to the end of the war. His lightly fictionalised war memoir *The Middle Parts of Fortune*, probably the best book about ordinary soldiers in the Great War, was published anonymously in 1929 in an edition limited to 520 copies; a year later an expurgated edition went on general sale under the title *Her Privates We* by 'Private 19022'. Manning's name did not appear on the book until 1943, eight years after his death, and the unexpurgated book did not go on general sale until 1977. T.E. Lawrence, who admired the book greatly, recognised its authorship as being the same as that of *Scenes of Portraits.*

Marchbank, Miss Isobel
'Sinn Fein', 277
This poem appeared in *Punch* in 1918.

Menzies, George Kenneth, CBE (1869-1954)
'The General', 291
Born in Edinburgh, educated at St Andrews

University and Balliol College, Oxford. Worked as a Private Secretary in academic and political posts, 1893-1908; Assistant Secretary to the Royal Society of Arts 1908-17, Secretary, 1917-35. Contributed to *Punch* (where this poem appeared in 1917) for 20 years; his only other published work was *The Story of the Royal Society of Arts* (1935).

'M.C.D.H.' (*see* Strachey, Charles)

Milne, Alan Alexander (1882-1956)
'Gold Braid', 131; 'From a Full Heart', 315
Journalist and writer, educated Westminster and Trinity College, Cambridge, where he edited *Granta*. Assistant editor of *Punch*, 1906-14; commissioned into Royal Warwickshire Regiment, February 1915, and served in France (including on the Somme) until 1919. As well as journalism, wrote novels and plays, including adaptations for the stage of Grahame's *Toad of Toad Hall* and Saki's (qv) only novel, *The Unbearable Bassington* — Milne had championed Saki in his *Punch* days. Is best remembered, if not idolised, for his collections of verse for children — *When We Were Very Young* (1924) and *Now We Are Six* (1927) — and especially for *Winnie-the-Pooh* (1926) and *The House at Pooh Corner* (1928). Most of his war verse is to be found in *The Sunny Side* (London, Methuen, 1922); these two poems were published in *Punch*, 1917.

Mitchell, Miss G.M.
'The Nurse', 283
This poem was published in *Poems from Punch, 1909-1920* (London, Macmillan, 1922).

Moberley, Lucy Gertrude (b. 1860)
'Commandeered', 171
Poem from *Blue Cross Fund: A Book of Poems for the Blue Cross Fund (to help horses in war time)* (London, Jarrold, 1917); her work is also quoted in, among others, Donald (ed.), *A Garland of Patriotism: An Anthology* (1917).

Monro, Harold (1879-1932)
'Carrion', 152. See also p. 147, 'Killed in Action', and footnote.
Poet and writer, publisher, editor and, as proprietor of the Poetry Bookshop (1913), bookseller; founder (1912) of the *Poetry Review*, which he ran till his death. Born in Brussels, educated Radley and Caius College, Cambridge. Served in a Royal Artillery anti-

aircraft battery, and later in the War Office, during the Great War. Published all of the *Georgian Poetry* anthologies edited by (Sir) Edward Marsh, was a friend of Owen and Gibson (qqv), among many others, and all his life encouraged young poets – including Rosenberg (qv) – often publishing their work. Wrote a number of war poems, and produced several books of his own verse; his *Collected Poems* (London, Cobden Sanderson) was published in 1933 with an introduction by T.S. Eliot. Also wrote criticism and edited an anthology of twentieth-century verse.

Moore, Bernard (*see* Hunt, Sergeant S.S.)

Munro, Hector Hugh (*see* Saki)

Munro, Neil (pseudonym, Hugh Foulis, 1864–1930)
'Fingal's Weeping'. 182; 'Macleod's Lament', 305
Writer and journalist, born in Inveraray. Wrote a number of books, including novels, most with Scottish or Celtic themes. These two poems are from his collection *Northern Numbers* (London, T.N. Foulis).

Nankivell, Captain Austin Threlfall, RN
'Off Coronel', 231
This poem appeared in Trotter (ed.), *Valour and Vision: Poems of the War, 1914-1918* (1920). Nankivell's work also appears in Clarke (ed.), *A Treasury of War Poetry: British and American Poems of the World War, 1914-1919* (1919).

Newbolt, Sir Henry (1862-1938)
'Vitaï Lampada', 22
Barrister, author and poet, best known for his sea verse, which includes 'Drake's Drum' and 'Admirals All'. Wrote *Naval History of the War, 1914-18* (1920). Much anthologised, especially in the earlier part of this century. This verse is from *Poems: New and Old* (London, Murray. 1912).

Nichols, Robert Malise Bowyer (1893-1944)
'Comrades: An Episode', 105
'Georgian' poet, close friend of Brooke and Sassoon (qqv). Educated Winchester and Trinity College, Oxford. Commissioned into the Royal Field Artillery, October 1914, served on Western Front (including Somme

battle) until August 1916, when he was invalided home with shell-shock. Joined the British Mission (Ministry of Information) to the United States, 1918. Professor of English Literature, Imperial University, Tokyo, 1921-24. Poetry collections are *Invocation* (1915), *Ardours and Endurances*, from which this poem is taken (London, Chatto & Windus, 1917), and *Aurelia* (1920); otherwise wrote, among other things, plays and a novelette.

Noyes, Alfred (1880-1958)
'Kilmeny', 232; 'The Search-Lights', 234; 'A Victory Dance', 306
Prolific English poet. Educated Exeter College, Oxford; temporarily attached to Foreign Office, 1916-1918; Professorship of Modern English Literature on the Murray Foundation, Princeton University, 1914-1923. Verse much concerned with the sea and with 'faërie' (with the latter of which his war poems are somewhat at variance); otherwise wrote biography, drama, short stories, essays, articles, criticism, lyrics, a novel, and two volumes of autobiography. Some of his verse was set to music by Coleridge-Taylor and Elgar; several volumes of his *Collected Poems* were published from 1910, culminating with a single definitive *Collected Poems* published in 1950 (London, Methuen). Noyes was also a moralist and would-be censor, and was involved in some of the attempts to ban Joyce's *Ulysses*, which did not appear freely in Britain until 1937.

'Observer, RFC' (*see* Alchin, Gordon)

Owen, Everard
'Three Hills', 181
This poem appeared in his *Three Hills and other Poems* (London, Sidgwick & Jackson, 1916).

Owen, Wilfred (1893-1918)
'It Was a Navy Boy', 55; 'The Show', 83; 'A Terre', 111; 'Disabled', 142; 'Futility', 144; 'Conscious', 144; 'Apologia Pro Poemate Meo', 151; 'Spring Offensive', 158; 'Miners', 288; 'The Send-Off', 296
Born in Oswestry, educated at Birkenhead Institute and University of London, worked as a clerk to a vicar in Oxfordshire and from 1913-1915 was a private tutor near Bordeaux. Enlisted in the Artists' Rifles, 1915, and was commissioned into the

Manchester Regiment, 1916. Served on the Western Front, January to June 1917, when he was invalided home and sent to Craiglockhart psychiatric hospital, near Edinburgh. There met Sassoon (qv), who had a considerable effect upon him and his work, and who introduced him to Nichols (qv) and Graves. In November rejoined a reserve battalion of the Manchesters, and in September 1918 returned to the front and his old battalion. Awarded the Military Cross for gallantry in October, and on 4 November — one week before the Armistice — was killed by machine-gun fire while his company was crossing the Sambre Canal. Never completed the collection of poems he had planned; *Poems* by Wilfred Owen, with an introduction by Siegfried Sassoon (qv) appeared in 1920 (London, Chatto & Windus). A new edition, with notices of his (Owen's) life and work by Edmund Blunden (qv) was first published in 1931 (London, Chatto); *The Collected Poems of Wilfred Owen* edited with an Introduction and Notes by C. Day Lewis, with a Memoir by Edmund Blunden, was published in 1963 (London, Chatto); *War Poems and Others*, edited by Dominic Hibberd, was published in 1973 (London, Chatto). The most authoritative collection is *The Poems of Wilfred Owen*, edited by Jon Stallworthy (London, Hogarth Press, 1985), in which 'It Was a Navy Boy' was printed for the first time. See also Owen, Harold (Wilfred's brother), *Journey From Obscurity* (3 vols.; abridged single volume, ed. H.M. Gornall, London, Oxford University Press, 1968); Stallworthy, Jon, *Wilfred Owen: A Biography* (London, Oxford University Press and Chatto & Windus, 1974).

Oxenham, John William Arthur Dunkersly (1852–1941)
'The Burdened Ass', 167; 'A Telephone Message', 272; 'Where Are You Sleeping To-Night, My Lad?', 290
Prolific writer, principally of fiction; educated Old Trafford School, Victoria University, Manchester; went into business and lived for some years in France and the United States, and travelled over Canada and most of Europe. Returned to England, gave up business and took to writing, eventually publishing more than 50 books between 1898 and his death. A number of these are collections of verse; his Great War poetry is to be found in *All's Well* (1916), *The King's*

High Way (1916), *The Vision Splendid* (1917), *The Fiery Cross* (1917), *Hearts Courageous* (1918), and *All Clear!* (1919) (all London, Methuen). His daughter, Elsie Jeanette Oxenham, was an equally successful (more than 80 books) writer of fiction for girls, principally about schools in the Angela Brazil manner.

Pain, Barry (d. 1928)
'The Army of the Dead', 74
Educated at Sedbergh and Corpus Christi College, Cambridge. Served as a Chief Petty Officer in the Royal Naval Volunteer Reserve 1915–16, then on London Appeal Tribunal. This poem appeared in the *Westminster Gazette* in 1914. His poetry was also published in a number of other war anthologies issued between 1914 and 1920. He published much else — poetry, short stories, novels, non-fiction — between 1891 and 1921, and while at Cambridge was one of the best-known contributors to *Granta*.

Pocock, Guy Noel (1880–1955)
'Years Ahead', 244
Educated Highgate School and St John's College, Cambridge. Taught for 10 years at Cheltenham College, then at Royal Naval College, Dartmouth, specialising in English. Gave up teaching for writing, editing and lecturing, 1923; Cambridge University Extra-Mural lecturer, 1932; joined BBC 1934, retired 1940, and rejoined staff at Cheltenham. Wrote novels, essays and many books for the teaching of English; also produced many anthologies, including, with Sir Arthur Quiller-Couch, *The King's Treasury of Literature*. This poem appeared in Pocock, G.N. (ed.), *Modern Poetry* (London, Dent, 1920).

'Pontiff'
'The Rime of the Gentle Pacifist', 275
This poem was published in the *New Witness*, 16 December 1915.

Pope, Miss Jessie (later Mrs Babington Lenton, d. 1941)
'Profiteers', 278
Writer of light verse and fiction, and of many books for children. Born in Leicester, educated there and at North London Collegiate School; contributed more than 200 poems and articles to *Punch*; wrote humorous fiction, verse and articles for

leading magazines, newspapers and illustrated weeklies; edited *The Ragged Trousered Philanthropists*. Her three volumes of war poetry were *War Poems* (London, Grant Richards, 1915 — from which this poem was taken), *More War Poems* (Grant Richards, 1915), and *Simple Rhymes for Stirring Times* (London, Pearson, 1916). Owen's (qv) 'Dulce et Decorum Est', of which the drafts are headed either 'To Jessie Pope etc.' or 'To a certain Poetess', includes the lines:

… My friend, you would not tell with such
high zest
To children ardent for some desperate glory
The old lie: Dulce et decorum est
Pro patria mori.

The Latin tag, from Horace's *Odes*, means 'It is sweet and seemly to die for one's country', an attitude which Jessie Pope had promulgated in her verse.

Postgate, Margaret Isabel (Dame Margaret Isabel Postgate Cole, DBE, 1893-1980)
'The Veteran', 139
Author and lecturer. Born Cambridge, daughter of the Professor of Latin at University of Liverpool, educated Roedean and Girton College, Cambridge (where she took a First in Classics). Wrote many articles and books, notably on Fabian and socialist topics, and edited Beatrice Webb's diaries. OBE 1965, DBE 1970; also wrote many detective novels, and some political works, with her husband, G.D.H. Cole, and held a number of senior educational and administrative posts. Member of Fabian Society, and friend of Beatrice and Sidney Webb; *Margaret Postgate's Poems*, in which this verse appeared, published 1918 (London, Allen & Unwin).

Pound, Ezra Loomis (1885-1972)
'The Profiteer', 278
Prolific American poet, critic and composer. Born in Idaho, educated University of Pennysylvania and Hamilton College; a gifted linguist, moved to Europe, 1908, and eventually settled in London. Founded, with Richard Aldington and Hilda Doolittle ('H.D.'), the Imagist school of poetry; was a friend, and championed the work, of *avant-garde* writers like James Joyce, T.S. Eliot and D.B. Wyndham Lewis; also a friend of Robert Frost (qv) and Hemingway, among many others. First volume of poems, *A Lume*

Spento, published 1908; London Editor, *The Little Review*, 1917-19; formerly editor of *The Exile*; contributed articles and criticism to many papers and magazines. Left England, 1920, for Paris and then Rapallo, and worked for a time as W.B. Yeats's secretary; began his long poem, the 'Cantos', of which Nos. 1-109 appeared between 1925 and 1959. Apart from his verse, is best remembered for his translations, literary essays, and letters, and also for his influence upon European writers in the first 40 years of this century, to many of whom he gave unstinting guidance and encouragement. During the 1930s Pound became increasingly taken up with economic and social theories, and his views led him into anti-Semitism and some support for Mussolini. During the Second War he broadcast on Rome Radio even after America's entry into the war in 1942. In 1945 he was charged with treason, but was found unfit to plead and put in a mental institution. He was released in 1961 and returned to Italy, where he died. Wrote many books and two operas; was also an artist. Pound's influence on modern poetry was profound, although there is no agreement among critics as to the merits of his own contribution. These lines are from 'Canto XXXVIII' in *The Cantos of Ezra Pound* (London, Faber, 1954).

Powell, Sidney Walter (1878-1952)
'Gallipoli' (extracts), 209
Born in London, educated at Aldenham School, brought up in South Africa from his mid-teens. Entered the Natal Civil Service, but spent most of his time writing; left in 1899 and took up 'a life of profanity' for 18 years, chronicled in his memoirs *Adventurers of a Wanderer* (1928, new edn [including 'Gallipoli'] 1986). Travelled in Africa, the Far East, the South Seas, Australia and New Zealand; served a number of times in the British imperial forces (including during the 2nd Boer War), and with the Australian Army in the Great War. Wounded at Gallipoli, invalided from the service after a year in hospital, sailed again for Tahiti in 1916; left in 1918, married the woman who had nursed him after Gallipoli, and settled in Australia. Returned to England in 1925, and lived there for the rest of his life, earning what he could from writing novels and reviewing. Two years after 'Gallipoli' came to public notice (see text p. 209) in 1932 a

collection of his verses, *One-Way Street and other poems* (London, Harrap) was published. Wrote a number of novels, most with a South Seas setting, and *South Sea Diary*, a remarkable account of his time in Tahiti. These extracts are taken from the full text of 'Gallipoli' in *One-Way Street*.

Read, Sir Herbert, DSO, MC (1893-1968)
'The Happy Warrior', 128; 'To a Conscript of 1940', 325
Poet, writer, art historian, and critic of both literature and art. Born in Yorkshire, where he lived for much of his life, educated Crossley's School, Halifax and at the University of Leeds. Commissioned into the Yorkshire Regiment (Green Howards), January 1915, promoted Captain 1917, fought in France and Belgium (DSO, MC, Mentioned in Despatches). At war's end considered a career in the Army, but left (1919) and joined the Treasury as a civil servant. Assistant Keeper, Victoria and Albert Museum, 1922-31; Professor of Fine Art, University of Edinburgh, 1931-3; Lecturer in Art, University of Liverpool, 1935-6; Editor, *Burlington Magazine*, 1933-9; Leon Fellow, University of London, 1940-2; Norton Professor of Poetry, Harvard University, 1953-4; Mellon Lecturer in Fine Arts, Washington, 1954; Senior Fellow, Royal College of Art, 1962; made a Trustee of the Tate Gallery, 1965; knighted, 1953. Many books on art and literature, and collections of verse; *Collected Poems* published (London, Faber) 1946, 1966 (although there are other earlier collections); his war verse is principally to be found in *Naked Warriors* (1919).

Rhodes, Anthony (b. 1916)
'Repetition', 324
Novelist, travel writer, biographer, writer on art and on history, critic. Served as a Regular officer in the British Army from 1935-47, when he was invalided out: his experiences in France and at Dunkirk, 1939-40, are recorded in his classic war memoir *Sword of Bone* (1942), in the new edition (1986) of which this poem appears (London, Buchan & Enright). Has written four novels and three travel books; his other non-fiction includes biographies, art history, and a triology, *The Power of Rome*, a study of Vatican diplomacy in the twentieth century.

Rickword, (John) Edgell (1898-1982)
'Moonrise Over Battlefield', 187
Poet, essayist, writer and editor; served on the Western Front and wrote many war poems. Editor, the *Calendar of Modern Letters*, 1925-27; Associate Editor, *Left Review*, 1934-38; Editor, *Our Time*, 1944-7. Wrote on poetry, social history, politics, Rimbaud, Wordsworth; translated two of Ronald Firbank's books; also wrote short stories, novels and verse. His war poems were published in *Behind the Eyes* (1921); *Collected Poems* (London, Bodley Head, 1947). Also edited *Soviet Writers Reply to British Writers' Questions* (1948).

Robertson, Corporal Alexander (k.i.a. 1916)
'"We Shall Drink to Them that Sleep"', 322
Served with the York and Lancaster Regiment, and was killed in action on 1 July 1916, the first day of the Battle of the Somme, during which the British Army suffered some 57,000 casualties. Two collections of his were published: *Comrades* (London, Elkin Matthews, 1916), and *Last Poems* (Elkin Matthews, 1918).

Ronald, C.J.
'In Memoriam J.H.H.', 58
This poem appeared in Ronald's collection *Spring's Highway*.

Rosenberg, Isaac (1890-1918)
'The Dead Heroes', 60; 'The Troop Ship', 72; 'Marching', 86; 'Louse Hunting', 119; 'The Immortals', 120; 'Dead Man's Dump', 155; 'On Receiving News Of The War', 164; 'Spring 1916', 176; 'Break of Day In The Trenches', 176; 'Returning, We Hear The Larks', 177
'Georgian' poet. Born in Bristol, family moved to East End of London, educated until aged 14 at Stepney Board School. Wrote first poems at 12, but also showed real promise in drawing. Apprenticed as an engraver, studied at art school in evenings, and (through the contributions of friends) attended the Slade School of Art, 1911-1914; exhibited paintings at Whitechapel Gallery. Encouraged as a poet by Binyon (qv) and Edward Marsh; first collection, *Night and Day*, published 1912. Weak lungs caused a visit to South Africa, 1914-1915; enlisted in King's Own Royal Lancaster Regiment, 1915, despite poor health, small stature, and

acute absentmindedness. Sent to France, 1916, and killed in action on 1 April 1918. His work, much of it influenced by his Jewish background, is widely regarded as among the best of Great War poetry. Rosenberg's *Collected Poems*, edited by Bottomley (qv) and with a Memoir by Binyon (qv) was published in 1922 (London, Heinemann); *The Complete Works* in 1937 (London, Chatto & Windus); *The Collected Poems of Isaac Rosenberg*, with a Foreword by Sassoon (qv), in 1949. The definitive edition is *The Collected Works of Isaac Rosenberg*, edited by Ian Parsons (London, Chatto, 1979).

Rose-Troup, Captain J.M.
'What is War?', 75
Served in the Queen's Regiment, and was later a POW in Germany. This poem appeared in Andrews (ed.), *From the Front* (1918); other verse in Osborn (ed.), *The Muse in Arms* (1917).

Rutter, Major Owen (pseudonym, 'Klip-Klip', 1889-1944)
'Joining Up', 50; 'Rumour', 52; 'Trenches', 101; 'Salonika Campaign', 196; Extract, 313 – all from *The Song of Tiadatha*.
Son of an RNR officer, educated at St Paul's School, spent five years as magistrate and District Officer with North Borneo Civil Service. Served in France and Macedonia with the Wiltshire Regiment, and was Mentioned in Despatches; *The Song of Tiadatha* first published, under pseudonym 'Klip-Klip', in Salonika, 1919, and in a general edition (London, Fisher Unwin) in 1920. Travelled widely in Europe, America and Far East; editor *The Writer* 1922-1924; organised publicity campaign for Society of Authors, 1927. Author of many books, travel books and articles, including *The Travels of Tiadatha* (1922), and a study of the HMS *Bounty* mutineers.

Saki (Hector Hugh Munro, 1870-1916)
Carol, 117
Best remembered for his collections of satirical stories, began his literary career as a political satirist for the *Westminster Gazette*, and from 1902 to 1908 was a correspondent in Russia and then Paris for the *Morning Post*. *Reginald*, his first pseudonymous collection of stories, was published in 1904, followed by *Reginald in Russia* (1910), *The Chronicles of*

Clovis (1911) and *Beasts and Superbeasts* (1914); his only novel, *The Unbearable Bassington*, was published in 1912. When war broke out he enlisted in the Army, refused a commission, and served in the ranks. He was killed as a sergeant on the Western Front, his last words reportedly being 'Put that bloody light out!' Among his best-known stories are 'Tobermory', 'Shredni Vashtar', 'The Unrest Cure' and 'The Open Window'.

Sargant, Edmund Beale
'The Cuckoo Wood', 41
'Georgian' poet, whose traces have been almost wholly covered. This poem appeared in one of the *Georgian Poetry* anthologies (London, the Poetry Bookshop).

Sarson, Private H. Smalley
'The Shell', 152
Canadian; this poem appeared in Kyle (ed.), *Soldier Poets: Songs of the Fighting Men* (1916). He seems also to have published a collection, *From Field and Hospital* (London, 1916).

Sassoon, Siegfried, CBE (1886-1967)
'Night on the Convoy', 73; 'To Any Dead Officer', 114; 'The Death-Bed', 140; 'Stretcher Case', 141; 'The Dug-Out', 145; 'Concert Party', 195; 'Picture-Show', 301; 'Everyone Sang', 301; 'Reconciliation', 302; 'Repression of War Experience', 310; 'Aftermath', 311; 'To One Who Was With Me in the War', 312
'Georgian' poet. Born in Kent into the wealthy, aristocratic, well-connected and cultured Sassoon and Thorneycroft families, educated Marlborough and Clare College, Cambridge. Enlisted as a trooper in the Sussex Yeomanry when war started, in May 1915 commissioned into Royal Welch Fusiliers (in a different battalion – the 1st – to his friend Robert Graves). An exceptionally brave officer, won the Military Cross in June 1916 when he single-handedly bombed and captured a German trench. Invalided home with trench fever in August, returned to France in February 1917, and joined 2nd Battalion RWF on the Somme front in March. Wounded in the shoulder on 16 April and sent to hospital in England. In June sent to Craiglockhart psychiatric hospital, where he met and encouraged Owen (qv), and where his critical views of the war's continuation hardened. On 30 July his statement against the continuation of the

war was read out in the House of Commons, and reported in *The Times* on the following day. After leaving hospital, he threw his MC ribbon into the Mersey and became an outspoken public critic of the war, which was then tantamount to treason. Passed fit for general service on 26 November, and on 7 January 1918 posted to 25th Battalion RWF in Palestine. Battalion arrived in France on 9 May, and on 13 July Sassoon was wounded in the head and sent back to England, where he remained on indefinite sick leave. Retired from the Army officially on 12 March 1918. By the end of the war was acknowledged as the leader of the younger war poets. After 1918, was Literary Editor of the *Daily Herald*, and began upon his trilogy of autobiographical Great War novels — *Memoirs of a Fox-Hunting Man* (1928), *Memoirs of an Infantry Officer* (1930), and *Sherston's Progress* (1936; all London, Faber). These, as much as his poetry, established his reputation as one of the greatest writers to come out of the war. Other books include *The Old Century* (non-fiction, London, Faber 1938), *Siegfried's Journey 1916-1920* (non-fiction; London, Faber, 1945), and a life of Meredith, as well as volumes of verse; his *War Poems* appeared in 1919 (London, Faber), and *Collected Poems* in 1947 (London, Faber); his *Diaries 1915-1918* (ed. and introduced by Rupert Hart-Davis) appeared in 1983 (London, Faber). An updated *Collected Poems 1908-1956* appeared in 1961, and there are other editions and selections, including his *Diaries 1920-1922* and *War Poems* (both ed. Rupert Hart-Davis, London, Faber, 1981 and 1983). His post-1918 verse has been much neglected, unlike his prose.

Scannell, Vernon (b. 1922)
'The Great War', 319
Poet, novelist, critic and broadcaster. Educated at the University of Leeds; served with the Gordon Highlanders, 1940-45, in the Middle East and North-West Europe. Held various posts after the Second War, including prep-school master; Southern Arts Association Writing Fellowship, 1975-6; Visiting Poet, Shrewsbury School, 1978-9; Resident Poet, King's School, Canterbury, 1979. Fellow of the Royal Society of Literature, 1960; Cholmondeley Poetry Award, 1974; granted a Civil List pension for services to literature, 1981. Has published ten novels and written or edited thirteen

books of poetry; also books of criticism and two volumes of autobiography. His *New and Collected Poems 1950-1980* was published in 1980; this poem appeared first in his collection *A Sense of Danger*, (London, Putnam, 1962). See also his *New and Collected Poems 1952-1980* (London, Robson, 1980).

'Scots Greys'
'An Appeal', 171
This poem was part of an advertisement for the Blue Cross which appeared in the *New Witness* of 7 October 1915. The Blue Cross was, and is, a charitable organisation operating hospitals for animals. The Royal Scots Greys (2nd Dragoons) was a heavy cavalry regiment famous for its use only of grey horses; it was amalgamated in 1971 with the 3rd Carabiniers (Prince of Wales's Dragoon Guards) to form the Royal Scots Dragoon Guards (Carabiniers and Greys). Napoleon at Waterloo, watching the charge of the Greys, remarked: '*Qui sont ces terribles chevaux gris?*'

Scott Moncrieff, Captain Charles Kenneth Michael, MC (1889-1930)
'Au Champ d'Honneur', 183
Served on the Western Front as a Captain with the 3rd Battalion, the King's Own Scottish Borderers, winning the Military Cross. He is best known for his translation of Marcel Proust's complex seven-part novel, *À la recherche du temps perdu (Remembrance of Things Past)*, of which Scott Moncrieff completed all but the final section before his death. The annual Scott Moncrieff Prize for the best translation of a twentieth-century French work published in Britain was established in 1964. This poem appeared in the *New Witness*, 23 December 1915.

Service, Robert William (1874-1958)
'The Volunteer', 62; 'A Pot of Tea', 66; 'Grand-père', 136; 'Going Home', 138
Born in Preston, educated at Hillhead High School, Glasgow, and apprenticed to Commercial Bank of Scotland. Emigrated to Canada in 1894, where he farmed for a time. Joined Canadian Bank of Commerce, transferred to the Yukon, and travelled extensively in the sub-Artic. Wrote novels and a great deal of verse about life in the wilderness. War correspondent for *Toronto Star* during Balkan War of 1912-13, and again during the Great War; he also served as

an ambulance driver (despite his age) in the Canadian Army Medical Corps on the Western Front for two years. His war verses, like Kipling's (qv), are much concerned with the ordinary soldier. His Canadian poetry was immensely popular, earning him the sobriquet 'The Man with the Ice in His Voice' – as such, he was somewhat pilloried in Blunden's (qv) *Undertones of War* ('cantering rhetoric about huskies and hoboes on icy trails'). Service's *Collected Verses* was published in 1930 (London, Ernest Benn); *Rhymes of a Red Cross Man* (in which these poems appeared) published in 1916 (London, Fisher Unwin).

Shanks, Edward Richard Buxton
(1892-1953)
'The Halt', 302
Born in London, educated at Merchant Taylors' School and Trinity College, Cambridge; editor of *Granta*, 1912-13. Commissioned into the South Lancashire Regiment in 1914; invalided out, 1915, and worked in the War Office until the war's end. Was involved to a certain extent with the Georgian movement; first volumes of poems, *Songs*, published 1915, followed by *Poems* (1916) and *Queen of China and other Poems* (1919); was the first winner of the Hawthornden Prize in 1919. Assistant Editor of the London Mercury, 1919-22; Lecturer in Poetry, University of Liverpool, 1926; Chief Leader Writer, *Evening Standard*, 1928-35. Besides verse wrote many other books, including novels, lives of Poe and Kipling (qv), and essays on English literature. This poem appeared in *Poems 1912-32* (London, Macmillan, 1933).

Sitwell, Sir Osbert, CH, CBE (5th Baronet, 1892-1969)
'Judas and the Profiteer', 277; 'The Next War', 323
Poet, essayist, novelist, writer of short stories and art criticism. Educated 'during the holidays from Eton'; commissioned as a Regular officer into the Grenadier Guards, 1912; served in France and fought at Loos; left the Army 1919. Some of his autobiography (5 volumes, 1944-50) covers his military service. Extremely prolific writer, knew many of the war poets, including Sassoon and Owen (qqv); devoted his life to conducting 'with his brother and sister [Sacheverell and Edith] a series of

skirmishes and hand-to-hand battles against the Philistine ... occasionally succeeding in denting the line, though not without damage to himself'. This sometimes led to the Sitwells being accused of pretentiousness and intellectual arrogance; Noël Coward parodied them as Gob, Sago and Hernia Whittlebot. Succeeded his eccentric father, Sir George, as baronet, 1943, and was in turn succeeded by Sacheverell on his death. His war poems – including the two above – are mostly found in *Argonaut and Juggernaut* (London, Chatto & Windus, 1919) and *Selected Poems Old and New* (London, Duckworth, 1943).

Smith, Miss Cicely Fox
'Admiral Dugout', 243
Daughter of a barrister, travelled in Canada and spent some time on the Pacific coast. Wrote many books, almost all about the sea and ships, including collections of songs, ballads and shanties, and books for children. This poem appeared in *Punch*, to which she contributed regularly, as well as to other periodicals; her *Songs and Chanties 1914-1916* was published in 1919 (London, Elkin Matthews).

Sorley, Charles Hamilton (1895-1915)
'A Call To Action', 36; 'Barbury Camp', 38; 'Stones', 39; 'Rooks', 40; 'Sonnet', 69; 'All the Hills and Vales Along', 80; 'A Hundred Thousand Million Mites', 82; 'To Germany', 84; 'Two Sonnets', 87
Born in Aberdeen, brought up in Cambridge, and educated at Marlborough. Spent six months in Germany after leaving school, returning as war started; immediately enlisted in Suffolk Regiment, was commissioned, and sent to France in May 1915. Killed on 13 October 1915, aged 20, during the Battle of Loos. The body of his work is very small, but Masefield and Graves thought him the most promising of all the war poets. *Marlborough and Other Poems*, his only, and posthumous, collection (Cambridge, Cambridge University Press, 1916), was an immediate best-seller. See also Spear, Hilda D. (ed.), *The Poems and Selected Letters of Charles Hamilton Sorley*, Dundee, Blackness Press, 1978

Spring-Rice, Sir Cecil Arthur, GCVO, KCMG (1859-1918)
'I Vow To Thee, My Country', 316

British diplomat. Born in London, a grandson of the 1st Lord Monteagle, educated at Eton and Balliol College, Oxford (where he contributed once of the verses of *The Masque of Bailiol*, a satire on prominent Oxford people composed by and current among members of his college). Entered the Foreign Office, 1882; Private Secretary to Lord Granville, 1884; précis-writer to Lord Rosebery, 1885; then served in embassies in Washington, Berlin, Tehran and Cairo. Served in St Petersburg (now Leningrad), 1903-5, then in Persia (Iran) again, 1906-1908, and in Denmark, 1908-12. Appointed British Ambassador to the United States in 1912, and served in that post until January 1918; he died in Ottawa, 14 February 1918, while on his way back to Britain. 'I Vow To Thee My Country' was originally known as 'Last Poem' (or, in hymn-books, 'The Two Fatherlands'); it was written on 12 January 1918, the last night Spring-Rice spent in the Embassy in Washington. The poem is nowadays famous as a hymn set to music by, notably, Gustav Holst.

Squire, Sir John Collings (1884-1958)
'To A Bulldog', 165; 'Homœopathy', 279; 'The Survival of the Fittest', 280
'Georgian' poet. English anthologist, parodist and writer, especially of light verse. Educated Blundell's and St John's College, Cambridge. Literary Editor, then Acting Editor, *New Statesman*, 1913-18; Editor, *London Mercury*, 1919-34; had strong interests in architecture, the theatre, and the preservation of traditional English ways of life, customs, and buildings. Succeeded Sir Edward Marsh as leader of the Georgian poetry movement, and upheld its aims. Published many collections of verse, light verse anthologies, parodies, editions of other poets' work and books on many other topics; edited the 'English Men of Letters' and 'English Heritage' seried. These poems are from *The Survival of the Fittest* (London, Allen & Unwin, 1916). Knighted, 1933.

Stein, Major Sir Edward de
(1887-1965)
'Chloe', 121; 'Elegy On The Death Of Bingo, Our Trench Dog', 169
Educated Eton and Magdalen College, Oxford; served in France with the King's Royal Rifle Corps (60th Rifles), 1914-18. Director of Finance (Raw Materials),

Ministry of Supply, 1941-6; Chairman of Finance Committee, British Red Cross Society until 1963; Director, Lazard Bros, 1960-2; President of the tobacco concern Gallaher Ltd. Knighted 1946. Both these poems appeared in *Punch*, 1918; also published a collection, *Poets in Picardy* (London, Murray, 1919).

Strachey, Charles
'A Revised Version', 259
This poem appeared in the *New Witness*, 14 January 1915. Its author may have been Sir Charles Strachey, KCMG, CB (1862-1942), educated King's College, Cambridge; served Foreign Office, 1885-99; represented Colonial Office at Paris Peace Conference, 1919; Assistant Under-Secretary of State for the Colonies, 1924-27. The author of the first poem, 'M.C.D.H.', is untraceable.

Swan, Robert
Untitled poem, 206; 'Trench Fever', 207
Canadian; both these poems are quoted in *The Great War and Canadian Society* (Toronto).

Thomas, (Philip) Edward (1878-1917)
'This is No Case of Petty Right or Wrong', 84; 'No One Cares Less Than I', 153; 'A Private', 172; 'As the Team's Head-Brass', 173
'Georgian' poet, born of Welsh parentage in London, educated St Paul's School and Lincoln College, Oxford; married his remarkable wife Helen while still an undergraduate — her support was to prove crucial both to his writing and to his reputation after his death. In 1912, Thomas started writing for Monro's (qv) *Poetry Review* and other literary magazines. Wrote mainly biographical, topographical and historical prose, and some fiction, until 1914, when, at the age of 36, and encouraged by his friend Robert Frost (qv) (to whom he was introduced by Ralph Hodgson [qv]), he wrote his first poetry. For many years he was much plagued by both depression and money worries, writing being his main source of income; but his wife's tireless support and encouragement, as well as that of poets like Abercrombie, Brooke and Frost (qqv), helped him to overcome many trials. Enlisted, 1915, in the Artists' Rifles; promoted Corporal, March 1916, and

applied for a commission in the Royal Artillery in June. In November he was commissioned into the Royal Garrison Artillery, was posted to 244 Siege Battery, and went on active service in France in March 1917. Although then nearly 40, he was remembered by his fellows as a fine officer who performed his duties with courage, skill and efficiency. He was killed by a shell-blast at Arras on 9 April 1917. Despite the fact that Thomas wrote very little actual 'war' verse, his reputation has steadily climbed, not least because of his poetry's evocation of the English countryside; his best-known war poems are much anthologised. Thomas's *Last Poems* was published in 1918, and *Collected Poems* (foreword by Walter de la Mare, London, Selwyn & Blount) in 1920, with subsequent editions of the latter in 1928, 1944 and 1948; in addition, there were a number of short editions published containing some of his verse. The definitive collection is *The Collected Poems of Edward Thomas,* edited by R. George Thomas (Oxford, Oxford University Press, 1978, 1981). There have, too, been a number of biographies, studies, and collections of letters published. See especially Helen Thomas's 2-volume biography, *As It Was* (1926) and *World Without End* (1931 – both London, Heinemann); combined edition 1956 (London, Faber).

Turner, Walter James Redfern (1889-1946)
'Soldiers In A Small Camp', 186
'Georgian' poet; born in Australia, educated Scotch College, Melbourne; travelled in South Africa, Germany, Austria, Italy, 1910-14; served in the Royal Garrison Artillery, 1916-18. Music critic, *New Statesman,* 1916-40; drama critic, *London Mercury,* 1919-23; Literary Editor, *Daily Herald* (after Sassoon [qv]) 1920-23; latterly Literary Editor of the *Spectator.* Wrote novels and essays as well as poetry and books on music. *Selected Poems 1916-36,* in which this verse appeared, published in 1939 (Oxford, Oxford University Press). 'Death's Men' is probably his best known war poem.

Tynan, Katharine (Mrs Katharine Tynan Winkson, 1861-1931)
'The Vision', 125
Prolific poet and novelist, educated at an Irish convent, began writing at seventeen

and published first volume of verse in 1885. Most of her books were romantic novels, many with an Irish setting; *Collected Poems* published 1901, but other collections came out in 1911, 1913 etc. Much of her Great War verse appeared in magazines, in this case in the *New Witness* of 27 January 1916.

Waugh, Alec (1898-1981)
'From Albert to Bapaume', 180
Son of the critic and publisher Arthur Waugh, elder brother of Evelyn; educated Sherborne and RMA, Sandhurst; gazetted to the Dorset Regiment, 1917, and served in France until 1918, when he was captured, ending the war as a POW (about which he wrote in *The Prisoners of Mainz,* London, Chapman & Hall, 1919). Rejoined the Dorset Regiment, 1939, served with the BEF in France, 1940, then in the Ministry of Mines, 1941, and finally in the Middle East, 1942-5, retiring as a major in 1945. Writer in Residence, Central State College, Edmond, Oklahoma, 1966-7. Wrote more than 50 books, principally fiction and many of them best-sellers: his novel *The Loom of Youth* (London, Chapman & Hall, 1917) caused a scandal for its treatment of homosexuality in a boys' public school. Also wrote *My Brother Evelyn and Other Profiles* (1967). This poem appeared in *Resentment* (London, Grant Richards, 1918).

Webster, Mary Morison
'Gallipoli (Anniversary)', 202

West, Arthur Graeme (1891-1917)
'The Night Patrol', 103
Educated at public school and Oxford, enlisted in the ranks in 1914, having been turned down for a commission because of poor eyesight. Served in France, November 1915 to March 1916, then underwent officer training in UK until August. A 'spiritual crisis' altered his attitude to the war, but he accepted a commission in September 1916 and went back to France. Killed by sniper fire, April 1917. *Diary of a Dead Officer: Posthumous Papers* (ed. C.E.M. Joad), in which this poem appeared, published 1918 (London, Allen & Unwin).

Whitmell, Lucy
'Christ in Flanders', 77
Her work appeared in Clarke (ed.) *A Treasury of War Poetry* (1919), Eaton (ed.), *The War in*

Verse (1918), Foxcroft (ed.), *War Verse* (1918), and Holman (ed.), *In The Day of Battle* (1916).

Wilkes, H.E.
'The Q-Boat', 240
This poem appeared in *Punch*, 4 September 1918.

Wolfe, Humbert, CB, CBE (1886-1940)
'A Thrush In The Trenches', 178
Poet and civil servant. Educated Bradford Grammar School, Wadham College, Oxford — First in Greats. Principal Assistant Secretary, Ministry of Labour. Published verse, light verse, parodies etc. as well as essays and criticism, studies of poets, and translations from Heine; also edited the Sixpenny Augustan Poets series. This verse is from *Requiem* (London, Ernest Benn, 1927).

Young, Edward Hilton (1st Baron Kennet of the Dene, GBE, DSO, DSC, PC, 1879-1960)
'Mine-Sweeping Trawlers', 235
Son of a baronet, educated Eton and Trinity College, Cambridge; called to the Bar 1904. Was a Lieutenant, RNVR on the outbreak of war, and served throughout, mostly in ships but at one time with the Naval guns in Flanders (DSC); wounded at Zeebrugge, 1918, and promoted Lieutenant-Commander. Saw action on the Archangel front in Russia against the Bolsheviks (DSO), 1919. Liberal MP for Norwich, 1915-23 and 1924-29; Conservative MP for Sevenoaks, 1929-35. In the Treasury, 1921-2; Secretary of the Overseas Trade Department, 1931; Minister of Health, 1931-5; in addition,

attended or chaired many inquiries, commissions etc., and was a delegate several times to the League of Nations. Married Kathleen Scott, widow of Captain Robert Falcon Scott, RN, the Arctic explorer. This poem is from *A Muse at Sea* (London, Sidgwick & Jackson, 1919). He wrote six other books, including another collection of poems.

Zangwill, Israel (1864-1926)
'Oliver Singing', 303
Novelist, essayist, poet and playwright; ardent pro-Zionist. Born in London and 'practically self-educated' (in fact he attended the Jews' Free School, and eventually taught there), was first a teacher, then a journalist; founded and edited *Ariel*, and was a prominent member of Jewish literary society in England. While teaching gained an Honours degree at the University of London. Lectured in Britain, Ireland, Jerusalem, Holland, and the United States; founder and President of the International Jewish Territorial Organisation, Vice-President of the League of World Friendship. Novels include *Children of the Ghetto* (1892, which he dramatised in 1899), *Merely Mary Ann* (1893), *Ghetto Tragedies* (1893), *The Master* (1895), *Dreamers of the Ghetto* (1899), and *Ghetto Comedies* (1907); plays: *Six Persons* (1892), *The Melting Pot* (1908), *The War God* (1911), *Too Much Money* (1918), and *The Voice of Jerusalem* (1920). This poem appeared in *The War for the World* (1916). His brother, Louis, was also a prolific writer.

INDEX OF TITLES AND FIRST LINES